Classroom Teaching in the 21st Century

Classroom Teaching in the 21st Century

Directions, Principles, and Strategies

Clive Beck and Clare Kosnik

Open University Press

Open University Press
McGraw Hill
8th Floor, 338 Euston Road
London
England
NW1 3BH

email: enquiries@openup.co.uk
world wide web: www.openup.co.uk

First edition published 2022

A catalogue record of this book is available from the British Library

ISBN-13: 9780335250271
ISBN-10: 0335250270
eISBN: 9780335250288

Library of Congress Cataloging-in-Publication Data
CIP data applied for

Typeset by Transforma Pvt. Ltd., Chennai, India

Praise page

During a time of great disruption due to the COVID-19 pandemic, **Classroom Teaching in the 21st Century** *is a gift to school leaders and teachers who are looking for sound advice to improve teaching and learning (including online learning) in practical ways, backed by research evidence and theoretical foundation. Instead of teaching for subject knowledge or teaching for 21st-century relevance, the book wisely proposes a pedagogy of doing both, which is both down-to-earth and far-sighted. The book is a great source of clear pedagogical principles and inspiration for teachers!*

Pak Tee NG, National Institute of Education, Nanyang Technological University, Singapore

In this disquieting and uncertain time, Beck and Kosnik offer **Doing Both Pedagogy,** *21 principles for 21st century teaching that deliberately veer away from narrow conceptions of schooling as the engine of the economy. If you are looking for fresh ideas about teaching for meaning and well-being, as well as for competence and content, look no further. Through vivid examples and accessible suggestions, readers can learn from the example of practitioners who struggle with the same issues that all teachers face (even more so in this challenging period), but have found their path into educating for wholeness, connection, and joy.*

A. Lin Goodwin, Dean, Faculty of Education, The University of Hong Kong, Hong Kong

This is an important new book which will make a substantial contribution to the literature on education and schooling. It is unique in that it draws on - and is informed by - the authors' impressive fifteen-year longitudinal study of 40 teachers at work, giving the book a 'real world' grounding, which sets it apart. The book addresses directions needed for 21st century teaching and pedagogy, focusing throughout on both teaching for subject knowledge and teaching for 21st century relevance. I expect this important new book to find a central place both in the general literature concerned with education, teaching and the work of schools, and especially in the teacher education literature.

Keith F Punch, Emeritus Professor, Graduate School of Education, The University of Western Australia, Australia

Beck and Kosnik draw on their longitudinal research of teachers to articulate principles for successful 21st century teaching and classrooms. Practical language and descriptions move beyond "on the street" definitions and interpretations and link to sound rationales and theoretical foundations for the principles. The rich teacher quotes will draw you in and prompt you to think about your teaching and your learners. Their systemic perspective prompts consideration that what happens in classrooms can have broad reaching implications. The last three chapters are a must read for new teachers as they begin to navigate the challenges and delights of teaching.

Kathy L. Schuh, Ph.D., Professor of Educational Psychology & Learning Sciences, University of Iowa, US

At the heart of this book is a deep respect for and understanding of the important and complex work that teachers undertake every single day in their classrooms. By bringing together pedagogical theory, research and practice, the reader is encouraged to think critically and creatively about what it means to be a teacher and a learner in the 21st century. Interwoven throughout are valuable strategies which challenge and support professionals to develop their practice in both informed and innovative ways.

Kristine Black-Hawkins, Reader in Inclusive Education, University of Cambridge, UK

To the teachers who participated in our longitudinal study (2004–2019), welcoming us into their classrooms year after year, generously giving their time for interviews and offering thoughtful comments about teaching and their lives as teachers.

And to our research team, for their unfailing commitment to the longitudinal study, their warmth and sensitivity in interacting with the teachers, their invaluable input and guidance, their sense of humour and camaraderie, and their willingness to learn alongside us.

Contents

About the authors

Clive Beck is Emeritus Professor in the Curriculum, Teaching and Learning Department at OISE/University of Toronto, giving courses in the areas of teaching, teacher education, and ongoing teacher learning. He is a past Coordinator of Graduate Studies at OISE and a former President of the American Philosophy of Education Society. He has had many large-scale funded research projects over the years and recently completed a 15-year SSHRC-funded longitudinal study (2004–2019) of forty teachers. He is currently Co-Investigator in the SSHRC-funded study "Pedagogy of Literacy Teacher Education: Meeting the Challenges of 21st Century Literacies". Apart from doctoral teaching and supervision, Clive has taught and supervised in the pre-service teacher education programme at OISE for over twenty years. His books, many of them co-authored with Clare Kosnik, include *Better Schools* (1990), *Learning to Live the Good Life* (1993), *Innovations in Teacher Education* (2006), *Priorities in Teacher Education* (2009), *Teaching in a Nutshell* (2011), *Growing as a Teacher* (2014), and *Building Bridges: Rethinking Literacy Teacher Education in a Digital Era* (2016).

Clare Kosnik is Professor in the Department of Curriculum, Teaching and Learning at OISE/University of Toronto, previously Director of Elementary Teacher Education at OISE and a former Director of OISE's Jackman Institute of Child Study. She supervises doctoral and master's students and teaches graduate courses in areas such as teaching, teacher education, and thesis research. She has received University-wide Awards for Excellence in both teaching and graduate supervision. Clare has conducted many large-scale funded research projects over the years, including being executive director of the Carnegie-funded Teachers for a New Era research at Stanford (2003/6). She is currently Principal Investigator of the SSHRC-funded study "Pedagogy of Literacy Teacher Education: Meeting the Challenges of 21st Century Literacies". Her books, many of them co-authored with Clive Beck, include: *Primary Education: Goals, Processes and Policies* (1999), *Innovations in Teacher Education* (2006), *Priorities in Teacher Education* (2009), *Teaching in a Nutshell* (2011), *Growing as a Teacher* (2014), and *Building Bridges: Rethinking Literacy Teacher Education in a Digital Era* (2016).

Preface

This book is about new directions needed in teaching in the 21st century. As such, it is quite critical of past schooling: ours is a "critical" educational stance. At the same time, we are strong supporters of teachers, acknowledging the enormous contribution they have made in the past: all of us would be much worse off without them. The complexity and changing nature of life and reality means that teaching – like any profession – can stand in need of improvement even though it is already achieving a great deal.

In keeping with seeing the value in past schooling, we propose a pedagogy of "doing both": teaching for subject knowledge *and* 21st-century relevance. Doing both in this way is essential because students still need extensive subject knowledge in the 21st century, and because government and school-system pressures to teach subject content and prepare for standardized tests continue to be strong. In the strategy sections of each chapter, we look at ways to make such dual-focused teaching feasible and enjoyable, for teachers and students alike.

The teaching approach we are proposing in this book defies easy labelling. Though we talk of fostering 21st-century work and life skills, we do not advocate the narrow educational model sometimes referred to as "neoliberal", "individualistic", or "success-oriented". Our concern is with the whole of personal, communal, and global life. While individual development is very important (Part 1 of the book focuses on it especially), our position is that individual wellbeing is impossible without the social, inclusive, holistic approach to life explored throughout the book.

The book is both theoretical and practical. In each chapter we discuss the theory of 21st-century teaching and refer to relevant research literature, but the largest section of almost every chapter is on teaching strategies, with practical examples from the teachers in our 2004–2019 longitudinal study. Indeed, we recommend that in using the book teachers often go first to the strategy sections to get practical suggestions and see concrete examples of the general teaching approach we are proposing.

The book is intended for use by pre-service and in-service teachers alike. Because it has to address so many sub-topics (given the complexity of teaching), we encourage dipping into it on an interest and need-to-know basis rather than reading all at once. This is especially necessary for in-service teachers who are so busy with daily work activities. However, a sense of the general direction and pedagogy is also important. For this we suggest looking at the Introduction and Chapter 18, which is on overall 21st-century pedagogy.

We wish to note here with gratitude the support of Open University Press in the development of the book. Apart from editorial and technical help, they encouraged us from the beginning to address 21st-century teaching while avoiding a narrow interpretation of the term. They also agreed to drawing on our longitudinal study of teachers, which we see as a major strength and attraction of the book. As well as making the book more practical and appealing, it has enabled us to celebrate the dedicated teachers and researchers who were involved in the study.

Finally, it is important to mention that the book was completed in the midst of the Covid-19 crisis. We have become aware of many of the problems of teaching in a pandemic from our own experiences conducting Zoom-based university classes at this time, and from the reports of pre-service and in-service teachers in these classes. We share aspects of what we have learned in Chapter 13 and elsewhere. School teaching in this context is especially challenging. While all the same 21st-century principles and strategies apply (as argued in Part 4), many additional measures are needed. Our heartfelt wishes go out to those who are doing or have done practice teaching, practicum supervision, pre-service mentoring, and regular school teaching under these circumstances.

Acknowledgements

We are deeply indebted to our longitudinal study participants and research team, and have dedicated the book to these two wonderful groups of people.

We also acknowledge how much we have learned over the years from discussions with our pre-service students and with other graduate students of whom many are practising classroom teachers.

We wish to thank Open University Press for their support in developing the book (we say more about this in the Preface).

And finally, we are grateful to the Social Sciences and Humanities Research Council of Canada for its generous funding of our research over two decades on teachers, teaching, and teacher education.

Introduction

Since the turn of the 21st century there has been much talk about the need to teach "21st-century skills" and "bring schooling into the 21st century". Digital literacy, of course, is a key area mentioned, but so are many other work and life skills and values such as autonomy, resilience, teamwork, cultural responsiveness, and global and environmental commitment. After two decades, however, movement in many of these directions in schooling has been fairly limited. This book is about the new directions needed in teaching in the 21st century and detailed principles and strategies for going in these directions.

In speaking of the need for new directions, we do not wish to downplay teachers' past and present achievements. As noted in the Preface, we are strong supporters of teachers and believe they are already successful in a great many ways: the world would be much worse off without their contribution. Students are cared for, acquire basic academic and social skills and values, and learn a great many important things about the world, themselves, and other people. However, additional progress is needed – and it is being held back by two main challenges.

Challenges to going in 21st-century directions

In this book we talk often about the challenges teachers face and how to deal with them. Almost every chapter has a section on this topic. Here we note two major ways in which movement towards 21st-century teaching is being hindered. This will help explain the approach we take in the book.

The first challenge is the simplistic view of teaching typically held by governments and members of the public; namely, that good teaching is the straightforward transmission of a narrow band of subject content, without much attention to broader life concerns. This view leads to imposing on teachers a detailed academic curriculum and a cover-and-test pedagogy. Of course, subject learning is very important, as we will illustrate throughout the book. But the content should be carefully chosen and adapted so schooling *also* promotes general personal, societal, and global/environmental learning, and this is currently being made difficult by system policies and expectations. It is true that to some extent teachers can – behind their closed classroom door – "resist" these policies and teach in relevant ways (Santoro and Cain, 2018), but this is possible only to a degree: policy inevitably "has its effects" (Yandell, 2016: 39).

The second main obstacle to going in 21st-century directions is lack of clarity among teachers *themselves* about the changes needed and how to implement them. Many of the directions were in fact recommended in the 20th century (e.g. by John Dewey, Jean Piaget, Lev Vygotsky, Paulo Freire) but they were only partially understood. For many teachers, terms such as "critical teaching", "inquiry learning", and "inclusive education" are still largely buzz words. As a result, teachers have difficulty implementing them, even when they have freedom to do so.

A dialogue about 21st-century directions

One of our central goals in the book, then, is to clarify what the recommended 21st-century teaching is, both as a basis for influencing policy and as a foundation for greater movement by teachers in this direction. If teachers are to stand up to the pressure to continue with a traditional teaching approach, they need to understand what the alternatives are and why they are so important.

But we wish to stress immediately that, as well as seeking clarity about 21st-century teaching, we remain open to alternative ideas. Clarity, though essential, is not enough: the directions have to be sound. And all those involved – teachers, students, parents, academics, and policy developers – have to be part of the conversation about sound directions. We see writing this book not as a definitive pronouncement but as part of an ongoing dialogue with the outcome still somewhat unclear. We believe that what we are proposing would represent a major step towards a sounder approach to teaching and learning, but it is up to other participants in the dialogue to respond as they see fit.

Overall directions for teaching in the 21st century

What are the directions for the 21st-century teaching we are so keen to emphasize and be clear about? The five broad directions we will propose (while staying open to additions and modifications) are as follows:

1 *Teaching for personal development*, including autonomy, resilience, critical thinking, mental health, and overall wellbeing – in the workplace and so many other life contexts.
2 *Teaching for social development*, again for the workplace but also for community participation and social life generally.
3 *Teaching for equity, inclusion, and political and global/environmental commitment*, including multicultural, international, and ecological knowledge, outlooks, and skills.
4 *Teaching for digital knowledge and skills*, in ways that are not only technologically current but take account of the needs of individuals, groups, societies, the global community, and the environment.
5 *Enhanced teacher identity, professionalism, and wellbeing*, including taking a stand on what and how to teach, developing a 21st-century pedagogy, continuing to inquire and grow professionally, achieving work/life balance and wellbeing, and in general connecting teaching to life and the world as a whole.

We call these 21st-century directions for two main reasons. First, they are directions in which the world is going this century, so to be successful in work, society, and life generally, people have to achieve them more than in the past.

But second, not only is the world going in these directions, it is *important* to go in these directions because autonomy, resilience, community participation, inclusion, ecological responsibility, and so on are inherently necessary for individual success and wellbeing and for life on the planet. Admittedly, such skills and values have always been important: this is not new. But there is *increased* adoption of them and awareness of their importance in the 21st century, and for good reason: schooling has to support and speed up this movement.

The critical nature of the book

Because of the many references to individual development and the key role of information technology (IT) in teaching, the directions we are proposing might be thought at first glance to be uncritical of the world "as it is" and supportive of a narrow, materialistic "success" orientation often referred to as "neoliberalism". As noted in the Preface, however, this is far from the case.

On the contrary, the book is extremely critical of current society and schooling (though we avoid being *too* negative, acknowledging the many good things teachers already do). We are proposing very extensive modification of teaching and schooling, far beyond what has been achieved to date. And our approach is very broad and socially (*as well as* individually) oriented, with material wellbeing just one goal among many. We are strongly opposed to reproducing current unequal, exclusionary approaches to society, life, and schooling: so much of the book is concerned with how to achieve an inclusive education and way of life.

We do emphasize the individual, partly because this dimension has been neglected in the past and partly because attending to it is so important, not only for individual wellbeing but also for general societal wellbeing. (Please see the Amanda Gorman tweet near the beginning of Chapter 1 that deals directly and brilliantly with this point.)

Principles and strategies for going in 21st-century directions

For each of the five parts of the book corresponding to the five overall 21st-century directions, we have identified several subsidiary principles with a chapter for each (see the Table of Contents). We are proposing a total of 21 such principles – and hence chapters – for the 21st century! For ease of reading and discussion, we use the same format for nearly all the chapters, with sections on:

- the principle, its importance, and some challenges;
- theory and research underlying the principle; and
- strategies for implementing the principle.

In addition, each chapter has a brief conclusion and a set of questions for reflection and discussion.

We invite readers to visit the chapters and sub-sections in whatever order they find useful, but we suggest early reading of the strategy section of each

chapter. This is always the most extensive section, in keeping with our commitment to make the book practical (as well as theoretical). We hope many of the
strategies will be of immediate help to pre-service and in-service teachers as
they negotiate the school classroom.

Although of practical relevance, however, we believe the strategies also
help further clarify the five overall directions and 21 principles. This is in line
with John Dewey's famous observation:

> [A]ll principles by themselves are abstract. They become concrete only in the
> consequences which result from their application. [While they are] funda-
> mental and far-reaching, everything depends upon the interpretation given
> them as they are put into practice in the school and the home. (*Experience
> and Education*, 1938: 20)

Principles are valuable in suggesting general directions – as Dewey says they
are "fundamental and far-reaching" – but extensive reference to practice is necessary to clarify what principles ultimately mean.

The strategies presented are in some cases quite concrete but in others
rather general (though with concrete examples). We summarize here the main
general strategies we recommend throughout the book so readers get a sense
of the overall pedagogical approach we are proposing. These strategies are
brought together and discussed in an integrated way in Chapter 18 as a 21st-
century pedagogy.

The 21st-century pedagogy we are proposing

1 Combine teaching for subject knowledge and relevance ("Do both")
2 Learn with and from your students
3 Build community and inclusion in the classroom
4 Get to know your students
5 Give students choice
6 Individualize learning
7 Plan and be flexible
8 Set up routines and recurring activities
9 Model what you teach
10 Collaborate often with other teachers

This pedagogical approach is perhaps not as distinctively "21st century" as the
21 principles recommended. However, in our view a comprehensive, integrated
pedagogy of this kind helps a great deal in implementing the principles. For
example, Strategy 1 – *combining* teaching for subject knowledge with teaching
for relevance – is necessary if we are to foster students' personal and social
development while *also* teaching much of the subject content the system
demands and that indeed students need. And Strategy 2 – learning with and

from your students – is essential if students are to develop the kind of autonomy and problem-solving ability the 21st century requires.

Examples from teachers: Drawing on our longitudinal study of teachers, 2004–2019

A key method we use to clarify the nature of 21st-century teaching is presenting examples and quotations from teachers. We do this mainly in the strategy section of each chapter. The examples and quotations are from a study we have just completed of two cohorts of teachers from the time they began teaching – twenty in 2004 and twenty in 2007 – until 2019; that is, for their first 15 and 12 years of teaching respectively.

This extensive longitudinal study was based solidly in the 21st century – the participants were clearly 21st-century teachers. Providing access to this material is in our view a major positive feature of the book. All the teachers were from North America (most from Ontario, Canada and eight from the US: four each from New York and New Jersey). However, many educators from other countries who have seen material from the teacher interviews have spoken of its strong international relevance.

Highlighting examples and quotations from practising teachers in this way is in line with our emphasis throughout the book on the expertise of practitioners. We believe teachers' views and practices should be referred to much more than in the past. As Schön (1983), Cochran-Smith and Lytle (2009), and many others maintain, informal on-the-job learning by teachers is a key source of ideas about education. Every year teachers have a sizeable "sample" of students and the opportunity to study them – week in and week out for close to 10 months – that would be the envy of many academic researchers. Moreover, they have strong motivation to "get it right", since they typically care a great deal for their students and also have to get along with them (and their parents) on a daily basis. In Chapter 17, we discuss at some length why it is appropriate to take very seriously input from teachers.

How to use the book

This book is designed for use as a text or major reference in both pre-service and in-service teacher education programmes. We ourselves have had extensive experience teaching and conducting research at both these levels. Given the wide range of topics covered by the book, instructors would normally only draw on certain chapters and sections. We have tried to lay out the contents clearly so the selection process is relatively easy.

Helpful though we think the book will be in course contexts, we wish to emphasize that in our view a great deal of teacher learning takes place informally "on the job". Accordingly, we want *also* to advocate its use by student teachers and in-service teachers in support of their on-the-job learning. If they are interested in a particular area of practice, they can refer to relevant sections of the book and try out what they see as promising.

As we say throughout the book, teaching is an enormously comprehensive and complex field with a great many issues and areas of inquiry; and as pre-service and in-service teachers refine their ideas and practices, it is difficult to know when and how a particular issue will arise. We would encourage readers, then, to dip into the book in whatever order is most appropriate for them.

Finally, we want to say again that we see teacher education as a dialogue. We feel strongly about these directions, principles, and strategies but present them as grist for the reader's mill. We would appreciate hearing from you and getting your frank feedback so we continue to be part of the conversation. Good luck with your ongoing journey!

Part 1

Direction I: Teaching for Personal Development

As noted in the Introduction to the book, schooling in previous centuries focused on academic learning almost exclusively. Now in the 21st century, for reasons we will discuss throughout the book, much emphasis is *also* needed on several other areas of student development: personal, social, cultural, and so on. In Part 1, we address the *personal* development of students, in particular the following aspects:

Aspects of teaching for personal development

Chapter 1: Teach for autonomy and resilience
Chapter 2: Foster critical thinking and problem-solving
Chapter 3: Support mental health development
Chapter 4: Promote overall wellbeing

Stressing personal development is perhaps controversial because it seems to lead towards "individualism" and away from longstanding norms of social responsibility. But in this and other parts of the book, we make the case that individual development and social responsibility are not in competition. Personal development is crucial not only for individual wellbeing but also for vibrant and caring communities and societies. It is difficult (though not impossible) for people to care effectively and continuously for others if they are not themselves strong and well.

Another concern about promoting students' personal development may be that it gets in the way of teaching subject content, something that is widely expected of teachers. However, in our view there is again no necessary conflict here, and in fact personal development is a crucial basis for academic learning. As stated in the UK Department for Education report, *Character*

Education: Framework Guidance, "there is no tension between a rigorous and stretching academic education on the one hand and outstanding wider personal development on the other" (2019: 4). With careful selection of subject content and pedagogy, academic and personal development can strongly support the other.

Personal development in the fullest sense overlaps with social development, the focus of Part 2 of the book, and with cultural, political, environmental, and other forms of development, as discussed in Part 3. Accordingly, the elements of personal development addressed in Part 1, though crucial, are just a beginning: a more complete picture will emerge as the book progresses. In Chapter 1, we begin by looking specifically at the need for students to develop autonomy and resilience, areas of development emphasized in the literature on 21st-century teaching.

1 Principle 1: Teach for autonomy and resilience

I want my kids to be excited about learning, and not read every night because I or their parents tell them to. I want them to realize the value of reading: that it can be for entertainment or pleasure or they're really curious about something.
— Jeannie, a Grade 1 teacher in her fourteenth year

The Principle, its importance, and some challenges

According to many, teachers in the 21st century should place more emphasis than in the past on student autonomy and resilience. Students need to become autonomous so they can take charge of their studies, perform better in the workplace, and enhance their life generally; which, in turn, will help them develop the resilience they require to survive and thrive in a complex, often challenging, and ever-changing world.

It is true that in the past teachers often urged their students to be personally responsible and persistent in their studies. However, the focus was mainly on academic learning rather than life more generally, and their autonomy was limited. They were given constant and detailed direction on what and how to study, rather than being supported in developing their own academic and life path, adapted to their individual needs, talents, and circumstances.

What are autonomy and resilience?

Being *autonomous* involves having a strong sense of self, an awareness of what is important for oneself, and an ability to work towards it largely on one's own. Autonomy in this sense is a balanced concept: it does not mean being individualistic in a selfish way. Rather, it requires that students think about their distinctive needs and develop a way of life – academic, occupational, social, etc. – that works for them *as well as* having many advantages for others.

Being autonomous, then, does not exclude having close relationships, working with teams, and drawing on others' ideas; and it certainly does not mean being self-centred and uncaring. Much autonomous behaviour is directed towards helping others. It is just that even when helping others autonomy is exercised because we choose to help and interact with others, rather than simply being told to do so.

Being *resilient* involves having the motivation, energy, and skill to persevere and flourish in the world. It is closely related to autonomy because to persevere and flourish individuals have to know what they value and how to pursue it, and exercise personal initiative in doing so. Being resilient is like having "grit", often mentioned as a 21st-century skill (Duckworth, 2016), and "will power", to use a more traditional term.

But with all three terms – resilience, grit, and will power – we need to avoid the suggestion that a mysterious "inner strength" is required that carries all before it. While personal strength is indeed necessary for persistent action, such strength is not mysterious: we can cultivate it by building a comprehensive, well-designed life, one with "enabling contexts" (Dolan, 2014) that "nudge" us (Thaler and Sunstein, 2009) in certain directions and so make persistence possible.

Why are autonomy and resilience important?

In the past, the moral values emphasized in schooling have largely been living for others and fulfilling our civic duty. However, just focusing on what we owe to others is problematic because it often leaves individuals without sufficient strength or motivation to help those others. Greater autonomy in thought and living is needed if individuals are to figure out how to establish a feasible overall way of life that includes helping others and doing one's public duty generally. As poet Amanda Gorman wrote in a recent tweet (2021):

> Remember that self-love is also revolutionary and world-changing. We cannot fight for others when we are fighting a war inside ourselves. Compassion is reflexive, a power that we first bestow on ourselves and then give away through our actions – to people, to our planet.

Of course, people in the past did often think about their own interests: this is basic to human nature. But they tended to do so secretly, sporadically, and with a sense of guilt, thus undermining both their own wellbeing and their effectiveness in helping others. In a highly complex, ever-changing world, individuals need to engage in conscious, systematic life planning if they are to act appropriately, both for their own wellbeing and that of other people.

Accordingly, at the school level learning by individual students has to be adapted to their distinctive needs, interests, talents, and circumstances if it is to be relevant and useful – as constructivists have long maintained (e.g. Piaget, 1968). This is not to deny the great importance of social learning goals and processes, which we will discuss at length in Part 2. But individualizing learning *to a significant degree* can in fact strengthen community life by making students feel safe and accepted and providing them with a solid basis for helping others. To summarize:

Reasons for teaching for autonomy and resilience

- Learning is more relevant
- Learning is more enjoyable and effective
- Engagement is increased and learning deepened
- Students can contribute more in class
- Everyone gets to know each other better
- Students become more able to help others

What are the challenges of teaching for autonomy and resilience?

Teaching for autonomy and resilience is not easy, especially given the top-down educational tradition from which we are emerging. It is important for teachers to be aware of the challenges so they are not demoralized by them and can begin early working to address them. The challenges include the following:

The widespread belief that we should live only for others. A challenge to teaching for autonomy is the common belief that living for others is our primary moral responsibility and that attending to our own wellbeing somehow diminishes us morally. Teachers will often encounter this view among parents, administrators, and other teachers – and even within themselves.

A detailed, mandated, society-oriented curriculum. The curriculum teachers have to implement usually focuses much more on society than the individual and, moreover, is normally so extensive in its academic learning requirements that it is hard to find time to foster students' general autonomy and resilience.

Scripted teaching mandates. Increasingly today, the modest shift that took place in the second half of the 20th century towards personalized, "child-centred" teaching is being eroded, with teachers strongly pressured to follow a top-down, uniform pedagogy the makes a more individualized approach difficult.

Standardized testing. Teachers are being told to teach-to-the-test in a way that, again, leaves little room for fostering student growth in autonomy and resilience.

The belief that everyone should learn the same things in the same way. In line with the emphasis on scripted, test-focused pedagogy, teachers who seek to promote student autonomy and resilience come up against the widespread assumption that all students should be taught the same things in the same way, and if you do not do this you are short-changing students.

Teachers' own education was standardized and top-down. It is difficult for teachers to overcome their own "apprenticeship of observation" (Lortie, 1975) in standardized, top-down teaching in school and higher education and develop ideas and approaches suited to supporting student autonomy and resilience.

As we will discuss throughout the book, we strongly believe that such challenges can, to a considerable extent, be overcome by teachers as they explore alternatives, individually and with others. We do not wish to add to the demoralization of teachers. But meeting the challenges requires a great deal of reflection, learning, and steady effort over the years.

Theory/research basis for teaching for autonomy and resilience

Many researchers report that autonomy is a crucial 21st-century skill, for the workplace and life generally. For example, Trilling and Fadel state that students need to develop "initiative and self-direction" in a world where "[t]he amount of time busy managers have for mentoring and guiding employees is quickly diminishing". Today's students "must prepare for the reality of 21st century work and develop deeper levels of initiative and self-direction skills as they progress through school" (2009: 28).

Some authors maintain that the traditional emphasis on a narrow band of academic knowledge and skill brought success to socially advantaged students but failure to disadvantaged ones (Banks, 2016; Gee, 2015). Moreover, such learning was of limited value even to privileged students. As Meier says:

> [S]chools ... present at best a caricature of what the kids need in order to grow up to be effective citizens, skillful team members, tenacious and ingenious thinkers, or truth seekers. They sit, largely passively, through one after another different subject matter in no special order of relevance. (2002: 12)

Acting autonomously requires seeing oneself as having many distinctive needs, abilities, and circumstances, and taking these into account in everyday life. According to Tranter, Carson, and Boland, "[Students have to] develop a stronger sense of who they truly are [and] form an identity that is their own, [coming] to appreciate and support the similarities and differences between themselves and others" (2018: 117). This does not necessarily mean students become selfish or isolated – indeed, Tranter et al. call their whole approach to teaching "relationship-based". But they have to learn to take initiative even in forming relationships, making sure they are in line with their personality and circumstances *as well as* the needs of others.

As noted above, autonomy is closely related to resilience, and this is also emphasized in the literature as a key goal of schooling. For example, the UK Department for Education document *Character Education: Framework Guidance* talks of ensuring that "our curriculum and teaching develop resilience and confidence", thus furthering students' lives in "wider society" (2019: 5). And Day and Gu (2014), while focusing on teacher resilience, speak generally about what resilience is, why it is important, and how to attain it. They say resilience is not a "quality that is innate" (p. 11) but rather a contextual quality (Dolan, 2014) that relies on developing personal and social values, structuring our environment and gaining the support of others.

Along the same lines, Tranter et al. (2018) take issue with Duckworth's popular book *Grit: The Power of Passion and Perseverance* (2016) for promoting a vague notion of grit and then stressing it too much. This can actually undermine people's resilience by not making clear how to achieve it and placing too much emphasis on conventional "good" behaviour such as "sitting still", "having manners", "cooperating", and "following rules". While such behaviours have their place, they "may not actually be skills for success" and emphasizing them too much can lead people to blame themselves for a lack of moral fibre when they fail (Tranter et al., 2018: 122).

Finally, at a general level, the individualization of learning needed to develop autonomy and resilience has been advocated by many educational theorists and researchers (e.g. Gardner, 1999; O'Meara, 2010; Tomlinson, 2001; Waring and Evans, 2015; West-Burnham and Coates, 2005). It should be noted that such individualized learning is also called "personalized" or "differentiated" learning (Waring and Evans, 2015), and these three terms have slightly different connotations. However, in this book we will use them largely interchangeably.

Strategies for fostering autonomy and resilience

We talk about … what they want to be when they grow up … and the biggest thing is to let them explore their interests; so if they love drawing, or love computers, give them the outlet to explore those fully, because they can learn so much at this age.
– Anna, a Kindergarten and Grade 1 teacher in her thirteenth year

The central approach we recommend for fostering autonomy and resilience is to individualize teaching and learning and, in that context, help students develop a sense of self and take charge of their learning and their life generally. As mentioned in the Introduction, the strategies section of most chapters will include many examples and quotations from teachers in our 2004–2019 longitudinal study of teachers. We believe this will help ensure the practical value of the book, and also clarify further the nature of the 21st-century directions and principles. Here is an overview of the specific strategies we advocate:

Strategies for fostering students' autonomy and resilience

1 Individualize the programme, including giving students choice
2 Individualize assessment
3 Helping students develop their individual interests, identities, and career paths
4 Encouraging students to take responsibility for their learning

---

Individualize the programme, including giving students choice

All students in a class share the same curriculum and learning community, but within that context there is need for choice and individualization if students are to develop autonomy and resilience. This is illustrated by Paul, a Grade 7/8 teacher in his fourteenth year who gives his students "a fair amount" of choice, especially in history:

In their research project on New France they can choose one of the historical figures we have talked about and do a more in-depth project on that person. And they can present their work in a number of ways. Some of them just like to write essays, others like to make a PowerPoint, and others make a poster. One made a replica of a rifle and wrote about it, another made some traditional clothes.

Kira, a Kindergarten teacher in her seventh year said:

> You have to individualize everything. For example, some kids will need pencil grips to write whereas others won't; to keep calm, a student may need a squishy ball under the desk or a little stretch band; if we give a math assessment, a child might need to go to the carpet instead of doing it at their seat.

Linda, also in her seventh year and a teacher of lower elementary students reported:

> When I meet and conference with the kids, I have my index cards ready to record the individual goals they are working on. I quickly jot them down and then make sure they have what they need in their book bag, whether it is sight words they're working on or a word family ... [And when] we had a non-fiction unit on animals and informational writing, I had a lot of photos of animals and non-fiction books and the kids could choose which animal they wanted to study. They were very interested and engaged, it was one of their favourites.

Individualize assessment

If students are to grow in autonomy, they have to feel they are being assessed in a way that respects their individual talents and academic and life directions. This helps them develop their own learning style and approach to life. For example, a student who is strong in non-fiction reading and writing should be able to get as high a literacy mark as a student whose talent lies more in fiction reading and creative writing. Jody, an elementary teacher in her tenth year, said:

> Over time you realize that everybody is at a different place, and you should be celebrating the kid who went from writing one to two sentences as much as the one who went from five to ten sentences. It's like how some of us learn to walk in a year and others in two years, but we're now all walking. With reading and writing, we're now all readers and writers ... it's just a matter of when it happens.

Of course, classroom assessment is time-consuming. But traditional assessment methods are also very labour-intensive; and time can be saved by doing much of the assessment incidentally while engaging in other teaching activities, and by doing it during class time rather than in evenings or on the weekend. Serena, a Grade 5/6 teacher with 15 years' experience, described such an approach: "Much of the assessment I do is observational and anecdotal ... it's very holistic and individualised". She gave an example of how she goes about it:

> We ended the year with a heritage fair and one thing the kids had to do was write essays. And I gave them a lot of choice. The topic was communities,

but the kids could interpret that however they wanted. And one kid was hugely ambitious, writing an extensive essay … And it wasn't well edited, for example he didn't capitalise well … But we can't look at only those things and discredit his really ambitious effort, how much he learned, and how much his understanding had changed.

So everyone receives individualized feedback, and it's very much about the intangibles, like "You took a really ambitious topic and sometimes that means it doesn't work out the way you want, but please keep that ambition, and maybe we need to work on some time management".

Helping students develop their individual interests, identities, and career paths

As well as individualizing teaching and assessment, there are other ways to support students in developing a sense of themselves and possible life directions. This can be done through discussion – individually or in class – and giving students opportunities to pursue such questions on their own. Nancy, a Grade 6–8 art teacher in her thirteenth year, commented:

Schools tend to teach you to fit in and listen rather than think outside the box, push your limits, and take those risks an entrepreneur needs to take. So I talk with my students about possible options. And in art classes I talk about what they are good at and how maybe if you are not in a sense "good" at art, it might still be involved in your career. Just like with English or math, it may be something you have to work hard at but it is still important, because whatever your career you need to be able to communicate and to use math to some extent. And I talk about perseverance and trying to get work in on time, and we reflect on different career possibilities.

Similarly, Anna – also in her thirteenth year and teaching Grade SK/1 – reported:

We talk about being "community helpers" and what they want to be when they grow up … and that is going to change a million times, but the biggest thing is to let them explore their interests; so if they love drawing, or love computers, give them the outlet to explore those fully, because they can learn so much at this age … And there are children who love to be creative, so I let them do art until the cows come home. They are so young and have a lot of time to figure out what they want to do, but at least those crucial skills are being developed.

Encouraging students to take responsibility for their learning

Another strategy for fostering autonomy and resilience is to support students in taking charge of their own learning and development, rather than constantly telling them what to do. Jeannie, for example, with 14 years' experience, spoke of her approach to her Grade 1 students:

I want my kids to be excited about learning, and not read every night because I or their parents tell them to. I want them to realize the value of reading: that it can be for entertainment or pleasure or they're really curious about something – sharks, for example – or they think Captain Underpants is hilarious so they want to read more of his books. I want them to develop a love of learning, to seek understanding and be curious.

Similarly, Felicity in her tenth year and teaching combined Grade 7/8 students observed: "Often I find I'm working harder than the kids, which is not right. So I think of ways to transfer the responsibility onto them, to help them develop a feeling of motivation and self-worth and knowing when they've done a good job and wanting to do well". And David, now a high school principal in his fourteenth year said:

Students need to have a level of accountability for their learning, and I'm not talking about this or that assignment or the grade they get, but seeing that learning is not done to them but is an action they take. They need to understand that a teacher will take them to a certain point but if they want to move beyond that, they have to become actively involved.

Students need to learn their "fit" in the world; and that is going to change over the years, but they need to understand how their interests are reflected in the world and how they are going to move forward. What opportunities am I going to have? Where am I going to be? They need self-exploration and knowing themselves, and recognizing that it's okay not to be good at certain things.

Chapter summary

Autonomy is an area of personal development often mentioned by writers on twenty-first-century learning. If young people are to achieve wellbeing and be contributing citizens, they have to hone a personal way of life that is suited to their individual needs, talents, and circumstances, as well as the needs of others.

A good communal and societal way of life is important too, but schooling in previous centuries focused almost entirely on the larger society, to the neglect of individual health and wellbeing. What we are proposing is a balance of the two. This is not a selfish approach but one that recognizes the essential role of strong individuals in meeting the needs of other people and society generally.

Promoting student autonomy need not be at the expense of academic knowledge. While fostering autonomy requires going well beyond academic topics, it can in fact strengthen academic learning by helping students see the relevance of subject content and develop skills of individual inquiry.

Developing *resilience*, another key twenty-first-century learning goal, is dependent on acquiring autonomy. If people are to have the strength and motivation to persist in particular activities and in life generally, they need to have an individual way of life that makes sense to them and provides for their personal wellbeing.

How can teachers promote student autonomy and resilience while also fostering the subject learning that the system requires? Strategies include: individualizing teaching and learning; giving students choice; individualizing assessment; helping students develop their own interests, identities, and career path; and encouraging students to take responsibility for their own learning and behaviour.

Questions for reflection and discussion

1 Why is autonomy important?
2 How are autonomy and resilience connected?
3 How can teachers promote autonomy and resilience in students while also teaching sufficient subject content?

2 Principle 2: Foster critical thinking and problem-solving

Inquiry learning is ... not just them doing whatever they want ... it's teaching them how to learn, so once they've done it enough times they can say: "I wonder about this, I'll do some research and get some books and figure it out".
— Paul, a Grade 3/4 teacher in his twelfth year

The Principle, its importance, and some challenges

As we continue to explore teaching for personal development, we turn to skills of critical thinking and problem-solving. Students may be autonomous and resilient, as discussed in the previous chapter, but not realize how disputed and open to interpretation much knowledge is. In the 21st century, students need to learn to think critically and solve problems. This is important in the workplace and many other life settings.

In the past, schools focused mainly on transmitting to students what the "experts" think. But knowledge is complex and tentative, and often partly personal or local; so while expert knowledge is useful, it is seldom clear-cut or sufficient on its own. Students need to become aware of this and learn how to critique existing ideas – both their own and other people's – and go on to build new knowledge.

What are critical thinking and problem-solving?

The emphasis on critical thinking by education academics in recent times is an important advance. But the word "critical" has not always caught on with teachers: in our research we have found that, after their preparation programme, they tend not to talk about it much. It is a rather technical term, and also can have negative connotations: calling someone "critical" is usually not a compliment in the everyday world. While keeping the basic idea, then, it is sometimes best to use other current terms such as "reflective" or "thoughtful". Whatever term we prefer, however – and we often use "critical" – the important thing is to be clear about the underlying issues.

Being *critical* in the sense we propose involves resisting adopting ideas just because they have been articulated – by experts or others – and rather continuing to explore and think carefully about them. Applied to schooling, this is the opposite of the traditional approach where students had largely to memorize and regurgitate expert knowledge regardless of what they thought of it. Of course, learning what experts have said is very important, but students also have to learn how to critique it and go beyond it.

Sometimes what is referred to as a "critical" position is in fact guided by a rather narrow and fixed approach to a set of issues. Use of the term critical to privilege a particular position in this way has again given some people a negative view of the term. Teachers have to realize that such usage is incompatible with the basic concept of being critical, which implies weighing many points of view and being open to revising our position: this is the outlook students need to be helped to acquire.

Problem-solving has a meaning closely related to critical thinking. With problem-solving the focus is on actions as well as ideas, but in either case careful reflection – often combined with experimentation – is required instead of simple reliance on expert opinion. The role of learners in this context is sometimes referred to as "construction" of ideas and courses of action, rather than just acceptance of the ready-made. "Construction of knowledge" is again a rather technical term that we may not always wish to use in everyday conversation, but the underlying idea is crucial.

In attempting to promote a problem-solving or "inquiry" approach, some educators advocate a very open pedagogy where students come up with nearly all questions and answers on their own. This is not the interpretation we are proposing. We believe teachers should often suggest questions for problem-based and inquiry learning, as well as possible answers: a considerable amount of teacher input is important for optimal learning. However, students should *also* be allowed input and *in the end* be able to reach their own conclusions. The solution to mindless inculcation is not to avoid teacher input but rather to encourage students – and give them time and opportunity – to critique and modify ideas, whether from the teacher or other sources.

Why is it important to foster critical thinking and problem-solving?

Thinking critically (or reflectively or carefully) and being a problem-solver results in students arriving at sounder and deeper understandings and has a great deal of payoff in the workplace and life generally. It enables young people to go beyond passive "book learning" or just looking things up online to being able to function effectively in a wide range of situations.

Not only are the ideas and practices arrived at through critical thinking and problem-solving sounder at a general level, they are better adapted to the individual needs and insights of students. Knowledge should in part be constructed (or built) by individuals in order to draw on their own experience and adapt it to their distinctive needs and life situation. Critical thinking and problem-solving are essential to this construction process.

A critical, problem-solving approach to teaching and learning is also more enjoyable and engaging, for students and teachers alike. As well as acquiring knowledge of what experts think, which can be enjoyable in itself, students are actively involved in knowledge development, again an often satisfying pursuit. There are widespread reports today of students being bored much of the time in school. We believe this is due partly to the lack of relevance of what they are studying, but also the absence of challenge and personal involvement.

As well as helping the individual, a critical, problem-solving approach enhances classrooms, local communities, and whole societies. Immediately it helps the classroom community, as students and the teacher listen to each other, get to know each other better, and acquire closer relationships. Beyond the classroom, prejudices are reduced and students are open to broader and more fruitful relationships as they go into the world. To summarize:

Reasons for fostering critical thinking and problem-solving

- Students develop sounder ideas and understand them more deeply
- They acquire essential problem-solving skills and habits
- Learning is better adapted to student needs, talents, and experiences
- Learning becomes more enjoyable and engaging
- The classroom community and teacher–student relationship are enhanced
- Students are better prepared to be open, inclusive, contributing members of society

---

What are the challenges of fostering critical thinking and problem-solving?

Promoting critical thinking and problem-solving in students involves challenges teachers need to be aware of and work to overcome. They include:

Largely uncritical views of knowledge. Parents, politicians, education administrators, and many others often assume that academic knowledge is an established fact and hence there is little need to spend time on critical assessment and inquiry learning. It is thought that the great works of literature have been identified, history has been accurately recorded, and the science in textbooks is clear and beyond dispute. Questioning this outlook can open teachers to criticism and even professional disadvantage.

A detailed, mandated curriculum. Even where public authorities and school administrators see the need for elements of critical thinking and problem-solving, they often still insist that teachers cover so much subject content that it is challenging to find time to go in these directions.

Teachers' own education was not like this. Most teachers were themselves educated in a largely transmission-oriented way. This means that not only have they not seen a more critical, problem-oriented pedagogy in action, they often at some level retain many of the traditional assumptions about knowledge and its transmission.

Teaching in this way involves more time and work, at least initially. We believe it is often possible *both* to teach mandated content *and* foster a critical, problem-oriented approach to learning, but acquiring the ability to do this takes time. It is usually only possible to shift one's pedagogy in this direction in a few major areas each year.

Once again, we believe these challenges can be overcome to a considerable extent, but pre-service and in-service teachers need to be aware of them and helped to deal with them.

Theory/research basis for teaching critical thinking and problem-solving

Critical thinking is often seen as an essential 21st-century skill. Bellanca refers to "the promotion of critical thinking, problem solving, and collaboration as the heart of a 21st century school transformation" (2010: 11). He traces this approach back to classical Greek times when "Socrates peppered his students with question after question", and also to late 19th-century Deweyan "experimental education" and "project-based learning" (pp. 11–12). He sees the shift beyond 20th-century uncritical memorization of subject content as necessary for "advanced learning and living in the global information society" (p. 10).

Authors do not always use the word "critical" to refer to this way of thinking. A common alternative is "reflective" (Pollard et al., 2019; Zeichner and Liston, 2014). As noted earlier, we believe it may sometimes be better to use another term because of the technical and often negative connotations of "critical". As well as "reflective", other terms used for the same basic idea are "innovative", "creative", and an "inquiry" approach.

The justification of a critical approach to teaching and learning is closely related to the reasons for adopting a "constructivist" outlook, a widely embraced position in education today. Even with respect to natural science, Belova, Stuckey, Marks, and Eilks maintain that in top-level scientific texts, the content is "still under debate" pending recognition by the scientific community, and "[e]very step away from the science core entails further steps of selection, simplification, and interpretation" (2015: 187). This means that the great majority (perhaps all) of those who teach science in university and school settings already have a simplified, interpreted, and possibly disputed version of particular subject content, and their students need to be made aware of this and helped to develop a similar critical, constructivist approach to knowledge, whether scientific, moral, personal, social, or ecological.

Problem-solving is also widely regarded as a 21st-century competence. It is closely tied to critical thinking and autonomy, as discussed in Chapter 1, as it involves questioning, arriving at new solutions, being innovative, and relating solutions to one's own needs. Trilling and Fadel maintain that the 21st-century global economy requires "higher levels of imagination, creativity, and innovation to continually invent new and better services and products for the global marketplace ... Beyond meeting the new demands of 21st century work [such skills] have long been at the heart of what it takes to become a self-reliant life-long learner" (2009: 49).

Strategies for fostering critical thinking and problem-solving

[W]e did a lot of independent research projects where, for example, they had to do writing but they could write about any topic they wanted.
– Gail, in her eleventh year and in a resource role,
previously a teacher of Grade 1

As discussed, helping students become critical thinkers and problem-solvers involves going beyond the top-down teaching and rote learning so common in the past. Instead of just learning content, students need opportunities to make judgements and build new ideas and practices. Here is an overview of the strategies we propose:

> **Strategies for fostering student critical thinking and problem-solving**
>
> 1 Making teaching and learning relevant
> 2 Inquiry learning and problem-based learning
> 3 Extensive talk by all students
> 4 Choice in projects, assignments, and activities

Making teaching and learning relevant

If students are to think critically and learn to solve problems, the topics and issues dealt with in class should as far as possible be ones they can relate to. Only then can they learn to make judgements about ideas and practices and genuinely solve problems. They need to be exploring the "real world" – their own and other people's. Along these lines, Grade 5 teacher Kelly in her tenth year said she takes students on a lot of field trips, "... so they can connect to the 'mess' of wherever we are going through. They learn how to engage with the public, share space, and be part of a bigger city instead of just their neighbourhood". She also works to foster social skills such as building friendships and navigating relationships, because "at this stage (age 10) they are starting to care about who and what is cool and build friendships and the whole puberty thing; and one thing I do is encourage them to identify feelings and tell their peers how they feel when they act in certain ways".

Similarly, Marisa, a Grade 1 teacher in her thirteenth year commented: "I'm getting better at implementing a real-world emphasis, and it depends on the grade you're in: a real-world experience for Grade 5 is going to be different than for Grade 1". She elaborated on how she makes learning relevant to her students:

> For the last three or four years we have been an eco-school and many of our real-world experiences have been around eco-literacy ... I'm getting better at accessing readings and videos and using human resources like inviting people to come into the class and share their expertise ... And some social studies topics are not very relevant to my students, so you have to weed some of them out and choose learning expectations relevant to your group.

Along the same lines, Wanda, also in her thirteenth year and a Grade 2 teacher stated:

> In science when I give them a unit on animals and the different types and species and how they exist and change ... we go to the African Lion Safari and the students are asking, why do certain animals look the way they do and have these and these characteristics, and this leads into the curriculum topic we're studying. And I ask them about their own experiences with animals, owning or caring for them.

Inquiry learning and problem-based learning

As discussed before, inquiry learning and problem-based learning facilitate growth in critical thinking and problem-solving. Students need to see themselves as thinking and investigating rather than just learning what others believe and have said. It is important for the teacher to realize, however, that the questions do not all have to come from the students; and also that inquiry and problem-based learning can be combined to a large extent with teaching-required curriculum content.

Sophia, a Kindergarten teacher with 10 years' experience strongly advocates the "Reggio-inspired" inquiry approach developed by the Reggio Amelia school district in Italy. She commented:

> I'm still loving teaching [partly because] I've implemented the Reggio-inspired philosophy over the years. This is an inquiry-based programme where the child constructs their own learning, based solidly in what they are interested in. For example, my students were interested in snow and snowflakes, so we investigated snow to the *n*th degree based on their questions and ideas. And the teacher documents what students learn, both to inspire further learning and to celebrate their learning: the children and also the teacher, the administration, and the parents see what they have learned.

Paul, with 12 years under his belt and a teacher of Grade 3/4 students emphasized the need for a balance between open-ended inquiry and teacher planning:

Inquiry learning is where you basically present the topic and then they come up with questions they want to know about and do research on, and also ways of presenting it. It's student-led but does need some guidance, it's not just them doing whatever they want. But it's teaching them how to learn, so once they've done it enough times they can say: "I wonder about this, I'll do some research and get some books and figure it out".

Similarly, Nina, now in her tenth year and teaching Grade 2 made clear the extensive role the teacher plays in inquiry learning:

So, we're studying Picasso as part of our art appreciation theme. We've read books about him, and at this point in the year (the final month) we've done so much that when I say I want them to generate their questions, they're all up for it. Basically what we're doing is trying to write Picasso's biography, because I often find that's what the kids are interested in ... And I have some books about him ... One is about how he had a little Dachshund dog called Lumpito, and it is called *The Boy who Bit Picasso*, which is a true story. And within the story there is a wonderful explanation of cubism. And we also look at some of his sculptures, which I'm finding the kids are also very interested in. But I listen to their questions. I could have said this is what we are going to learn about him and we will do this and this, and I do have a general lesson plan; but until I listen to the kids I don't know exactly what direction we're going in.

Extensive talk by all students

Learning to be critical and solve problems is helped greatly if *all* students (not just a vocal few) have many opportunities to express their views in class. Such an approach means the teacher doesn't have as much time to talk, but that in turn can boost the ownership students feel; and teacher input can still be substantial through frequent "mini-lessons" and providing students with print materials and links to internet sources. Vera, a Grade 3 teacher in her fourteenth year spoke of the importance of student talk:

Over the past few years I've shifted in terms of recognizing that I am not the one with all the answers. And I guess that came when I started teaching Grade 3, because they are the leaders in primary ... So when I talk to my kids now, I very rarely have a teacher tone. I am pretty real with them: this is me and this is how I interact with everyone, including you. If I have to use my teacher voice, then you know you are out of control; otherwise I am just going to talk to you like the teacher over there, or the principal over there, like this is who I am. Because I want the kids to feel safe and comfortable enough in our classroom to be who they are in front of everyone.

Marisa, a Grade 5 teacher with 8 years' experience, maintained that students should be allowed to talk quite a bit in class, even while they are doing other things:

Every teacher has a different tolerance level, but I give my students permission to talk a fair amount; it's partly so they can help each other out but also because developmentally it's right. They're ten or eleven years old and it's important to them to be able to talk to their friends. So if I can get them to work and talk at the same time, everyone's going to win.

Anita, in her twelfth year and a teacher of Grade 8 stressed the importance of everyone talking, whatever their personalities:

Some students are very introverted or shy but I think it is important for them to speak in class – although I am also okay with just going and talking to them one-on-one, or making sure they talk when they are in a group ... And I think it is important for them to talk with each other and develop communication skills. As you saw today I was choosing people to talk by pulling popsicle-sticks with names on them, because otherwise I have the same two students putting up their hand all the time ... And when they're working in a group I have them all talking by using "think-pair-share". And I tell them, "everyone in your group needs to know what you talked about because I'm going to call on one person from each group to tell the whole class"; and I don't tell them who it is going to be ahead of time.

Choice in projects, assignments, and activities

If students are to learn to inquire and solve problems, they have to be given a lot of choice in what they do. The teachers in our study grew over the years in the amount of choice they gave students and the strategies they used to promote choice. Tanya, serving as a K-8 instructional coach in maths and social studies in her fifteenth year, commented:

I'm much more comfortable now saying to them, "these are the curriculum expectations and this is broadly what you need to do to show you have met them, but you can do it in any way you feel most comfortable with" ... Giving them choice shows you respect them and see them as competent and helps with that positive relationship you have with them ... it shifts the power structure in the classroom.

Gail, now in her eleventh year and in a resource role but previously a Grade 1 teacher said she gave a lot of choice to students, explaining how she did it:

[W]hen I taught Grade 1 we did a lot of independent research projects where, for example, they had to do writing but they could write about any topic they wanted. And in terms of how they were going to get information for what they were going to write, they had a lot of choice. Do you want to go to the library and get a book? Do you want to go on the iPad and find something? Do you want to watch a documentary?

So trying to help them to figure out what works best for them and who they are as learners, how they learn best and what they like. I always go back to parenting or even just to people in general: if we're doing something we're interested in we're going to do a great job, and we're going to stay focused on it a lot longer. We're not going to dig our heels in and there will be less behavioural issues. And I think it's on the road to helping them be independent, when they start to figure out these things for themselves and advocate for themselves.

Chapter summary

Critical thinking involves avoiding adopting ideas just because they have been stated – by experts or others – and instead thinking carefully about them. Other terms can be used such as "reflective" and "thoughtful" – and may be preferable in some contexts – but the same basic idea needs to be preserved.

Problem-solving is closely related to critical thinking. It focuses on actions as well as ideas and often includes practical experimentation. But as with critical thinking, there is weighing of ideas and practices rather than simple acceptance.

Schools in the past often focused mainly on memorization of "expert" and "established" ideas. In the 21st century, teachers need to move strongly towards critical thinking and problem-solving because people are now expected to have these abilities in many settings and have many more opportunities to do so.

A critical, inquiry approach does not mean that "anything goes". Teachers should continue to share their ideas and those of experts with students and propose questions for consideration. Some ideas and practices are better than others – which is precisely why being critical is important. However, students should be encouraged to reach their own conclusions.

Many strategies are available to teachers to foster critical thinking and problem-solving, while also teaching subject content. These include: choosing relevant topics and content (so grappling with the issues is meaningful to students); encouraging inquiry learning and problem-based learning; ensuring that all students talk often in class (so they can develop their own ideas and share them with others); and supporting choice in projects, assignments, and other learning activities.

Questions for reflection and discussion

1 What is critical thinking and why is it important?
2 What are problem-solving, problem-based learning, and inquiry learning and why are they important?
3 How are critical thinking and problem-solving connected?
4 How can teachers promote critical thinking and problem-solving?

3 Principle 3: Support mental health development

I just remind them that everybody is different ... always telling them that we can't be good at everything, but we will definitely find our niche ... we all have different abilities and skills.

— John, a teacher of K-6 health and physical education and dance in his thirteenth year

The Principle, its importance, and some challenges

An area of student personal development often emphasized in the 21st century is mental health. However, the time classroom teachers actually spend promoting mental health is often quite limited, for various reasons: they feel it is not really their role; they are not adequately trained for it; and they do not have enough time for it given the amount of subject content they have to cover. In this chapter, we will make the case for teachers attending to their students' mental health while also addressing these concerns.

Apart from its direct benefits, fostering the mental health of students is important as a basis for other necessary 21st-century attainments, such as resilience explored in Chapter 1, overall life satisfaction and motivation to be talked about in Chapter 4, and general social development to be discussed in Part 2.

Many studies have concluded that the mental health of young people today is declining steadily (and of course Covid-19 has exacerbated this situation). This was certainly the overwhelming view of the teachers in our longitudinal study. So it is today an even more pressing learning need than in the previous century. But precisely what is meant by mental health, and what can teachers do to promote it in their students?

What is meant by supporting mental health development?

If we are to see fostering student mental health as an integral part of teaching in mainstream classrooms, we need to have a rather broad understanding of what it is. We cannot view it simply as a medical area, with medication and formal therapy the only solutions (although teachers are sometimes asked to distribute medication or help with some aspect of formal therapy).

One task often mentioned by those who suggest mainstream teachers should have a role in fostering mental health is the promotion of "mindfulness", both as a classroom activity and a life skill students can take with them into the future. Mindfulness includes meditation and certain ways of reflecting about oneself, life, and the world generally. While some people may not see the practice of mindfulness as mental-health related, it is very widely described as such – and we agree, assuming the broad definition of mental health noted above.

Another type of mental health support often discussed is assisting students with general life management. Teachers traditionally have helped students with aspects of their life such as keeping a diary, work habits, and so on. This can be taken further and used to support students in mental health-related areas such as stress management and developing a positive sense of self.

Yet another way to help students with their mental health is teaching them how to focus their attention, such as on realities rather than (too many) fantasies, on positives rather than (too many) negatives. This has similarities to cognitive behavioural therapy (CBT) and is often referred to as such, but it certainly need not take a strongly "therapeutic" form. Passing on wise sayings from various sources and promoting certain kinds of "self-talk" have been done for millennia by teachers and others.

Why support students' mental health development?

Fostering students' mental health in the broad sense discussed is important simply from a practical point of view. It helps ensure that students interact well with the teacher and their fellow students and attend to their academic work. However, in keeping with the general 21st-century directions we are advocating, we believe teachers should think beyond the immediate context and also consider the general life benefits to students.

Teacher support of students in the mental health area is especially important today because of cuts in special education funding that have brought increased integration of students with "special needs" into mainstream classes (also rightly justified on other grounds). Students often do not have specialists to help them, thus requiring classroom teachers to step in. Even where teachers see this as unfair or inappropriate, they have little choice but to take up the task to some degree, given their concern for the wellbeing of their students and the everyday functioning of their class.

Another reason for teacher involvement in this area is that parents and health professionals need their help. Even if we define mental health in largely medical and therapeutic terms, there will often be parts of it that require teacher assistance. And beyond this, teachers spend more time with students than is possible for health professionals or even, in some cases, their parents, and so have to be relied on for certain kinds of mental health support. Furthermore, teachers sometimes develop a rapport with particular students that places them in a strong position to help in this area.

Finally, helping students with their mental health can enrich the professional experience of teachers and their own life generally. It can make their relationship with their students more enjoyable and fulfilling, and enable them to learn a great deal about the problems people encounter in life and various ways of dealing with them. In summary:

Reasons for supporting students' mental health

- Students get more work done
- The classroom functions more smoothly
- The class community is enhanced
- Students with "special needs" are integrated more fully
- Parents and healthcare professionals are assisted in their roles
- Teachers' own lives are improved
- Above all, students' mental health is enhanced in the present and future

---

What are the challenges of supporting students' mental health development?

Assisting students with their mental health presents many challenges for teachers. We think these can largely be met, but teachers need to be aware of them and of possible ways of addressing them. The challenges include:

Detailed curriculum expectations and standardized testing. Students' mental health issues are enormously varied, as are the ways of addressing them. With standardized curriculum and testing, it is difficult to explore with individual students their distinctive concerns and the types of insight and practice each of them needs.

Scripted teaching approaches. The teaching practices mandated are equally standardized. On the whole, teachers are expected to present explicitly the subject content students are required to know. Fulfilling this agenda of curriculum presentation leaves little room for individual discussion with students or open-ended discussion with the class of mental health concerns that may not even be on the curriculum.

Belief that everyone should learn the same things in the same way. Parents, administrators, and even students themselves often believe that all students should learn the same things, and if they do not, then some of the students are being short-changed. However, with distinctive mental health needs, different students need to learn different things to a considerable extent and be able to pursue them with their own style.

Beliefs about everyone having the same talents. As with learning content, so with talent cultivation and recognition, many of the same goals are pursued for all students. But the mental health problems students encounter often come from failure to recognize their distinctive talents – that everyone is talented in their own way – and the need for each person to embark on their own path of talent development.

Teachers' own highly academic and standardized education. Most teachers have got where they are in part because they succeeded in traditional high school and higher education study. It takes a great deal of re-thinking and re-education to develop new goals and modes of learning of the kind needed to support their students' mental health.

Inadequate understanding of how to pursue and promote mental health. The field of mental health is still greatly under-developed. Teachers share in this general professional and societal deficiency, making it difficult for them to devise ways of supporting their students' mental health.

Theory/research basis for supporting students' mental health development

The UK Department for Education document *Character Education: Framework Guidance* states that: "Schools with clear expectations on behaviour and with well-planned provision for character and personal development can help promote good mental wellbeing" (2019: 4). Similarly, Holt and Grills (2016) maintain that teachers can play a crucial role in "screening," "identification," and "referral" in this area. They can serve as key "student advocates," provided "they receive appropriate education and training around how to recognize warning signs of mental illness and distress" (2016: 2). And beyond identification and referral, the authors say, teachers can support students with mental illness by enhancing the school environment in which they "spend a significant amount of time". Improving this environment "can serve to promote psychological health [and reduce] psychological distress" (ibid.).

In keeping with the purpose of their book, Holt and Grills focus mainly on "students with mental illness" as a sub-group. But in a broad sense of the term, *all* students need to experience mental health and be prepared for a healthy future. For example, all students at times experience bullying and loss of self-esteem – leading to anxiety and low-grade depression – and so need to learn how to stand up to people and value their own distinctive qualities and achievements. And all students struggle at times with lack of motivation in their schoolwork, and can be helped by general discussion of where academic achievement fits into their lives and how to increase their motivation. Phillippo, while concerned in particular with students with identified "autism, learning disabilities, communication disorders, cognitive disabilities, and behavior disorders" (2013: 115), maintains that ordinary classroom teachers can help *all* students as they foster "life skills development" (p. 154) and general "student wellness" (p. 164).

Many researchers believe that promoting student mental health is vital in fostering other 21st-century competences, as we discussed in an earlier section. For example, Goleman and Senge maintain that resilience is increased when students attain greater emotional wellbeing (2014: 29). Similarly, Murphy says that mindfulness "strengthens the part of the brain that controls self-regulation and promotes ... resilience and a variety of positive mental and physical outcomes" (2019: 12).

In promoting mental health it is important to avoid simplistic solutions. For example, according to Oettingen (2014), just teaching "positive thinking" is not enough. Throughout her book, significantly called *Rethinking Positive Thinking*, she advocates the practice of "mental contrasting", which involves seeing both positives and negative at the same time rather than just dwelling on the positives (important though that is at times).

Similarly "mindfulness" (Kabat-Zinn, 2013), a practice proposed in many schools and school systems today and with proven benefits in focusing people's minds on certain things (e.g. their breathing) and away from others (e.g. particular stressors), needs to be supplemented by a complex set of values, insights, and strategies if students are to experience mental and other forms of wellbeing across the spectrum of their lives. Dolan, while agreeing that mindfulness "definitely has its place", says it "only goes so far" (2014: 153), since *many* aspects of our life context need to be attended to if we are to achieve wellbeing. Of course, the definition of mindfulness can be expanded to include all this (Murphy, 2019), but as often described and developed its impact on mental health only goes so far.

Strategies for supporting mental health development

We talked a lot about managing stress, but with the whole class. It was good for the boy with anxiety but also for everyone else: we discussed managing stress, getting enough sleep, taking stress breaks.

– Kelly, a Grade 5 teacher in her tenth year

As we have said, to become substantially involved with mental health teachers have to adopt a broad concept of their role, one that goes beyond just subject teaching. While recognizing the limits to what they can do – since they are not health professionals – they need to see mental health as a vast and complex area in which they can in fact contribute significantly. Here is an overview of the strategies we propose:

Strategies for supporting students' mental health

1 Discussion with individuals and the class about mental health and way of life generally
2 Teaching mindfulness, self-management strategies, etc.
3 Supporting self-esteem development
4 Establishing a safe, predictable, relaxed classroom
5 Connecting to families

Discussion with individuals and the class about mental health and way of life generally

Teachers need to discuss with their students the nature and importance of mental health, strategies for achieving it, and the role of a sound overall approach to life in mental health. Kelly, a teacher of 34 Grade 5 students in her tenth year reported: "I had a few girls with eating issues and awkward body issues, which was tough; and I had a student on the autism spectrum, although he actually fit right into the classroom. Also there was a boy who had anxiety and whose mother had severe anxiety". One of her main strategies in approaching these and other mental health matters was discussion with the class as a whole:

> We talked a lot about managing stress, but with the whole class. It was good for the boy with anxiety but also for everyone else: we discussed managing stress, getting enough sleep, taking stress breaks. We also talked about zones of regulation, and soon without me even asking them the kids started saying, "I'm in the blue zone" if they needed to do something to cheer them up. And two girls were in the school's Stop Stigma Club and they told us, "Oh today we are going to do pushing the clouds away, a strategy for pushing your stress". So they taught all the kids that, it was talked about and discussed, it wasn't this hidden thing in the corner.

Teaching mindfulness, self-management strategies, etc.

As noted earlier, mindfulness is being spoken of a lot today as a means of promoting mental health among students, along with other ways to manage emotions, outlooks, and behaviour. Teaching Grade 2/3 in her thirteenth year, Nina reported that she participates in a school-wide effort to teach mindfulness: "This year our school started a daily 5-minute mindfulness session. We have a teacher who is also a yoga instructor, and she does it over the PA for 5 minutes just before lunch". Nina supports this initiative, although the logistics are still being worked out. She also spoke of other techniques she uses, some of which perhaps fall under mindfulness:

> One thing I've started over the last few years is breathing. When they are starting a really important task and need to focus, they do their breathing. They breathe in through the nose, and out through the mouth. And it works, especially for the Grade 3s when they are starting their year-end standardized testing. And because we've done it all year, they are used to it. Another thing we do is the pat on the back, give yourself a pat on the back – or a hug; and it's awesome. And I say to them, give yourself a little self-love. And these are little things they can do by themselves as well.

Supporting self-esteem development

Self-esteem is a key factor in mental health, with implications for depression, anxiety, bullying, and so on. To help in this area, Kendra, a Grade 8 teacher at a lower SES school and with 12 years' experience gives her students opportunities to succeed at sports:

> At this school many kids don't have a lot of parental support in some ways, so I've had to think about how to approach that and get kids involved who go straight home after school and don't join extracurricular sports. What I do is organize lunchtime intramural games to build up skills; and this year I've amped it up, and for Grades 7 and 8 I run every sports team except basketball. Often I let them take ownership of the team and I just do the permission forms ... And you feel a sense of accomplishment. They may not get the best grades and you may never get any teacher gifts from them, but you've taught them how to play something and they're so happy to have learned it.

John, the teacher with 13 years' experience we came across earlier in the chapter, talks directly with students about their self-image:

> I just remind them that everybody is different. And we talk sometimes about football, soccer, hockey perhaps. Everybody has a different ability or body size. Maybe you can run all day, so you're a midfielder in soccer. Or you have an intense streaking speed and always know where to position yourself, so you're a striker. Or you can really pounce, jump, focus, so you're a defender or a goalie: you might not be the fastest, but you're a smart person and don't crumble under pressure. Just always telling them that we can't be good at everything, but we will definitely find our niche; just reminding them that we all have different abilities and skills.

Establishing a safe, predictable, relaxed classroom

A key to reducing anxiety is creating a supportive classroom. Linda, who teaches lower primary students and is in her tenth year, talked about how she helps her students feel safe by telling them personal things: "I share family things with them, like that I have a baby, and they love to see a picture of him and hear stories about him. And it's partly to let the kids know that they're safe". And Deirdre, also in her tenth year and who teaches Kindergarten said:

> One thing I do, especially at the beginning of the year when they don't fully trust their teacher, is spend one-on-one time with a few kids each day. And I still do that at the end of the year. Also, I have a special moment with them during choice time, like I go into their centres and engage in play with them and discuss what they're doing. And also using informal assessment and supporting them ... I'm a strict teacher, but even when I'm telling them to sit down and being strict with them, they know that I love them and I'm not afraid to show and talk about those emotions.

Connecting to families

Some people object to classroom teachers helping with mental health on the ground that it is the realm of the family. One way to address this concern while also increasing student support in this area is to work closely with families. Gail, in her tenth year and a Grade 1 teacher noted:

> In parent interviews I talk with the parents about their child and the direction they're going in. There was one student in particular whose parents were aware that he probably had ADHD and had taken him to the doctor but didn't want to medicate him. And he was the best kid, the nicest, would share any- thing, always happy, but he just couldn't sit still and struggled to read. But we were able to get him into a special programme halfway through the year, and whereas he started the year as Not Yet Reading he finished at 16! He is a brilliant thinker and an amazing writer, but he can't read his own writing. And I would say to his parents, he is going to do great things, and I sent home a great report card.

Similarly, Anna, a teacher of SK/1 in her thirteenth year said:

> I definitely consult with parents on mental health issues, like if a child is having anxiety attacks or can't deal with transitions like going to church or the gym. And over time as I get to know the children I can figure out whether I can deal with it or should call mom and dad and talk through it with them. Of course it is a real juggling act when parents are at odds with each other, and I sometimes look at school support and see if we can get a social worker to help with whatever is going on.

Deirdre, a Kindergarten teacher with 10 years' experience reported:

> With one parent it was just incredible. I was at an IEP [individual education plan] meeting about a little boy and his mother turned to me and started crying. And she said: "It's a beautiful thing. I was so scared at the beginning because he is autistic, and he cried every day for 3 months about going to school and still has issues and throws tantrums, but he has made such gains in terms of his social and linguistic skills ... When he was in Pre-K they thought he would have to go to a District 75 school, but by the end of the year his interacting was fine ... He's really bloomed, and I'm so happy you're such a mom to him because I work all the time ... And you've given me so many resources and shown me not to give up and just keep going, because it's going to be okay.

Chapter summary

Mental health is an increasingly pressing concern in certain parts of the world and sectors of society, especially among young people. And apart from being an issue in itself, mental health is an important basis for *other* 21st-century attainments such as resilience and wellbeing.

If teachers are to become involved in supporting student mental health, however, it must be understood quite broadly. It cannot be seen as simply a medical area, with medication and formal therapy the only treatments: it has to include everyday solutions such as mindfulness and cognitive behavioural techniques that ordinary teachers can become involved in promoting.

Mindfulness, cognitive behavioural techniques, and so on are increasingly recommended to teachers for use with their students. They are strategies that have been employed for millennia by teachers, philosophers, religious professionals, and others. They are of value to all students, but can also bring at least some relief to those who have been diagnosed with formal mental illness.

In our view, although mindfulness and cognitive behavioural strategies can be of great assistance to students, even more approaches are needed, especially the development of a sound overall way of life. As several writers have stated, wellbeing requires not only thinking differently in the moment but structuring our environment differently so that it "nudges" us in sound directions and also brings enjoyment and satisfaction in itself.

Strategies teachers can use to help promote mental health among their students include: discussions with individuals and the class about mental health and way of life matters; teaching mindfulness, self-management strategies, etc.; helping students build self-esteem; establishing a safe, predictable, relaxed classroom; and connecting to families regarding mental health issues and strategies.

Questions for reflection and discussion

1 What is mental health?
2 What definition of mental health makes it a legitimate domain for teachers to operate in?
3 How is mental health important for other areas of 21st-century development?
4 How can teachers promote mental health while also meeting system demands for extensive subject teaching?

4 Principle 4: Promote overall wellbeing

Knowledge today is at anyone's fingertips, so now I'm shifting to teaching them skills of how to become successful in life. What are the learning skills you need and the personal skills?

– Anita, a Grade 8 teacher in her thirteenth year

The Principle, its importance, and some challenges

As well as helping students in the specific areas of personal development discussed in Chapters 1–3, teachers need to promote students' *overall* wellbeing. This is important because young people, like people generally, naturally want enjoyment, satisfaction, and "happiness" as much as possible across all their life. Moreover, overall wellbeing is necessary for development in particular areas. For example, resilience and mental health require at least a minimum general level of satisfaction and happiness.

Helping students develop overall wellbeing is an ambitious task, but it is one teachers should embrace. Young people spend so much of their life in school – up to 18 years if pre-school and college/undergraduate university are included – that it is inappropriate, even cruel, to restrict them just to academic learning and then send them out into the world to learn how to live. And besides, even academic learning can be more effective and enjoyable when combined with general life learning and wellbeing.

What does it mean to promote overall wellbeing?

Traditionally, success in life has generally been seen in terms of just one or a few attainments – for example, knowledge, pleasure, wealth, doing one's duty, helping others. But in fact life is very complex and interconnected, so people have to succeed in many ways in order to experience wellbeing. Accordingly, students need to develop a comprehensive understanding of and approach to life. For example, reading novels can be a great source of insight and enjoyment, but students are unable to appreciate novels very much unless they are familiar with many of the things being explored in them. Similarly, it is difficult for students to understand historical events if they cannot make connections to somewhat similar phenomena in their current everyday reality.

But having a comprehensive understanding of and approach to life is not enough. People's way of life must include many enjoyments, satisfactions, and so on – often called "positive states" or "happiness" – if they are to be sufficiently motivated and energized. Of course, when students begin school they usually already have a way of life that motivates and satisfies them to a degree, one they have been building since birth and that fits their personality, circumstances, etc. Teachers need to respect this foundation, while exposing students to new ideas and pursuits to enhance their life further.

In this chapter, we will talk primarily about *individual* wellbeing, as distinct from that of sub-groups and societies. In schooling, individual wellbeing has often been neglected, the focus instead having been on helping others and being good citizens – which of course are important. But as noted in Chapter 1, unless students develop a sound individual way of life within which they experience enjoyment and satisfaction, they will not have the insight, energy, and motivation to contribute substantially to the welfare of others.

While developing a satisfying individual way of life needs to be emphasized, however, there are many similarities across individuals. For example, good relationships are probably important to everyone, though in varying forms and degrees. Accordingly, there should be joint as well as individual learning about wellbeing.

Why promote student wellbeing?

Helping students develop a satisfying individual way of life is somewhat controversial because it can be seen as too self-centred, and also as getting in the way of academic learning. But we believe it is essential for several reasons, and it is something that is increasingly advocated today by educators, social scientists, and popular writers.

The main reason for helping students with their overall wellbeing is to enhance their life, both now and in the future. Academic learning is just one aspect of life. Accordingly, given that students are in school full-time for so long, they should not have to spend all that time solely on academic learning, to the neglect of life learning.

Even from the point of view of academic learning, attention to wellbeing is important because it increases students' engagement and satisfaction, which in turn ensures that they concentrate and participate more fully. Just "covering" subject content does not necessarily mean they will learn it. Again in terms of academic learning, a wellbeing emphasis deepens students' learning by helping them connect their ideas to the real world, including their own needs and circumstances. In other words, it aids their "construction" of knowledge, which is widely advocated today.

A focus on student wellbeing improves the general atmosphere in the classroom, since students have a sense of belonging and ownership. As a result, the class community is enhanced, collaborative learning is strengthened, and students' social skills are improved. A wellbeing emphasis also improves the teacher–student relationship, as students see that the teacher cares about their happiness and is working to enhance it. In addition, teachers' own wellbeing is increased. They enjoy being in the classroom more, and they themselves learn about how to live, both as they prepare lessons in the area and from the ensuing class discussions. In summary:

Reasons for promoting students' overall wellbeing

- Students' lives are improved, both now and in the future
- Student engagement in academic learning is increased
- Academic learning is deepened by greater connection to their lives
- The classroom atmosphere and community are enhanced
- The teacher–student relationship is improved
- The teacher's own wellbeing is increased

What are the challenges of an emphasis on student wellbeing?

Some people see promoting student wellbeing as encroaching on the role of the family, and so may oppose teaching in the area. Even if most parents approve, just one complaint can be a problem.

What constitutes human wellbeing is somewhat controversial, so teachers often have to take a stand on matters seen as personal, "subjective", or a matter of opinion. They have to develop a rationale for teaching in this area, one that satisfies both themselves and other people to the extent possible.

Teachers have so much subject-teaching to do, it is hard to find time for matters of wellbeing. Even if "doing both" – teaching for subject knowledge *and* relevance – is possible, going down that path takes time and effort.

Teachers have usually not had much experience or training in this area, and funding for in-service training is limited – partly because teaching is seen as a straightforward task requiring little training. Once again, it takes time to for teachers to develop the necessary strategies.

Given traditional views of the role of the teacher, teachers who spend time in this area may get less professional recognition, except from students and some parents. Teachers who are very successful at traditional academic teaching will tend to receive more acclaim.

Once again, we believe these challenges can be met to a considerable degree, but doing so requires additional time and effort, at least initially.

Theory/research basis for promoting overall wellbeing

Many educational theorists and researchers maintain that student wellbeing should be a central goal of schooling, or even *the* central goal. This position of course pre-dates the 21st century, going back for example to Aristotle in ancient Greek times and William James and John Dewey in the nineteenth and twentieth centuries. Late in the 20th century, renowned educational philosopher John

White argued in *Education and the Good Life* that education has "a single over-arching aim: the promotion of the pupil's wellbeing" (1991: 12).

Now in the 21st century, the importance of overall wellbeing is stressed even more. In *Education for Social Justice: Achieving Wellbeing for All*, Chapman and West-Burnham maintain that "social justice means wellbeing [for all], which in turn means happiness; so the role of society, and particularly for government, is to secure happiness" (2010: 37). And in *The Triple Focus: A New Approach to Education*, Goleman and Senge say: "As more parents, educators, and students bring social and emotional learning and systems thinking into schools, we will see happier, calmer, and more personally mature students succeeding in their lives and contributing to vital societal changes" (2014: 12).

As these quotations illustrate, prominent in many scholars' conception of wellbeing is "happiness" or what some call "positive experiences": enjoyment, satisfaction, and so on. However, it is crucial to note that the same writers often speak of the limits to such positivity. Important though wellbeing is as a goal, expecting *too much* of it can in fact undermine happiness by resulting in constant disappointment (Dolan, 2019; Oettingen, 2014). Moreover, the amount of happiness needed varies somewhat from person to person, depending on our personality, circumstances, and other factors. According to Seligman, we should not aim at complete positivity but rather seek to move to "the upper part of [our] set range of happiness" (2002: 120).

Furthermore, what constitutes wellbeing is a complex matter (as we saw with mental health). As Smith and Wilhelm (2002) point out, achieving a "flow" state of happiness is not just a matter of focusing on one thing, such as our work – it requires friendship, achievement, discovery, meaning, and more. In most situations, many conditions need to be fulfilled if we are to be satisfied or happy; and what we do and experience in each situation should as far as possible feed into other aspects of life in order to ensure that it is feasible to be happy.

Another important qualification is that wellbeing should be experienced in the present, not just in the future. Dewey (1916) famously argued that, whereas education has often focused primarily on preparation for the future, if students do not experience a sound approach to life and learning while in school, they will not know what it means or how to achieve it in the future.

Strategies for promoting overall wellbeing

Teachers can promote wellbeing by prioritizing it in the classroom routines. And that doesn't just mean putting on a video and having students dance to it. It has to be bigger than that.

Tanya, a Grade K-6 consultant now in her fourteenth year

As mentioned earlier, teachers need to foster not only the particular skills and healthy mental states discussed in Chapters 1–3 but also students' *overall* wellbeing. Life is complex and comprehensive and has to be addressed across a broad spectrum of areas. Here is an overview of the strategies.

Strategies for promoting students' overall wellbeing

1   Discussing what is important in life and the need for an overall way of life
2   Modelling a good way of life by the teacher and the class community
3   Exploring students' individual identity, goals, career, and way of life
4   Integrating exploration of overall wellbeing into the study of subjects

Discussing what is important in life and the need for an overall way of life

Achieving overall wellbeing requires students to be aware of the *many* goals that are important to human beings and developing a comprehensive way of life that goes in these directions. Discussion with students – both individually and as a class – is a key strategy for helping them develop such goals and life patterns. Nina, a Grade 2 teacher in her tenth year, spoke about how she discusses way of life matters with her students:

> I really don't want kids to have bad manners, and I know that sounds trite but it's important for their wellbeing. So I model it and tell them I expect them to do it in class and with their friends. Similarly, I'll say to them, "it's not really a good thing for you to be sitting with your dirty shoes on your chair: are you going to do that in somebody's living room?" Those are just basic life values and life skills, because you want to get along with people and have them think well of you. And I don't want to sound like I'm a real hardliner or anything, but I talk with them about the need to treat people the way you want to be treated.

John, in his thirteenth year and teaching K-6 physical and health education and dance, highlighted conversations with his students about life matters:

> Obesity is on the rise, and children's physical activity just isn't there. Many students are very comfortable sitting in their house playing on their iPad and using technology to remove them from the real world, whereas I'm trying to bring them back to the world. And I do it through simple things like encouraging them to have pastimes and hobbies, like riding a bike.
>
> I leave school quite late, and often kids are riding by saying, "Look Mr. S, I'm riding my bike today", or their skateboard. And I make a big deal out of it. I stop them and comment on their bike and how much I like it, and how proud I am of them that they're out doing it.

And I put it out there to every student that if there's anything in the way of sports events or dance competitions, I'm willing to attend. And I connect with them about healthy eating as well, through my health programme. So I use enthusiasm and encouragement.

Modelling a good way of life by the teacher and the class community

Apart from discussion about having a positive overall way of life, teachers need to model it in the classroom. Marisa, a Grade 1/2 teacher in her fifteenth year, spoke about how she prioritizes wellbeing and builds it into her classroom:

[The key thing is that] the kids want to be in your class and the parents want their children to be there. Especially now, as a mother, I know the anxiety parents feel the month before school begins – which teacher is my child going to have for the next ten months? And parents have a lot of hope that you're going to welcome their child and yes, educate them, but also just make them happy, every day.

Tanya, now a Grade K-6 consultant in her fourteenth year observed:

Teachers can promote wellbeing by prioritizing it in the classroom routines. And that doesn't just mean putting on a video and having students dance to it. It has to be bigger than that. You need to support children by things like going outside with them and modelling the importance of that with them. And I model it in just how I talk with them: "How was your night, did you play a game with someone, and where did you play?"

And Nina, a Grade 2 teacher in her ninth year said:

I like fun, laughing, watching comedies, seeing the humour in things, just having that enjoyment. So I have that in my own life and I bring it to my classroom. I reflect on it, especially on a stressful day, and ask myself: did we laugh today, did we have that collective group experience of laughing and having the instant vacation laughter gives you? And either I think yes we did or, if I'm not sure, I've got to remember to make sure we do tomorrow. Because we are a community of learners, we're all those wonderful things you read about in books on teaching; and they are kids, they don't want to feel heavy and stressed out.

Exploring students' individual identity, goals, career, and way of life

As well as discussing and modelling wellbeing and way of life at a whole-class level, teachers need to help individual students build their own distinctive good life. Paul, with 13 years' experience and a teacher of Grades 7/8 reported:

Last year we had classroom circles quite often, where we all sat together and people had chances to share; and also students would often come and talk to me about things. And in literacy we did a project called, "Getting There from Here", a kind of career project, where they wrote about what they wanted to do in the future.

I had them describe what they think their adult life will be like, where they are going to live, what kind of home, and are they going to have a family. Then they actually had to price it out: to do that, you need to first do this and that; and they did some writing about it. And a lot of them were surprised, it was a wake-up call.

And I think Grade 7 and 8, it's a good time to realize you have to start working hard, you can't wait till Grade 12 … [But rather than a specific job] I say to them your goal is to create choice for yourself, so then you can make the choice that makes sense to you.

Karen, a teacher of Kindergarten and in her thirteenth year said:

We talk about our strengths. Some of the kids are amazing at puzzles, so I say to others who are not so good, "Why don't you ask Candy for help, she is the puzzle master"; and that further emphasizes their strengths. And some are amazing at drawing but not so good with their letters and writing, so it's really important to highlight their talent in drawing.

And Marisa, also in her thirteenth year and a Grade 1 teacher reported:

I give them a lot of time for unstructured play, exploring things that interest them and practising their communication skills … Also, self-regulation and responsibility are big in our classroom: everyone has a job or works with others to do things, whether it's stacking chairs or getting the snack ready or cleaning up. Teaching them to be independent and responsible is very important to me, right from the beginning of the year. By the end, they are teacher assistants and help me handle papers and things like that. So they're building independence and responsibility but also confidence, because they come to feel, "I can do this and I can do it on my own".

Integrating exploration of overall wellbeing into the study of subjects

Because time is limited, a key strategy is to address overall wellbeing in the context of subject teaching. This is the "doing both" strategy we present in Chapter 18 when describing 21st-century pedagogy in general.

We saw in the previous section how Paul used essay writing to help students explore possible life directions. In the same way, Anita, a Grade 8 teacher in her thirteenth year said:

Knowledge today is at anyone's fingertips, so now I'm shifting to teaching them skills of how to become successful in life. What are the learning skills you need and the personal skills? Of course I teach curriculum content, but there are ways of relating that to what they are doing.

And Vera, in her tenth year and a teacher of Grade 1, talked about how she addresses way of life matters while teaching literacy:

At the beginning of the year, I decided to address character issues in my literacy programme, delving deeply into texts that lend themselves to discussing character traits: respect, responsibility, integrity, and so forth. And it's been eye opening for me because I always thought those concepts were too complicated for Grade 1. But when you discuss those things with them they take them on. They can look at a character in a children's book, like a Franklin book, for example the story about Franklin finding a camera and using it and not giving it back, and then come up with the most amazing things about integrity – and they're only 6!

Chapter summary

Student personal development, the direction for teaching explored throughout Part 1, covers many areas including autonomy, critical thinking, and mental health. *Overall wellbeing*, the topic of Chapter 4, brings these and other elements together.

The complexity of life requires a comprehensive "way of life" in which the various pieces fit together and support each other. Only with a total way of life can overall wellbeing be achieved. And without a significant degree of wellbeing it is impossible for students to have the engagement and resilience needed for optimal learning and a satisfactory life generally.

Wellbeing is commonly understood to include "positivity" or "happiness". Many people avoid the word happiness on the ground that it promises too much. They prefer terms such as enjoyment, satisfaction, or positivity – or simply wellbeing, with enjoyment and satisfaction assumed. But whatever term we use, the reference to positive experiences is very important, as this is a strong and probably universal aspiration.

What constitutes wellbeing and brings satisfaction varies considerably from one person to another, so people need to develop their own individual way of life. It is important, then, to avoid imposing on students a uniform life approach. However, there are also many overlaps and commonalities in what brings people wellbeing, so students can benefit greatly from discussion of way of life matters with fellow students and the teacher.

Strategies for promoting wellbeing among students include: discussing what is important in life and the need for an overall way of life; modelling a way of life characterized by wellbeing by the teacher and in the class community; supporting students to explore their individual identity, goals, career, and way of life; and exploring ways to achieve wellbeing in the context of studying subject content.

Questions for reflection and discussion

1 What is wellbeing, what are its limits, and how can it be enhanced?
2 Why is wellbeing important?
3 Why is a comprehensive, integrated way of life important?
4 To what extent are their differences and commonalities in wellbeing from one person to another?
5 How can teachers promote overall wellbeing among their students?
6 How can teachers combine helping their students in this area while also promoting their own wellbeing?

Part **2**

Direction II: Teaching for Social Development

Development of the individual person, as discussed in Part 1, is an extremely important dimension of 21st-century learning. But a key aspect of individual development is growth in *social* values, understandings, practices, and skills. In Part 2, we turn to an exploration of social dimensions of development, notably:

Aspects of teaching for social development

Chapter 5: Teach interaction and communication skills
Chapter 6: Teach teamwork and leadership skills
Chapter 7: Promote community participation
Chapter 8: Foster overall social development

The social development we look at here is still largely at a more personal level. However, we will discuss life in institutional settings (including teamwork and leadership) and broader cultural contexts (including community participation). In Part 3, we will address the wider and more public aspects of the social.

In social matters, there is sometimes a tendency to go to either of two extremes. On the one hand, the importance of the social in human wellbeing is underestimated, with educators and others focusing almost exclusively on academic learning and career success. On the other, and especially in popular culture, the importance of the social is often overstated, with those who are socially able being universally acclaimed and those who lack social skills and appeal feeling inferior to the point where it affects their mental health. In Part 2 – and indeed throughout the book – we try to steer a middle course, stressing the importance of social skills and relationships but also the value of many other goals and achievements.

5 | Principle 5: Teach interaction and communication skills

In Grade 5 we should do a lot to assist our students with their social skills and friendship navigation ... helping [them] identify feelings and communicate with their peers ... And it gets easier and [they] get better at it and start doing it without me, which is the whole point.

— Kelly, a Grade 5 teacher in her tenth year

The Principle, its importance, and some challenges

In the past, much of the time in school was spent listening to the teacher, with minimal speaking by students except in response to teacher questions or making formal presentations. In the 21st century, there should be a shift to much more student talk, both formal and informal. This would help students develop the interaction and communication skills now typically needed for the workplace and life generally.

As well as helping with development of these skills, speaking is often more enjoyable and engaging for students than passively watching or listening. Furthermore, it need not detract from subject learning, since students listen more carefully when they have a chance to respond. Underlying lecture-style teaching has been the belief that "if we cover it they will learn it", but this is often not the case, as students' minds are only partly on what is being said.

It might be thought that with all the online exposure today, young people do not need much interaction in school. Rather, they should be given lectures, PowerPoint presentations, and guided reading to teach them the basics. But in fact many of the digital messages students receive – blogs, podcasts, newscasts, etc. – are quite "top-down", just like lectures. Interaction in the classroom is very important if students are to achieve deep learning of how to engage with others and jointly solve theoretical and practical problems.

What is meant by teaching interaction and communication skills?

The classroom *interaction* we are talking about here includes some formal elements but goes beyond them to informal exchanges, more like in daily life. It is true that in some ways interaction in the classroom will always be different from everyday life – for example, students in the classroom have to meet higher standards of respect and inclusion (Paley, 1992). Nevertheless, an everyday quality should be more in evidence in the classroom than in the past, with more friendliness, humour, and personal sharing. This will help students learn how to interact in real-life settings and make learning more enjoyable. Even subject learning will be enhanced, provided it too is more connected to everyday matters than in the past.

Communication skills are closely related to interaction skills, and the processes for acquiring them are similar. Once again, communication *in the classroom* cannot always be exactly the same as in everyday life but can still be more like it, with many informal and personal elements. And these elements are essential if the communication is to be "real" enough to promote real-world skills. The communication experiences that help in this way take various forms: face-to-face, via the internet, one-on-one, and in small or large groups.

Informal interaction and communication with *the teacher* as well as other students is also very important (though again with limits). It helps students to become more engaged, since they usually see teachers as key players in schooling. Students also learn how to interact and communicate with adults as distinct from their peers.

For all this to occur, the class must be a genuinely social community, not just a "learning community" or "community of practice" – although these elements are also very important. For this reason we usually avoid such qualifiers, speaking simply of the class collective as the class or the class community.

Why are interaction and communication skills important?

In the past, work structures and other institutional settings tended to be organized in a top-down way, but in the 21st century they are increasingly interactive. In the workplace and elsewhere, people are not as often now simply told what to do. Courses of action are frequently arrived at through back-and-forth dialogue, with input of many questions, suggestions, and explanations by all parties involved. This approach may seem complicated and unclear but it can actually be more efficient, enabling people to focus on what the real issues and tasks are rather than constantly trying to work out what the hierarchy expects of them.

In the school setting in particular, interaction and communication increase student interest, engagement, and enjoyment. Students learn from each other and the teacher, and they learn how to learn. They come to see knowledge and action as more complex than they had thought, and more dependent on varying circumstances and points of view. Simple, "strong," "decisive" action, previously viewed as the benchmark of efficiency, can in fact leave out many key variables in a decision.

Apart from resulting in deeper insight, communication in the classroom leads to the acquisition of the skills necessary to explain ideas to others and encourages students to join in a course of action. These skills are essential in the workplace but also in everyday life, in shared activity with family, friends, and others. Such communication also makes learning more enjoyable, and enables students to get to know each other and themselves, and to increase their self-respect. In summary:

Reasons for teaching interaction and communication skills

- Workplaces increasingly allow and require these skills
- An interactive approach to decision-making is more effective
- Interaction and communication make learning more engaging and enjoyable
- Such an approach helps students get to know their talents and grow in self-respect
- Class members, including the teacher, get to know each other better

---

What are the challenges of teaching interaction and communication skills?

It is difficult to find time to teach skills of interaction and communication, given the amount of subject content teachers have to "cover". Whether in fact covering all that material in a top-down way is effective is questionable, but developing an alternative pedagogy that combines subject teaching and student interaction and communication is a challenge.

Teachers did not experience this kind of schooling, and so in many cases do not understand what it is or how to implement it. The lecture method – including using PowerPoint – is what they are familiar with, and often what their administration expects.

Parents, and even students, may not see teaching for interaction and communication as central to schooling. Accordingly, teachers have to develop ways to explain to everyone the importance of these skills.

A new kind of teacher–student relationship has to be worked out, involving constant dialogue rather than the teacher telling students what to think. This can undermine parents' and students' respect for the teacher and the teacher's own self-respect.

Theory/research basis for teaching interaction and communication skills

Based partly on the SARS research project, Trilling and Fadel state: "The ability to work effectively and creatively with team members and classmates regardless of differences in culture and style is an essential twenty-first century life skill" (2009: 80). They mention specifically the skill of being able to "interact effectively with others", including knowing "when it's appropriate to listen and when to speak" (p. 81). They emphasize skills of "cross-cultural interaction" in an age when such skills are "more important than ever" (p. 90).

Similarly, Bellanca highlights "communication" as one of the main 21st-century skills that schools need to foster (2010: 1). To facilitate such learning, he advocates an "enriched learning project" approach that "differs from direct instruction and other stand-and-deliver models. [It is] geared to producing standards-aligned outcomes not only for content, but also for critical thinking, collaboration, and communication" (ibid.). He is careful to note that while use of digital tools can enhance student learning under this model, "they are not required – teachers can create highly effective projects without them" (ibid.).

The 2009 OECD report on 21st-century competences emphasizes the need to teach skills appropriate to an increasingly social work environment. "Developments in society and economy require that educational systems equip young people with new skills and competencies which allow them to benefit from the emerging new forms of socialisation" (Ananiadou and Claro, 2009: 5). In the workplace, these skills are "new" because work is going beyond "an industrial mode of production", where the main form of interaction and communication is telling and being told what to do. Young people's education now must help them develop "social values and attitudes [needed for] these new spaces of social life" (p. 5).

The 2019 UK Department for Education *Character Education: Framework Guidance* report states that good schools "contribute to forming well-educated and rounded young adults ready to take their place in the world". This involves overall personal development, including "the acquisition of social confidence and the ability to make points or arguments clearly and constructively, listen attentively to the views of others ... and speak persuasively to an audience" (2019: 7). Such development requires many in-class opportunities to speak. Similarly, Pollard et al. (2019) state that as a key principle of "education for life", "effective pedagogy fosters both individual and social processes and outcomes. Learners should be encouraged and helped to build relationships and communication with others [which requires] giving them a voice" (2019: 115).

Strategies for teaching interaction and communication skills

I try to build their social skills just by talking kindly to kids, whether they want to be first in line, whether they need help with their backpack, whether somebody touches their toy or their tower or pushes them accidentally ... How you speak to them in the classroom really matters.

– Dina, a Kindergarten teacher in her twelfth year

As we have discussed, skills of interaction and communication are essential in today's world. But teaching such skills has not usually been a major focus of the school classroom. Here is an overview of strategies we propose:

Strategies for fostering students' interaction and communication

1 Discussing the importance of interaction and communication skills and how to develop them
2 Modelling good interaction and communication by the teacher and in the class
3 Extensive student talk in class
4 Parties, lunch clubs, etc.

Discussing the importance of interaction and communication skills and how to develop them

As with other skills, individual and class discussion of the importance of inter-action and communication skills and how they can be acquired is helpful in fostering them. Dina, a Kindergarten teacher in her twelfth year described how she goes about it:

> I try to build their social skills just by talking kindly to kids, whether they want to be first in line, whether they need help with their backpack, whether somebody touches their toy or their tower or pushes them accidentally, or kicks them on the carpet because they lack control of their gross motor skills. How you speak to them in the classroom really matters. I myself and some of my teaching partners have been in situations where you just want to snap at a kid; but if you establish that practice they're just going to be snappy back, or they're going to cry. And with parents it's the same: how I talk to them and what they expect of me and what I expect of them. If we're communicating in a nice, kind way from the get-go, we can accomplish anything.

Kelly, who has been in the profession for 10 years, talked about how she helps her Grade 5 students develop their interaction skills:

> In Grade 5 we should do a lot to assist our students with their social skills and friendship navigation because they need it. They're starting to really care about who and what is cool, how they're engaging with their friends, and the whole puberty thing. So I find I'm doing a lot on helping kids identify feelings and communicate with their peers.
>
> And I'm always saying, tell them how you feel, how you felt when he pushed you to the ground or when she didn't want to sit with you. And it's really powerful when you hear them say I felt hurt and the other kid immediately backs down or feels sorry or something that simple. And it gets easier and the kids get better at it, and they start doing it without me, which is the whole point.

Modelling good interaction and communication by the teacher and in the class

Just as important as discussing interaction and communication with students is modelling these skills in the classroom. Wanda, a Grade 3 teacher in her fifteenth year commented:

> I interact with the kids a great deal, because if I get to know them and have a relationship with them and we show respect for each other, and if the students feel they're valued and can trust me and that I'm there to support them, they're much more willing to take the risks I need them to take in the classroom … But if I don't know anything about my kids or about their passions or home lives, I can't gear my programmes to them.
>
> And one of the things I do is hang-out with them. So at recess when we're outside I play soccer with them, I take them outside and we run around and do silly things together. I ask them what they did on the weekend, and if they've had a hockey game, did you win? It's that kind of one-on-one communication and being something other than just their teacher.

Anna, a teacher of Kindergarten with 15 years' experience, mentioned discussions she had with her colleagues about modelling social interaction and communication:

> One thing we talk about as teachers sometimes is how you have to demonstrate to your students what you want to see in them. So just modelling for them how to talk to someone or respond to them appropriately, being mindful of how you interact with them, and not losing patience: always having time to talk and not dismissing them.
>
> Or if you see a child act inappropriately, talk about it as a group: How does it look to push and shove to the front of line? And I act it out, and they'll laugh and say, "Oh, that's bad". And then I get them to demonstrate it and they say things like "That's inappropriate" – they start using the vocabulary too, and learn to say things like, "It doesn't matter, you're only going to be there a second faster".

Extensive student talk in class

In Chapter 2, we saw the importance of student talk in promoting critical thinking and problem-solving, and obviously it is also beneficial in helping students learn how to interact and communicate. Yvonne, a Grade 6/7 teacher in her seventh year reported:

> The current department chair was impressed that I often spent just half an hour teaching a lesson and then for the last 15 minutes had the kids working in pairs. And now I'm really working on that, trying to limit my talk time even more so they have more pair time. It means that the quieter kids who don't raise their hands and often check out during whole-class discussions are getting a chance to talk.

A former Grade 7/8 teacher who became a coordinator, Lucy – with 7 years' experience – stressed the importance of creating a class culture in which students are not afraid to speak freely:

> One thing I pride myself in is that when students first came into my classroom they didn't want to share their writing, in fact they hated it because of the peer ridicule and how the kids would respond. And I told them that in my classroom people should feel free to share their writing, and in fact I'll share my writing. And the rule was that you're not allowed to comment or make a face or anything: if I saw it I would call the kid out because that was it. But after every person shares their reading, you will applaud. And I told them this is a safe zone, there is no judgement, you can share freely.

Parties, lunch clubs, etc.

Apart from formal class discussion, student interaction and communication can take place in other ways and on other occasions. For example, Jill, a Grade 1 teacher in her twelfth year said: "We do our weekly community circles where the kids have freezies and we meet and talk about the week and all of that kind of thing". Nora, in only her third year and a teacher of Grade 9 English reported: "I had a modified English class of just 15 or 16 students, and one thing we did was everyone picked a poem and we had a little mini party, everyone brought food and we sat in a circle and read our poems out loud, and it was great, we loved it".

Paul, with 15 years' teaching behind him and now teaching Grade 7/8 talked about a lunch club he recently established:

> On Mondays I do a kind of lunch club for our students called the Joy Lunch Club, and it's so kids if they want to can have a smaller, quieter setting for lunch. Because the main lunch room is loud and intense, and some of them just retreat into their phones for the whole lunch period. And it tends to be the quieter kids who come to the lunch club but not always; and some of them started bringing Dungeons and Dragons or card games.
>
> And it's honestly one of the highlights of my week, because it's just this room of really nice kids who are there to enjoy each other's company. And there are only two rules: that you make sure you and everyone around you is enjoying themselves, and that we don't use phones or other technology. There are usually at least twenty kids who come, sometimes thirty, and from different classes. The kids are really dedicated to it because they know it will be a pleasant environment with a pleasant vibe; it's totally worked.

Chapter summary

Interaction and communication are key 21st-century skills that people need increasingly in the workplace and other settings. They are an essential aspect of social development, which is the overall direction for teaching explored in Part 2 of the book. We can no longer support the common separation of the social from other dimensions of life.

In Part 1, we discussed the development of an individual way of life. Here we take this into the social sphere. People are distinctive in which people they like to be with and the types of interaction they prefer. Even though social life is intrinsically interpersonal, then, and requires many compromises, it does not involve giving up individual values and behaviour patterns.

In many ways, interaction and communication have become more feasible in the 21st century because of the widespread use of IT. However, the basic norms of social interaction and communication have to be learned and applied in the context of IT use. Students do not learn how to be social in appropriate ways simply by being on their devices.

In the past, most of students' time in school was spent listening to the teacher, with minimal student talk except in response to the teacher. This has to change. It undermines a whole area of learning, is less enjoyable for students and teachers, and deprives students and teachers of opportunities to learn from others and through dialogue.

Strategies for fostering the development of students' interaction and communication include: discussing the importance of interaction and communication and how to develop skills in these areas; modelling good interaction and communication by the teacher and in the class community; extensive student talk in the classroom; and parties, lunch clubs and so on.

Questions for reflection and discussion

1 What are interaction and communication?
2 Why are they important?
3 How do people differ in the place of these elements in their lives?
4 How can teachers support student development in these areas?

6 Principle 6: Teach teamwork and leadership skills

A lot of children come in without social skills, so that is an important area of development because collaboration is a key skill. So I'm helping them learn how to socialize and collaborate on a continual basis in the classroom.
— Sophia, a Kindergarten teacher in her thirteenth year

The Principle, its importance, and some challenges

Many theorists and researchers stress the need for students in the 21st century to learn teamwork and leadership skills in new forms. People today are increasingly working together in a variety of roles, influencing each other reciprocally rather than some giving directions and others following them.

Leadership is not an authoritarian role to the extent it used to be. Proposing a course of action remains important, but it is something everyone may do at certain times rather than just a few designated for this role. Even where certain people are "in authority", they tend to dialogue with those "under them", each learning from the other.

What are teamwork and leadership and how are they enhanced?

As just noted, teamwork and leadership today are more complex and nuanced than often understood in the past. Working effectively as a team involves everyone exercising judgement and doing what they are good at, acting sometimes as a leader and sometimes a follower.

In a sports team, for example, each player has a position and is chosen for it because of their distinctive talents. Playing in a position and being good at it gives each team member an authority and leadership role, although other team members have a say at certain points. The captain technically has final authority, but it is well known that some captains do not exercise very good judgement in certain matters and some overstep their authority. Team members then have to decide whether to just do what they are told or override the captain and face the consequences.

The role of the chair of a meeting is instructive here. It is important to have a chair, but the authority of that person is largely procedural, with substantive decisions made by vote and the chair serving as an expert primarily in meeting management. Teachers are in a good position to think about this. Like a chair they have authority in the classroom, but that does not mean they should always tell their students what to think and do. The role of a parent is somewhat the same: those who draw a line in the sand often find themselves having to move it.

Teamwork and leadership, then, are closely connected. Ordinary team members have to understand the designated leader role, abide by it in certain ways, and exercise leadership themselves in some ways. A team member needs to know how to be a leader and a leader how to be a team member. Each needs to have knowledge, wisdom, and skill regarding the other's role. Some of this is gained through instruction and some through experience and reflection.

Why promote teamwork and leadership?

Given traditional parental, school, and other authority structures, students may not have had much experience of teamwork and sound leadership, but in the 21st century they have to acquire these skills in order to succeed in school, the workplace, and other settings. However, they need to develop the skills in a different form than previously: both teamwork and leadership have to be flexible and interactive.

Even in family and friendship settings, skills of working together and taking the lead are often needed. No matter how good a relationship, a considerable amount of negotiation and taking of turns is involved, respecting and taking advantage of different needs and talents. As Dolan (2014) says, letting someone else make decisions in a given situation often saves time, reduces stress, and opens us to fruitful new directions. However, we all must learn how to take initiative of this kind in a positive, restrained way.

In the classroom, being good team members and leaders is important for learning, since individual students and the teacher have distinctive insights and talents to contribute. Also, working together is often more enjoyable and engaging than working alone: it can result in a kind of "flow" that carries everyone along. But once again, skills of collaborative learning and interactive leadership are often lacking, and have to be taught and modelled in the classroom. To summarize:

Reasons for teaching teamwork and leadership skills

- Teamwork and leadership skills are needed today in the workplace and other settings
- Working in a team can be more enjoyable than working alone
- Teamwork and interactive leadership allow many talents to develop
- They also increase our social experience
- Processes of collaboration and interactive leadership are not well understood

What are the challenges of teaching teamwork and leadership?

Interactive leadership does not come naturally to many teachers, since they do not have training or experience in it. Accordingly, going in this direction will require a great deal of time and effort.

Education systems usually expect teachers to transmit a pre-set curriculum, and it is difficult (though not impossible) to see how this can be reconciled with collaborative learning and interactive leadership.

Many parents, administrators, colleagues, and even students may not expect or appreciate an interactive approach, resulting perhaps in reduced respect, some professional disadvantages, and objections from time to time.

Some students are used to being "in charge" and respected for their superior knowledge, and will resist the move to a collaborative, interactive approach and want to dominate class and small-group discussions, at least initially.

This kind of "soft" leadership requires a different approach to behaviour management, requiring considerable learning and adjustment for teachers. Some students with "discipline problems" may not respond to it initially.

Students have to be prepared for other settings, both within and beyond the school, where a different approach to learning, decision-making, and leadership is followed. This requires a considerable amount of discussion.

Theory/research basis for teaching teamwork and leadership

Regarding *teamwork*, Goleman and Senge advocate educating "the whole child", with a particular emphasis on social and emotional learning (SEL). Focusing on other people, they say, "is the basis of empathy … along with social skill, cooperation, and teamwork" (2014: 29). They propose a "systems" approach to work and life that in their view is at the heart of "our capacity to collaborate [and] our appreciation for what it takes to get things done together" (p. 63). An education based on a systems outlook "builds on these innate capacities and shows how they could truly benefit today's students and society" (p. 63).

Goleman and Senge also talk about the teaching approach needed to foster skills of joint decision-making. Such skills cannot be taught "by traditional pedagogy, where teachers stand in front of classes and deliver information" (2014: 71). Rather, teachers have to use project-based and cooperative methods where students have responsibility and learn jointly with one another. They note, however, that although the value of such methods is widely recognized by educators, they are not often practised because teachers are not trained in them and their use is hindered by the constraints of school culture.

The 2009 OECD report on 21st-century competences includes among the knowledge management skills needed by young people in the 21st century, "analysis and sharing in socially networked environments", adding that "[f]or many young people, schools are the only place where such competencies and skills can be learned" (Ananiadou and Claro, 2009: 5). Bellanca sees collaboration as at "the heart of a 21st century school transformation", and speaks at length about how to create a "collaborative classroom culture" (2010: 11). And Trilling and Fadel, in discussing how to educate for 21st-century skills, stress learning how to "work effectively in diverse teams", including working "with people from a range of social and cultural backgrounds" and "respond[ing] open-mindedly to different ideas and values" (2009: 81). This openness to varied social and cultural backgrounds is important not only for social justice but because such differences can be drawn on "to create new ideas and increase innovation and quality of work" (p. 81).

Turning to *leadership*, again many theorists and researchers emphasize that it is a key 21st-century skill, closely related to teamwork but requiring considerable refinement of our understanding of how to exercise leadership. Trilling and Fadel say that in the 21st century, students should learn leadership skills in school, including how to "[u]se interpersonal and problem-solving skills to influence and guide others" while showing "integrity and ethical behavior in using influence and power" (2009: 85).

Falk talks at length about leadership within a school, arguing for "viewing everyone as a learner and leader". While most of her discussion in this area is about the principal and teaching staff, she includes everyone in the school community – "students, staff, and families alike" (2009: 161). The approach to leadership she advocates and illustrates in detail is one that "enables rather than controls others. It seeks to build the capacities of school community members, including them in decisions that are critical to their lives and their work. Leadership enacts the ideals that the community embraces" (p. 175).

Strategies for teaching teamwork and leadership

> [O]ne of my big things with the Grade 1s, because they are still so little, is giving them the words they need to solve problems, how to speak to someone respectfully while also disagreeing.
>
> Jill, a Grade 1 teacher in her twelfth year

If students are to learn the 21st-century skills of teamwork and leadership, they have to understand the nature and importance of these skills and have opportunities to observe and practise them in the classroom setting. The strategies we propose include:

Strategies for teaching students teamwork and leadership skills

1 Talking about teamwork and leadership
2 Modelling positive, interactive leadership
3 Giving all students experience in teamwork and leadership
4 Building community and inclusion in the classroom

Talking about teamwork and leadership

Students need to understand the nature and importance of teamwork and inter-active leadership because these have not always been emphasized in schooling. And they have to see how these skills connect to other 21st-century skills and approaches such as interaction and problem-solving. Jill, the Grade 1 teacher we met earlier, described how she talks with her students about the importance of being able to work together:

> In my teaching, every day, I work to build relationships with my students and have them learn how to build relationships with each other and work through problems together when they arise. And one of my big things with the Grade 1s, because they are still so little, is giving them the words they need to solve problems, how to speak to someone respectfully while also disagreeing ... And over the years in primary I've increased the time I spend on those basic social skills, because to be able to work and learn together they need to be able to co-exist."

Maria, a Grade 4/5 teacher with 13 years' teaching experience, illustrated how she talks about teamwork with her class:

> Their parents are going to tell them to be a lawyer, a doctor, an engineer, or whatever but they can come to that sort of conclusion later. Meanwhile what we can teach them is teamwork. And I tell my students, whatever you want to be in life it will involve teamwork; even if you want to be the next Drake, he has to work with the sound people and the lighting people, getting ready for his concerts. There are people who travel with him, he has a team of people. And if you don't have the teamwork skills and the social skills to get along with people, no one is going to want to work with you. Even if you want to be an engineer, nobody works alone. Unless you're George R. Martin writing "Game of Thrones" – but even then he had to work with the creative people to make the show. You have to have those skills.

Modelling positive, interactive leadership

As in a sense the "leader" of the class, the teacher is in a good position to model how to lead other people while working with them, rather than just telling them what to do. Anita, a Grade 8 teacher in her fifteenth year, spoke of how to set a certain leadership style:

> You can say the same thing in a very different way, and you can build com-munity by being a role model for positivity. I was talking with a teacher about how a particular student in her class has a problem with authority and expresses it by doing silly things like hiding in the closet, even though he's in Grade 6; and he doesn't respond well to being told "no, don't do that all the time". And we agreed that just rephrasing it can change things for a student. So instead of saying, "stop that, get out of there", we should say things like,

"is everything okay?" So just changing it around, creating that more caring, nurturing environment.

Paul, a Grade 5/6 teacher in his eighth year described how he works to avoid a top-down teaching approach:

> I've been giving my kids quite a bit of independence lately. I have periods of the day that are called flex-time, which basically means they can decide what to work on. And although there are always a few I have to chase around a bit, the majority know that they have to finish their short story (or whatever) because it's due next week. And I do this because I want them to figure out what they need to work on, not just what the teacher said they have to do.

Along the same lines, Grade 5/6 teacher Serena with 14 years' experience said:

> I tell my students that at the end of the day it's their choice; there is very little I can do to make them learn. I can lay out the options but then they are accountable to themselves for their choices ... I had two children this year who cannot sit. And I had talks with them and said, "You can't walk around the classroom and annoy other students", but there are other options: we have a standing desk (and one of them liked that); or, "if you need to go for a walk, just signal me and go, by yourself or with a friend" ... If you make all the decisions in your room things are simpler in a way, but you're taking away their autonomy.

Giving all students experience in teamwork and leadership

Related to the "all students talking" strategy discussed in other chapters, *all* students should have experience in both team membership and leadership roles – for example, all should participate in small groups, report back from groups to the whole class, prepare and deliver debate arguments, and give and respond to (brief) class presentations. Again Maria, the Grade 4/5 teacher with 13 years' teaching experience, commented:

> I think they're too young to know what career path they want to take, but we need to prepare them with the teamwork skills and problem-solving they'll need. It's great that they're learning the basic math, reading, and writing skills required in the workplace, but they should do more working together and problem-solving. That will ultimately prepare them for when they find out the kind of work they enjoy and are good at.

And Jill, the Grade 1 teacher in her twelfth year, spoke of how she teaches interaction skills through the everyday life of the classroom:

> I have high expectations for the kids of how they behave in the classroom, how they treat and talk to each other, and how they treat me; and we do a lot

of talking about those things. But honestly, classroom play is probably the biggest way you get to see how they naturally communicate and what kind of habits they have. So helping them develop through that is a major strategy I use, and they don't even realize they're working on those skills when I pipe in here and there and give them a little nudge ... And because my Grade 1 programme is focused on helping kids learn through play, I use play a lot in their subject learning as well. So they have many opportunities to work with different tools in open spaces and collaborate with each other, which gives them further ways to learn all these skills.

Building community and inclusion in the classroom

Teamwork and interactive leadership require having a social, inclusive approach to other people and a positive concept of oneself. Developing in these ways is facilitated by building community and inclusion in the classroom. Several strategies for going in these directions are presented in other chapters; here there are just a couple of additional examples. Sophia, a Kindergarten teacher in her thirteenth year said:

A lot of children come in without social skills, so that is an important area of development because collaboration is a key skill. So I'm helping them learn how to socialize and collaborate on a continual basis in the classroom. We have community circle twice a day where we talk to each other about what we're interested in, something we've observed, something we've succeeded at, or a strategy we have learned ... So it is sort of celebrating them, building their self-esteem, making them realize that their interests matter and that we can all learn from them.

Miranda, another Kindergarten teacher with 12 years' experience, talked about how she builds community in the classroom and uses the process to foster skills of collaboration:

At the beginning of the year I talk about the zones of regulation and the different feelings, sometimes asking students to share their feelings. And I tell them that we don't always come into the classroom in a happy (green) zone, but we can work to help each other get into that zone from a different zone. (The red zone is angry or frustrated; the yellow is confused or excited; the blue is sad or hurt or hungry; and the green is happy and calm and ready to learn.) And we also talk about family, which is something they can share.

So through this kind of sharing they can feel more confident, stand up and talk to the other students and the teacher, and have a sense of ownership in the classroom. And as they get better at it, we do more sharing time on the carpet and hear different things they're interested in. And that's how we begin to build inquiries in the classroom, by listening to what they have to say, and as they feel more comfortable we can build more inquiries throughout the year.

Chapter summary

Teamwork and leadership are also often cited as areas of 21st-century learning. They are increasingly important and possible in the workplace and other life settings. However, they are more complex and nuanced than often understood in the past. Within teams, different people exercise leadership at different times; and designated "leaders" have to be careful how much authority they exercise if they are to keep team members on board and take maximum advantage of their expertise.

Teamwork and leadership are important components of the social development of students. In order to become effective team members and leaders, students have to learn how to bring social values and skills into teamwork and leadership contexts. Too often in the past these domains were kept separate. As well as being more effective, a social approach to teamwork and leadership can be more engaging and enjoyable.

Strategies for promoting development of teamwork and leadership include: talking with students about teamwork and leadership; modelling of positive, interactive leadership by the teacher; giving all students experience in teamwork and leadership; and building community and inclusion in the classroom so that everyone is respected equally.

Questions for reflection and discussion
1 What are teamwork and leadership and how are they changing?
2 Why is it important to foster teamwork and leadership among students?
3 How do people differ in the place of these elements in their lives?
4 How can teachers support student development in these areas?

7 | Principle 7: Promote community understanding and participation

Classrooms are places where we should be teaching kids how to interact with each other ... how to have respectful relationships at a personal, family, and community level. And they need to understand their own rights ... but also how they should be treating others.

— Carrie, previously a middle-school teacher but
now a vice-principal in her thirteenth year

The Principle, its importance, and some challenges

So far in Part 2 we have focused on particular interpersonal skills needed for the 21st century, in the workplace and other settings. However, these specific skills in turn require broader community understanding, skills, and commitment. In the 21st century there is increasing need for people to have general "community literacy" as a backdrop to achieving workplace effectiveness and other aspects of wellbeing.

With the growing use of online communication and fewer chain-of-command institutional structures, people need more – not less – community literacy so they can participate in the varied types of community that are emerging. And the classroom – whether face-to-face or online – is an ideal setting for developing in the ways required.

At present, the opportunities for community experience and learning in the classroom are often not taken advantage of. Many children see their main relationship as that with the teacher, since he or she is the person they have to satisfy and they are given little time and encouragement to relate collaboratively and socially with their classmates. The opportunities of the classroom should be capitalized on to a greater extent; and this need not be at the expense of academic learning provided such learning is itself conducted in a social, interactive way.

What is involved in promoting community understanding and participation?

There has been a lot of talk in the education literature in recent decades of the need to create a "learning community" or "community of practice" in the classroom, and these are important concepts. But the focus should not be just on academic learning to the neglect of personal and social learning. As mentioned earlier, in this book we use more open-ended terms such as "classroom community" or simply "community" to allow also for the personal and social aspects of classroom life.

In our view, the teacher has a major role to play in building a classroom community, but that has to be done jointly with the students, both because they have a lot to offer and because they will learn a great deal through their joint role. It should not be just a matter of the teacher organizing games and other activities for the class, although there is a place for that.

A class community is different in certain ways from other types of community: neighbourhood, sporting, professional, religious, etc. However, many of the same insights and skills are involved, so rich classroom experiences of community will prepare students for these other contexts. This is another reason why the classroom community should not be seen too narrowly as a *learning* community.

The term "community" might suggest strong physical presence and connection, but as noted above a rich community experience can be created even in an online setting. This is largely a new aspect of teaching that many teachers have only recently begun to master in the context of the Covid-19 pandemic. However, some instructors (ourselves included) have found that with Zoom and similar technologies many of the strategies of community-building used in face-to-face settings can be reproduced online, such as assigning students randomly to small groups, moving to and from breakout rooms, random reporting back from small groups, and having all students in turn present briefly to the group/class as a whole and respond to each other's presentations.

Why promote community understanding and participation?

Building genuine community in the classroom and helping students (and oneself) develop the related understandings, skills, and commitments has immediate payoff for teachers and their students. Students look forward to coming to class and are more engaged at all levels, and teachers also enjoy their work more and find it more fulfilling.

Classroom dialogue and various forms of collaboration are facilitated, as students get to know each other better and come to respect each other as fellow community members. It becomes easier to mix up groups and seating arrangements, which in turn strengthens the community further. Students become more confident in speaking in groups and the whole-class setting and honestly saying what they think.

Social and emotional learning is strengthened. Social skills are developed and friendships are formed in ways that are inclusive rather than exclusive of other community members. Students' emotional wellbeing and mental health are supported as they feel safe and respected in the classroom. Bullying is reduced.

Beyond friendship and immediate social relationships, students acquire understandings of the nature and value of communities in general and what is required to make them possible. In summary:

Reasons for promoting community understanding and participation

- Students look forward to coming to class and are more engaged
- Teachers find their work more enjoyable and fulfilling
- Dialogue and collaborative learning are facilitated
- Social and emotional learning is enhanced
- Students feel safer, and bullying is reduced
- Broader community understandings and skills are developed

What are the challenges of promoting community understanding and participation?

Building community in the classroom requires fostering many skills and values among students. This of course is what we are aiming at and has considerable payoff in the long run, but it takes a great deal of work.

Given the time involved, fitting in required curriculum coverage is challenging. Ways of "doing both" can be developed to a considerable extent, but that also requires a lot of time and effort.

School authorities and local administration may wonder about the value of community-building activities, and see teachers as wasting their time and neglecting their more important tasks.

Teachers may wonder if they will be able to "keep control" in a class-community environment. Once again, we believe that in many ways a community culture can facilitate classroom management, but developing the necessary strategies and structures is a challenge.

Growing class sizes today make developing community and related skills and attitudes more difficult. This is especially so when teaching has to be online: the images on the Zoom checkerboard become very small.

Students often wonder how classroom-type community behaviour can be practised in the outside world, which can be much harsher. Again, it is an ambitious (though rewarding) task to help them learn how to adjust their behaviour to different settings and apply the same principles in a modified form.

Theory/research basis for promoting community understanding and participation

Beyond fostering collaboration as discussed in Chapter 6, many theorists advocate building a strongly social classroom community that is not only enjoyable in itself but also helps students develop community skills and commitments. Dewey long ago famously said: "[E]ducation is essentially a social process.

This quality is realized in the degree in which individuals form a community group". The teacher is a key member of the group, but when education is seen as a community process, the "teacher loses the position of external boss or dictator [and] takes on that of leader of group activities" (1938: 58–59).

Martin (1992, 2011) proposes thinking of the classroom as "the schoolhome", a place where there is a strong emphasis on teachers and students caring for each other and thereby learning how and why to have positive, caring relationships. Similarly, Tranter et al. recommend a "relationship-based approach" to schooling in which "educators work very hard to strengthen belonging in their students, and use a variety of ways to foster a sense of connection and community … [In this environment, students] are more eager to attend school and more willing to learn alongside their peers" (2018: 70).

As Tranter et al. suggest, community development is not just important in itself, it can also support academic learning. Along these lines, Gillies describes a classroom where "academically productive talk" took place "in a social environment that was supportive of students' discussions" (2016: 2). And Goleman and Senge say that we need to establish a caring classroom, in which "the teacher embodies and models kindness and concern for her students and encourages the same attitude among the students. Such a classroom culture provides the best atmosphere for learning, both cognitively and emotionally … In such a space children's brains more readily reach the state of optimal cognitive efficiency" (2014: 32)

Establishing genuine community in the classroom does not require reproducing the traumatic conditions often evident in communities in the outside world, with which many students are already only too familiar. Dewey spoke of the need for the school to be a "purified" environment that helps students develop a *better* way of life (1916: 24). Similarly, Paley (1992) describes how she implemented in her Kindergarten classroom the rule "You can't say you can't play" – that is, if a fellow class member wants to join your play group you have to let them – despite objections from many students on the ground that, in everyday life, you choose who you play with. Paley stuck to the rule and, even though there was not full compliance, it had a very positive impact on her class, year after year, and her students learned many skills and attitudes of positive community life.

Strategies for promoting community understanding and participation

Over the year I change the groupings three times so they experience sitting with different children rather than just in the same spot the whole time.
Felicity, a Grade 3/4 teacher in her seventh year

We have spoken in general terms about the nature and importance of promoting community understanding and participation among students. We now look at some practical strategies for doing this. Here is an overview of what we recommend:

> **Strategies for promoting community understanding and participation**
>
> 1 Explicit teaching of community and the skills involved
> 2 Modelling by the teacher through a strong teacher–student connection
> 3 Building community in the classroom
> 4 Students getting to know each other

Explicit teaching of community and the skills involved

In this area of 21st-century learning, as with others, explicit discussion is a key strategy. Students need to understand why community is important and how a middle path is necessary between overly strong individualism and unthinking adherence to community norms. Carrie, in her thirteenth year, now a vice-principal but previously a middle-school teacher, commented:

> Classrooms are places where we should be teaching kids how to interact with each other, how to get a job, how to work within a team environment, how to have respectful relationships at a personal, family, and community level. And they need to understand their own rights, how they should be treated, but also how they should be treating others.

Sandra, a Kindergarten teacher in her eleventh year, reported how she talked with her class about the role various workers and helpers have within a community:

> I wanted to do a unit on "community helpers" in social studies. And I planned to build it around the classic story Jack and the Beanstalk, tying it in with environmental issues as well, and I thought the kids would be so excited with the Jack and the Beanstalk theme. But in fact it just fizzled out! They weren't interested.
>
> So in place of that, we ended up building a city out of recycled things from home that they brought on Earth Day, and we started to ask questions about this city, like who lives in it and who contributes to it? And that essentially launched about six weeks of a fun, authentic discussion of community helpers, the people I originally wanted to study. Fire fighters and police officers, yes, but also coffee baristas and travel agents, and people in our community who have roles you don't necessarily see. And the kids put their own spin on it.

Maria, who taught Grades 4/5 prior to going on maternity leave and then returned to Kindergarten in her fifteenth year, talked about the importance of class community and the need to discuss with students the skills, attitudes, and behaviours required for community membership.

> In Kindergarten I'm definitely focusing on building community at the beginning of the year; I've always emphasized it, but now I'm spending more time

on it. It's pretty obvious that my kids love to share and need more opportunity to talk and be listened to. I still do the good old community circle where the person holding the talking stick gets to speak and then passes it on.

So within that they're learning how to be a good listener: a lot of it is about listening. I say to them, "listen with your eyes, your ears, and your heart". You're looking at the person who is speaking, that's your eyes, and obviously you're hearing what they're saying, that's your ears; but you also need to listen with your heart, show them that you care about what they're saying. Face them, look at them, maybe ask a question, or just sit quietly – all those things show that you're listening with your heart and that you actually care.

Modelling by the teacher through a strong teacher–student connection

If teachers model a close, friendly relationship with their students, it will make their own lives richer and more enjoyable and also get their students on board with community participation and skill development in the classroom. Paul, a teacher of Grades 7/8 in his fifteenth year commented:

One thing I've been thinking about this year is the need to remind younger teachers not to get drawn into that feeling: my students are a burden and I have to battle against them all the time. Because when teachers I know have gone in that direction I can see how problematic it is. It makes you feel bad about your work every day; and when the kids see that they're a burden to you, and for example you get frustrated and angry when they can't do something, they're not motivated to learn. Maybe in the old days kids would still be motivated, because there was a different social dynamic, but now they will just get angry and dismiss you ...

There are two teachers who complain to me a lot about how unfriendly and disengaged their students are. And I just think to myself, you have to find a way to get into them and make them have the feeling of "oh, wow, my teacher really cares about me and is trying hard to help me". Then they respond.

Building community in the classroom

As well as talking about the importance of community and modelling what it means through the teacher–student relationship, teachers need to work in other ways to establish community in the classroom. David, now a principal in his fifteenth year but previously a middle-school teacher, observed:

Most teachers do some form of community-building at the start of the year, but it should be a thread woven throughout the year. Some teachers start it and are excited, but then they get into teaching the curriculum and there's little follow-up. As a principal I do it partly through the monthly assemblies where certain kids are recognized: that serves to keep reminding the students as well as the staff that we are a community.

I find some teachers have to be reminded that it's okay to have fun in the classroom, it doesn't always need to be work-heavy. And I stop by their classroom sometimes and remind them of that, especially at times of the year when report cards are due and they're worried about meeting curriculum expectations and lose focus on everything else. And then they wonder why the kids are struggling so much. So community-building is very important, and as I said it has to be a year-long investment.

Students getting to know each other

Building community and fostering related skills and attitudes is helped if students are able to get to know each other really well. Ways to achieve this include students speaking often in class, classroom celebration of students throughout the year, and varying the seating arrangements.

Everyone speaking often in class. As we have noted with other personal learning, extensive talk by everyone is a key way for students to get to know each other and so become closer as a community. Unless they hear from each other, students will not be aware of each class member's distinctive ideas and personality and will likely form impressions of them based on stereotypes of gender, race, ethnicity, appearance, and so on. Serena a Grade 5/6 teacher in her fifteenth year described how she ensures that students talk often and so get to know each other.

In building community in your class … a key strategy is allowing all the people in your room to be who they are. And sometimes that means they're in a bad mood or they don't want to do what you think they should, but you have to allow them to feel comfortable enough to say things like, "I hate this assignment", in which case you say something like: "Okay, I get that you don't like it, I can see you're not happy. Is it just today, do you need a break from it, what is it about this? Because at the end of the day I do need to assess you on transformational geometry (or whatever). But this is not the hill we're going to die on, so how can we work through it?"

They have to feel they have a say in it, because a community is not just a one-way thing. It's allowing them to bring their opinions into the classroom all the time even if they differ dramatically from yours, thus allowing them to bring in their own ideas about politics or whatever and their own experience of the world in a meaningful way.

VIP for a day. Another way for students to get to know each other is by regularly celebrating individual class members. Mike, a lower primary teacher with 12 years' experience, described an activity he used for this purpose:

In the first month of school I do this VIP kind of writing exercise, where we pick a kid every day and they sit on a special chair and we interview them and get personal information from them about what they like, what their family is like, etc. And I like doing this at the beginning because you find out those little things about them and can engage with them more, and this in turn leads to more learning opportunities. Also, the closer the relationship the smaller the hierarchy, which again helps with learning. So if they know you know certain things about their hobbies and interests they can make little references to it, which makes them feel good.

Varying the seating arrangements. Another way to help everyone get to know each other is by regularly changing the seating arrangements. Felicity, a Grade 3/4 teacher of 7 years said: "Over the year I change the groupings three times so they experience sitting with different children rather than just in the same spot the whole time". And Kendra, a teacher of Grade 8 and in her twelfth year reported:

In my classroom they don't sit in rows, it's a big U; and especially at the beginning of the year I change the seating around quite a bit, or let them choose their seating. By the middle of the year it doesn't matter so much where I put them because they often shout across the room at somebody they want to talk to. And I sometimes say to them, "Okay, choose where you sit but at some point during the day if it's too much, I'm going to move you and you're just going to be okay with it". And they are okay with it.

Chapter summary

Students need to learn not only how to interact with individuals and work in teams, but how to participate in a larger community. Belonging to a community gives a wider sense of responsibility, but also a sense of identity and belonging. It can have a strong social component that is enjoyable and fosters many "acquaintances" as well closer relationships.

In order to belong to a community, one has to follow certain norms of caring and respectful interaction and behaviour. These can be experienced as constraints to a degree, but students need to learn that such limits are worth while given the gains of safety, belonging, and enjoyment a community affords. We can also learn a great deal from other community members about mundane matters as well as the finer points of human nature and conduct.

The classroom is an ideal setting for experiencing community and learning how to support and benefit from a community. Unfortunately, traditional schooling largely failed to take advantage of the possibilities of classroom community, the focus being largely on academic learning with a minimum of social interaction. It is because of the importance of the social in classroom life that we normally speak of the "class community" rather than using terms such as "learning community" and "community of practice" (valuable though these terms are in certain contexts).

Some strategies for teaching community understanding and participation in the classroom are: explicit discussion with students about the nature and importance of community and the values and skills it requires; modelling by the teacher through a strong connection with all students; building a genuinely social community in the classroom; and facilitating students getting to know each other.

Questions for reflection and discussion

1 What is community and why is it important for both students and teachers?
2 What are the similarities and differences between the classroom community and other communities (neighbourhood, workplace, religious, etc.)?
3 How do people differ in the place community has in their lives?
4 How can teachers support student development in community understanding and participation?

8 Principle 8: Foster overall social development

I talk with my students about bigger goals in life and the fact that, to be a really successful person, you need to be able to interact with people.
— Paul, a teacher of Grades 7/8 in his fifteenth year

The Principle, its importance, and some challenges

So far in Part 2 we have discussed fostering social development in particular areas; but to make progress in these areas and others, students need to be building an overall approach to social life. As with life in general, social life is complex and interconnected, so any one element is difficult to achieve without a broad set of goals and strategies. And overall social development is also important for overall personal wellbeing, as discussed in Chapter 4.

In traditional schooling there has been some attention to social matters. In literature, for example, students often read about the joys and struggles of relationships; and in history, students learn about the importance of social relationships in certain historical eras and the development of particular social groups over time. However, students need a more comprehensive understanding of the enormous importance of social relationships, what form they should take, and how to build and maintain them.

What is overall social development?

Social relationships are crucial to people's wellbeing. Our personal interactions can bring us a great deal of pleasure, knowledge, and support; alternatively, they can cause us much suffering and loss. Accordingly, it is important to learn how to build a solid network of relatives, friends, acquaintances, and so on, one that is integrated with and supports our overall way of life. Social development begins in early childhood and should continue strongly throughout the school years, when we have a unique opportunity to increase the range and quality of our relationships.

Developing social relationships is not a simple matter. It takes time and commitment of resources and so has to be weighed against other components of life, with efforts to integrate all the components in order to optimize our goals. With every relationship, even the most intimate ones, there are conflicting interests requiring negotiation and compromise. Traditionally and in popular literature and media there has been a tendency to see relationships as of absolute value and romanticize them, overlooking some of the challenges, complexities, and competing life goals. In our view the time has come to question this approach, while continuing to see the great value of the social in our lives.

Another area requiring discussion is individual differences in social life. People vary in the kinds of people they like to interact with and the type of relationships they prefer – for example, a few deep relationships versus a larger number and range. They also differ in the sheer amount of emphasis on the social in their life. Again, popular culture has sometimes presented social relationships as of absolute value, whereas they seem to have a larger place in the lives of some people than others. Such differences need to be explored and largely respected.

Why address overall social development in the classroom?

We spoke in Chapter 4 of promoting students' overall wellbeing, including helping them develop a comprehensive "way of life". With the help of classroom teaching and discussion, they can come to see the key role of the social within their way of life, and set about developing their social skills, choices, and relationships, thus enhancing their wellbeing.

As they explore in depth the social dimension of life, students come to see that people differ in the type and degree of social experience that works for them, and become more respectful of these differences in others. They also become more aware of their own strengths and weaknesses in social matters: things they can feel proud of (which increases their self-esteem) and things they need to work on.

An important aspect of learning in this area is coming to see how social relationships and experiences can be integrated into other pursuits, including formal learning, work life, and family life. Students then realize they have more time for "socializing" than they thought, and can embark on building the social more fully into various activities.

Reasons for fostering overall social development

- Students become more aware of the importance of the social in their life
- They work to develop their social skills, choices, and relationships
- They become more respectful of differences in people's social lives
- Students recognize their strengths and weaknesses in social matters
- They learn how to combine social life with other things

What are the challenges of promoting overall social development?

Many aspects of social life are somewhat controversial, so if teachers are to address the social they will have to negotiate some of these controversies. For example, issues of "morality" will arise, such as what place should be given to our own needs in social relationships.

Addressing social matters can take up a lot of time, and since these matters are not widely seen as central to schooling, tough decisions have to be made about how much time to spend on them – except where it is possible to integrate them fully with subject study.

Families may see the social as largely their domain, so apart from concerns about the time involved, they may object to the teacher interfering in this aspect of their child's (and the family's) life.

Even some students may think their social life is none of the teacher's business. As noted in Chapter 7, Paley (1992) found that many students believe their friendship life is for them to decide, including who they play with.

Teachers and students have different preferences and tolerance levels with respect to classroom socializing. The amount of talk that goes on during learning activities, for example, has been seen as a matter where teachers may need to do some negotiating, on behalf of themselves and their students.

Theory/research basis for promoting overall social development

Many writers have emphasized the importance of social relationships for human wellbeing. For example, Dolan says, "the evidence quite clearly shows a strong positive association between happiness and doing things with the people you like" (2014: 154). On this basis, he argues that people need to come to acknowledge the importance of positive social interaction and learn to prioritize it in their life decisions.

Renowned social psychologist Mihalyi Csikszentmihalyi (1990) stresses the importance of pursuing happiness in life, and in particular achieving the state of "flow", which is an ongoing condition characterized by happiness. The concept of flow has been widely adopted. However, educational researchers Smith and Wilhelm (2002), who have embraced the idea of flow and applied it to high school teaching, maintain that Csikszentmihalyi does not give enough place to the social dimension in his exposition of flow. Their study of male high school students of working-class background led them to conclude that such students require a more social approach to life and learning than is commonly proposed under flow. The boys they studied said that when they were with their friends, they could achieve greater intimacy and "be themselves" (2002: 42).

> In their logs the boys talked about the social in a variety of ways: how friends and family affected literate interests; the importance of relationships with teachers; their enjoyment of working in groups; and the importance of relationships they cultivated with textual characters, authors or directors. (Smith and Wilhelm, 2002: 142)

Chapman and West-Burnham observe: "Evidence shows that both introverts and extroverts have more positive feelings when sharing activities with other people" (2010: 86). Accordingly we need to create a school setting that supports developing good relationships: "[W]e cannot impose friendships, but we can develop cultures in which individuals value each other's perspectives and uniqueness. If shared understanding is to emerge ... then friendship must be valued as beneficial, not incidental" (p. 125).

As a basis for developing a more social approach to life, students need to have a strong respect for other people and greater recognition of their distinctive strengths. Meier, Knoester, and D'Andrea present a report of an early childhood teacher who developed a way to teach students to appreciate other people. "Each day, we would draw one student's name out of a can. For that day, we would collectively share good thoughts about that child – focusing on what the child was good at, what he or she liked to do, or other characteristics we had observed" (2015: 55). The teacher said that the purpose of the activity was to make students more aware of what other people have to offer.

Strategies for promoting overall social development

One concrete thing that's especially valuable – for students and me – is having [photos] of them in the classroom ... in some dramatic pose ... with their name on it as a classroom decoration, so they're all part of the class and it shows.
– Rachel, in her eleventh year, previously a Kindergarten teacher but about to move to K-8 music and drama

Promoting the development of the "whole child" has often been advocated in education, but we need more ideas about what it means and how to do it. Regarding overall social development, the teachers in our study mentioned the following approaches:

Strategies for promoting students' overall social development

- Discussion of the key place of the social in a way of life
- Teacher modelling a social approach to life
- Bringing the social into the classroom
- Relating subject areas to social life, including fiction and non-fiction reading
- Links to family

Discussion of the key place of the social in a way of life

Once again, teachers need to talk explicitly with students about the importance of having an overall approach to life, and the essential role of the social in this. Students have to be made aware of the complexity of life and how many components are necessary for a good way of life, including the social. Paul, a teacher of Grades 7/8 in his fifteenth year reported: "I talk with my students about bigger goals in life and the fact that, to be a really successful person, you need to be able to interact with people".

Teacher modelling a social approach to life

As well as talking about it, teachers should show through their own behaviour how much they value positive social relationships. With 7 years' experience, Lucy, now a consultant but having previously taught Grades 7/8, talked about her relationship with her students:

> I have much more compassion for students now, whereas when I first became a teacher I had so many expectations of them and was very strict. But now after those years of experience and also having kids of my own, I see that they're just kids. The expectations need to be there, but when a kid's going through something you have to take that into account. I realized too that a lot of the misbehaviour in your classroom either reflects on your own teaching or the fact that there is something else going on.
>
> So my overall demeanour has changed. Whereas I used to be so stressed about everything we have to do, now it's just: take everything as it comes. And the things you thought were so detrimental really don't matter ... I'll get to them tomorrow.
>
> And the kids respond to that. The "laid back" way I teach (not that I use that term with them!) is refreshing to them, because often they sit in classrooms and it's like, we've got to get this done and do this and that and that. Whereas you can actually stop and say to them, "how is everybody doing today?" And if you invest a little time to show that you care, they give a lot back in return.

Kendra, a teacher of Grade 8 and in her twelfth year, described the strongly social approach she has with her students:

> I'm always finding ways to connect with my students, especially those who are more withdrawn, trying to get them just to look up and say something. I even walk over during my prep periods and watch them in their other classes to see what they're up to. Sometimes I sit with them; the other teachers were a little put off by that at first, the French teacher in particular, but I said, "No, no, I love French and I just want to see what's going on", and after a while they were completely okay with it, I was like another kid in the class.
>
> And I go through my list and realize, oh I haven't talked to so and so in a long time, let's see what she's up to; and I'll see her in the hall and just comment, "Oh, what's your shirt say?" or something like that. And sometimes it's embarrassing because there's nothing important on their shirt, I'm not the most sophisticated conversation starter you'll find. But they just laugh and it's fine.

Bringing the social into the classroom

Closely related to the class community-building discussed in Chapter 7, it is important to support the development of social relationships in the classroom, with all students getting to know each other. This helps students see possibilities for the social in their personal lives and how to go about it. The development of a social relationship between students and the teacher is one dimension of this approach.

Nora, a middle school teacher with 5 years' experience, described how she developed a strongly social relationship with her students:

> I liked the fact that [the students wanted more than just a teacher]; that was a big part of why I liked coming to work. I had a great relationship with 99% of the students; I was pretty laid back with them and didn't get mad about stupid things. If only five students met a particular deadline I would think maybe I've missed something, and we would regroup and figure out together what happened.

In her eleventh year, Rachel, previously a Kindergarten teacher but about to move to K-8 music and drama, described how she takes steps to make sure students get to know each other and feel part of the community:

> One concrete thing that's especially valuable – for students and me – is having physical images of them in the classroom. In Kindergarten when we were talking about feelings I took photos of all of them, so we had black and white photos of their feelings; and when I was teaching them about numbers I took photos of them holding up a particular number of fingers, so they were all part of the learning. [Next year] with 300 students that would take a lot of time, but I'm still thinking of taking a picture of each kid in the first week in some dramatic pose, and having that there with their name on it as our classroom decoration, so they're all part of the class and it shows.

Relating subject areas to social life

Some school subjects lend themselves to addressing the social side of life while also teaching the required content. This is especially so of fiction reading, where social relationships are often at the heart of the story. The same is true of health education, physical education, and music. Candice, in her thirteenth year and teaching integrated arts in primary/junior, spoke of the social component in her music and dance programme:

> The Orff pedagogy I use in music is so much about social interaction. Because if you're making music you're probably not going to do it alone, and if you're doing it with somebody else you have to be able to pick up on their body language and many things they're doing. And today we're losing all those social skills. Even if kids are playing together with a television, they're losing that body language, talking, eye contact, all those skills.
>
> Much of what we do, then, is directly concerned with addressing that. Like the dance games we do, when you're finding a partner you have to make eye contact, watch body language, send signals: "Yeah I need a partner, let's do that". Often there's no time to talk because of the singing and dancing and

music, so it's doing this without talking to one another, just figuring it out. And maybe somebody gets there before you, so look for somebody else: all the big social stuff.

And back to music, if a student is conducting the group the others have to know when to start, when to stop: one group has the rhythm sticks and everybody else has to watch them to know where to be.

Links to family

As we have seen before, making connections to families is an important strategy in fostering personal development, and this is so in the case of their social life, especially for younger children. Jill, in her twelfth year, talked about how she links to family in her Grade 1 class:

I spend a lot of time building a relationship with my students, because without the relationship learning will be hindered, especially in early primary where you are asking them to take risks and do things they've never done before.

For example, I have a journal writing programme where the child and I write each other letters, back and forth, in a journal that goes home. It's very informal but I get to know more about them, their home life, and what they like to do, and they ask questions and do the same with me.

And this year the brother of one of my students who was in an older class said to me, "I heard you have a dog named Sadie", and I'm like, "Yeah, yeah"; so it became a family kind of conversation. So it's a great way to build a relationship with them and with the families as well.

Chapter summary

As well as particular values and skills of interaction and community participation, students need to develop an overall understanding of and approach to social life. Relationships with other people are crucial for both our own wellbeing and the wellbeing of others. But too often the social has been seen as an incidental rather than a fundamental dimension of a way of life.

People vary in the type of social relationships they prefer. Some like to have a few close friends and others a larger number of less intimate friends and acquaintances. Some focus more on family relationships, whereas other see family and friends as equally important in many ways. A key learning for individual students in this area is to develop a set of social relationships that works for them.

Once again, the classroom provides a great many opportunities to understand and experience the social, and this has not been capitalized on enough in the past. Too often, the classroom has been seen as a largely functional context.

But while it has a major functional purpose, it can be strongly social at the same time, and the two can reinforce each other. In many countries, school is one of the few contexts for broad, inclusive social experience remaining today.

Among the strategies for fostering overall social experience among students are the following: discussing the key place of the social in an individual way of life; the teacher modelling a social approach to life in the classroom and beyond; bringing the social into the classroom; relating subject areas to social life, including fiction and non-fiction reading; establishing links to the family.

Questions for reflection and discussion

1 Why are social relationships important to a way of life?
2 How do people differ in the place the social has in their lives?
3 How can people enhance their social life?
4 How can teachers support student development in this area?

Part **3**

Direction III: Teaching for Equity, Inclusion, and Political and Global/Environmental Awareness

In Parts 1 and 2, we discussed teaching in relation to mainly personal (including social) aspects of life. Here, in Part 3, we move to considering ways to help students understand and participate in the public domain. However, many of the matters we explore here – such as equity and inclusion, and political understanding – are also important at a personal level. We should not draw too sharp a line between the two.

The aspects of 21st-century teaching we focus on especially in Part 3 are:

Aspects of teaching for equity, inclusion, and political and global/environmental awareness

Chapter 9: Teach for equity and inclusion
Chapter 10: Promote political understanding and involvement
Chapter 11: Foster international outlooks and skills
Chapter 12: Teach for overall global/environmental awareness

Principle 9: Teach for Equity and Inclusion

I spend a great deal of time fostering equity and inclusion, and one of the ways I do this is through reading books ... Especially with the Grade 1s, it's hard to talk about things like residential schools, or slavery, or homophobia and have those big conversations, but there are a lot of great picture books that take those hard topics and communicate them in a way that's accessible and relatable to kids.

– Marisa, a Grade 1/2 teacher in her fifteenth year

The Principle, its importance, and some challenges

Equity and inclusion are 21st-century learning areas that are important for everyone's wellbeing. Treating people equally and inclusively has sometimes been seen as a way to graciously help people less fortunate than ourselves. But in fact, supporting growth and action in this area enhances everyone's *own* wellbeing. Much has been written lately along these lines (e.g. Joseph Stiglitz, *The Price of Inequality*, 2012).

It might be thought that talking about our own wellbeing is irrelevant when dealing with this topic: if equity and inclusion are morally right, we should promote them, regardless of self-interest. But people usually need several reasons to pursue a course of action, and it is well documented that many students at school and in higher education stop listening and even become angry when pressed to embrace equity and inclusion. If significant progress is to be made, the moral message – which of course is valid – has to be supplemented with reference to personal interests, natural empathy, environmental care, and other considerations.

What is meant by promoting equity and inclusion?

We discuss equity and inclusion together in this chapter because they are closely connected. If we see people as equal, we tend to include them more, and including them is a major way to treat them equally. Of course, there are some people we include more than others because they belong to our family, live near us, etc. But that is for special reasons, and not necessarily because we see them as superior. Much of the time we should mix with a very diverse range of people, both for their sake and ours.

In this book, we use the terms equity and inclusion in a broad sense that covers many kinds of difference: culture, race, nationality, language, class, gender, sexual preference, age, ability, and so on. Accordingly, we do not normally use the term "multiculturalism" to refer to equity and inclusion in general, given its literal emphasis on culture. Some prominent writers do often use the term multiculturalism when referring to the field, but increasingly they too are stressing that they are using the term in a way that goes far beyond culture (e.g. Banks, 2009a, 2009b, 2009c, 2016; Nieto, 2009, 2016).

Seeing people as equal does not mean that we think they are all the same. People vary enormously from one another, which is partly why inclusion enriches our lives: it opens us to new ways of seeing, acting, and being. But on the whole differences between people do not run along lines of race, gender, etc.; rather, they occur at an individual level *within* races, genders, etc. This is why stereotyping people based on these categories is so distorting and harmful. Moreover, there are enormous similarities and commonalities between people that cut *across* these categories. The central mistake in this area is to be biased against people based on such categories, a stereotyping that gives rise to much of the exclusion and discrimination that occurs.

In talking about the fostering of equity and inclusion in the classroom, we want to stress the importance of *both* discussion *and* modelling, since some teachers emphasize one to the neglect of the other. Modelling equity and inclusion without explicit discussion has only a limited effect because students do not understand what they are seeing. And equally, talking about equity and inclusion without practising them also has little impact, because again students do not understand what is meant and, moreover, do not think we are serious about it. Both discussion and modelling are needed.

Why discuss and model equity and inclusion?

The central purpose for addressing equity and inclusion in the classroom is so students and the teacher grow in this dimension of life. This, in turn, has an impact on their life beyond the classroom: in the school, the family, the workplace, and other settings. An immediate result is that all students feel safe and included in the classroom.

Because everyone feels safe, included, and respected, community-building is facilitated, whole-class and small-group participation are increased, and students are able to focus more on their academic and other learning. In addition, learning and life in the classroom become more enjoyable for students and the teacher and they look forward to coming to school.

In an equitable and inclusive classroom, students are able to develop further in this area as they see what it means and the positive impact it has, and as they get to know and appreciate students of different cultures, races, genders, income levels, and so on. In summary:

Advantages of promoting equity and inclusion in the classroom

- Students and the teacher grow in equity and inclusion
- All students feel safe and included
- Community-building is facilitated
- Students participate and learn more
- The class is more enjoyable for everyone, including the teacher
- Students learn inclusion through first-hand experience in the classroom

What are the challenges of teaching for equity and inclusion?

Parents and students are sometimes resistant to an equitable, inclusive approach, whether for general ideological reasons (e.g. belief in racial or ethnic purity or superiority) or because they come from societies or sub-groups where bias and inequity are widespread and deeply ingrained. Parents may object to teachers getting into this area.

Education has a long tradition of bias towards a narrow set of intellectual abilities and interests, ones that favour certain classes and cultural backgrounds. Most teachers are themselves heirs to this tradition, have succeeded in part because of it, and may have difficulty seeing through it. This bias is reflected in public tests, admission criteria, curriculum emphases, and teaching approaches. Teachers who adopt a different approach may be criticized and even penalized professionally.

Partly reflecting this academic bias, extensive study of equity and inclusion is often seen as a "waste of time" by superintendents, school administrators, parents, and others. It is thought that teachers should just "get on with it" and teach the basic content and skills. The way bias and prejudice undermine even academic learning is not understood, or is set aside because it only impacts certain students. Again, teachers who reject this position may be opposed.

In particular, inclusion of students with special needs in the mainstream classroom can be challenging, as it can increase teachers' workload (especially as class sizes grow) and lead to classroom management challenges for which teachers have not been prepared.

Theory/research basis for promoting equity and inclusion

Social justice is widely emphasized by educational theorists and researchers. For example, Zeichner and Liston in their 2014 book on reflective teaching include social justice as a key component of a reflective approach:

> Within our democratic society ... schools are supposed to help all students learn. But they don't. Our public schools tend to reproduce, not alter, the divisive divisions in our society ... Schooling for social justice attempts to right these wrongs. And the wrongs are many and varied and longstanding. (2014: 65)

Florian, Black-Hawkins, and Rouse argue for a broader concept of inclusive education than has often been used in the past. They say there is increasing agreement internationally that "inclusive education is one that extends to *anyone* who might be excluded from, or have limited access to [education]. This includes those living in poverty, newly arrived migrant children, and others who may not speak English or who have a different ethnic, cultural or religious heritage" (2017: 19). Similarly, Nieto says that scholars in the field of multicultural education "have in recent years broadened the scope of multicultural to include social class, gender, disability, and LGBTQI issues, among other social differences" (2009: 86). In the same way, Banks (2009a, 2009b, 2009c) advocates considerable breadth in defining multicultural education and related inclusion of all students.

While a broad concept of inclusion is being used today, the issue of inclusion of students with "special needs" in mainstream classrooms remains a major one. Some teachers question this practice because they see it as reducing the general level of learning. However, according to Florian et al., this does not have to be the case: "high levels of inclusion can be entirely compatible with high levels of achievement ... combining the two is not only possible but essential if all children are to have the opportunity to participate fully in education" (2017: 2). Many of the same teaching strategies work for all students.

Dolby (2012) maintains that a more positive approach to teaching for equity and inclusion is necessary than has often been used in the past. She argues that excessive preaching and blaming tends to undermine both the teacher–student relationship and the culture of the classroom; moreover, such an approach is largely ineffective because it leads to a great deal of resistance.

Her more positive approach, which she has experimented with extensively at the pre-service level, involves discussing with students the great potential of humans for empathy; exploring with them the ways in which an equitable, inclusive society is better for everyone, not just members of sub-groups; and studying with them the many commonalities between people of different sub-groups. This is in line with Trilling and Fadel's position that in the 21st century it is more important than ever to become "cross-culturally fluent," that is, develop "a better sense of how we are all different and all the same" (2009: 81). Going beyond humans, Dolby's approach also involves fostering a strongly ecological outlook that is inclusive of the whole of nature, with "empathy for all living things" (2012: 127).

Strategies for fostering equity and inclusion

I always read picture books about gender equality or LGBTQ matters in Grade 1, and the same in Grade 2 and Grade 4. With race, too, I always made sure there were images in the classroom of a variety of races, reflecting the students in my classroom.

– Tanya, a district consultant at the time of interview – her
fifteenth year – but returning to the classroom the following year

As we have said, teaching for equity and inclusion is challenging. Educators have often worked hard at it at different levels with disappointing results. However, we believe much more could be done. Key strategies include the following:

Strategies for fostering equity and inclusion

1 Discussing the importance of equity and inclusion
2 Modelling equity and inclusion by the teacher
3 Including students with special needs in the mainstream classroom
4 Mini-lessons, discussions, and assignments on historical and current bias and discrimination
5 Mixing everybody up

Discussing the importance of equity and inclusion

As we have said, a major reason for lack of progress in educating for equity and inclusion is lack of clarity about what the issues are and why they are important. Accordingly, extensive discussion of the area is a key teaching strategy (and also helps teachers become clearer about it themselves). Anita, a Grade 8 teacher in her fifteenth year said: "I had a big discussion with my class this year about sexist and homophobic language, and we delved into the history of it because they were really interested. And that is probably one of the things they remember most from the year, and that I remember most".

Similarly, Miranda teaching Kindergarten in her twelfth year described how she discusses equity and inclusion with her students:

> This year we had a student who was developmentally delayed, and at the beginning of the year the other students didn't notice it much but then they started to wonder: "How come he gets to do this and this and we don't?" So I talked with them about it and I said, "Well you know Jamie learns differently from you and me", and we talked about it. And sometimes I would say to them, "Jamie has done a really great job today, so now he gets to go and do such and such; but I know you don't need that special time". And I had another student who needed assistance in walking at the beginning of the year, and they noticed she had an educational assistant; but we talked about that and they understood it.

And Marisa, a Grade 1/2 teacher in her fifteenth year, talked about how she works to ensure that her students understand that everyone has strengths, and also that there are many commonalities between people of different sub-groups:

> In our reading and also our activities, like art activities and class celebrations, students look at their strengths but also the strengths in their peers. Also embedded in all those activities is looking at our similarities – not just our differences – and how, for example, we all love our family and we all have traditions that are important to us. They may look different, but they're all important to us. And respect for each other is embedded in that as well.

Modelling equity and inclusion by the teacher

As noted earlier in the chapter, modelling equity and inclusion is just as important as talking about it because it shows what it means in practice, and also that
we really mean what we say. Again, Anita, the Grade 8 teacher in her fifteenth
year said:

> It's important how you are in a classroom every day; for example, being
> careful how you speak, the pronouns you use. And also being careful what
> videos you show. Like if I'm showing a science video I don't always choose
> one with an old white guy, even if it's a good video. I look also for videos that
> show people with different ethnicities, accents, and skin colour, both women
> and men, and trans people. The same with choosing books to read, I con-
> sciously think about what I am presenting to students, books that represent
> them or a variety of people.

Maria, previously a Grade 3/4 teacher but now teaching Kindergarten in her
fifteenth year commented:

> I spend a lot of time building relationships with my students, it's probably the
> most important thing I do. Certainly that's true now that I'm teaching Kinder-
> garten, but I think it's crucial all the way up, because you see kids coming
> from broken homes and kids with attitude. And I don't say to them, "Why are
> you walking this way, or feeling that way?" Because it makes a huge differ-
> ence if you show them you care.
>
> And some of the older kids don't really know me this year, because they were
> very small when I was on maternity leave. And one of them said to me the
> other day, "You know my name!" – because I made a point of saying his
> name. And sometimes if you just stop and ask them how their day is, they
> will treat you completely differently. So I spend a lot of time on that.
>
> Last year I had a child in my class who was autistic, and I think the reason
> we worked so well together was because of the relationship I had with him,
> he felt safe. And I've made sure that this year he's with a teacher who has a
> similar approach, because I know he needs that. I mean they call you mummy
> a lot of the time in Kindergarten, so you know you've got to go with that kind
> of relationship. All of a sudden, you're the one there for them.

Including students with special needs in the mainstream classroom

As noted before, the term inclusion is now used more broadly; but a very important sub-group who need to be treated equitably and inclusively in the mainstream classroom are students with "disabilities" or "special needs": physical,
cognitive, emotional, etc. Gail, a Grade 1 teacher with 10 years' experience said:

> I think my classroom this year worked quite well for my students with special
> needs. Such inclusion can be challenging for the teacher because of the

demands it places on your time and attention. But one thing I've loved is seeing how tolerant and understanding the other students are.

Like if we had a student who would be insulting and yell and throw stuff, I would just pull a couple of students over and say: "I'm really sorry he's acting like this, can you just maybe go play with him somewhere?" And they'd be like, "Oh yeah, we get it". They were so understanding and inclusive. And sometimes I'd be working with another student who needed attention, and they'd be like: "Mrs. P has to be with someone else, so just give her a minute". They really got it, that some students have special needs. And I had some kids who had noise cancelling headphones or fidget toys or fidget seats or whatever, and the others didn't get to use that stuff but they were okay with it.

So having those students with special needs in my class affected me positively, because it brought out the tolerance piece. And I want my students to understand that we are all different and don't all get everything the same.

Rachel, now in her eleventh year, who taught Kindergarten for several years but is moving to K-8 music and drama, spoke of how she draws on the interests of everyone in the class:

Teaching Kindergarten in recent years I've realized how important it is to draw on students' interests. Like, watching them during free play and seeing they're into building rocket ships, and asking myself how I can use that as a springboard into a whole other inquiry? I'm not sure what that will look like next year in music and drama when I only have them for one period a week, but I'm hoping I can still find ways to draw on their interests and personalize their learning.

Mini-lessons, discussions, and assignments on historical and current bias and discrimination

Apart from the general discussion of equity and inclusion mentioned in earlier, there is a need for mini-lessons, discussions, and so on on specific injustices, past and present, so students are aware of bias and discrimination and the great suffering it brings to so many people. These matters are often painful, but should not be overlooked in the name of a "positive" approach to the area. Marisa, the Grade 1/2 teacher we met earlier reported:

I spend a great deal of time fostering equity and inclusion, and one of the ways I do this is through reading books. I'm very intentional with the books that I read to my students, especially picture books, because they have a great way of dealing with those more difficult topics. Especially with Grade 1s, it's hard to talk about things like residential schools, or slavery, or homophobia and have those big conversations, but there are a lot of great picture books that take those hard topics and communicate them in a way that's accessible and relatable to kids.

Tanya, the consultant who previously taught lower elementary and was returning to the classroom the following year commented:

> I've always done a lot to make my classroom inclusive but I'm more confident with it now because I have done a lot of study lately of equity issues; so I will do it to an even greater extent next year. But I always read picture books about gender equality or LGBTQ matters in Grade 1, and the same in Grade 2 and then Grade 4. With race, too, I always made sure there were images in the classroom of a variety of races, reflecting the students in my classroom.
>
> But now I have more knowledge and understanding and resources. Like I wasn't great at addressing indigenous issues but I've spent a lot of time learning about it the last three years – though I still have a lot to learn – and I will bring that into the classroom in a way I wasn't able to previously.

Mixing everybody up

We talked in Chapter 7 about regularly changing student seating arrangements in order to help build classroom community. This is also an important strategy for fostering equity and inclusion in the classroom. Vera, a teacher of 15 years, spoke about how, at her highly multiracial, multicultural school, she gives students a lot of choice about where they sit but combines it with considerable nudging on her part. Her approach is so remarkable and successful that we present here the whole of her lengthy description.

> I don't know if a lot of people would agree with my approach, but I kind of force kids to get to know one another and be around different people, and I tell them why. And every month we switch tables so nobody feels too comfortable anywhere.
>
> But I let the kids choose where they sit every month, even if I know it's a bad choice, because I want them to live out the consequences of their actions. At the beginning of the year no one really knows anyone, or they think they do but within a week of choosing a spot they're asking me to switch tables. And I'm like "no, you chose this spot, you live it out, you find a way to get along with the people here; you may not like them today but something could happen and tomorrow you're best friends. So just give them a chance. Here's my strategy for you in how to manage this, but if you really, really can't manage, I will move you".
>
> But I force them to move every month so they get a new opportunity, and over the year they gradually make better choices. And I give them parameters. I say, "okay, I need a balance of boys and girls, and of Grade 3s and 4s"; it doesn't have to be exactly the same number but fairly even. And an extra guideline is to sometimes pick someone [they've] never worked with before, or someone [they] know is going to help them, or someone [they] don't get along with. Every month I change that parameter.

And what if they choose someone and that student doesn't choose them? It doesn't matter. But before they go to their new spots, we sit altogether as a class and discuss. And I say, "okay, I see a balanced group here, this looks good. But we're missing a girl over here, would someone like to volunteer to go over here for the month?"

And I had one student this year who had undiagnosed anxiety and depression and just could not manage in any group, and so for three months I let him sit by himself. But then I said to him, "sweetie, I know this is what you needed for now but it's almost the end of the year and this is your last opportunity to sit with other members of our class and be a part of everything. I will let you keep on sitting by yourself, but just know this is your last chance". And at first he said he was fine where he was; but twenty minutes later he came to me and said, "I want to be in a group". And so for the last month he got to sit in a group of eight children. That's a triumph. I was floored that he came back to me.

And you might think that as a strategy switching groups isn't a big deal. But it became a monthly opportunity for the kids to re-evaluate the dynamics in our classroom, reflect on who they were or were not comfortable with, and challenge themselves. And you could see by the end of the year how the kids grew and knew what was going on. One child – because every month also I have them tell me two of their strengths, a need and their goal for the following month – one child in the final month wrote: "one of my strengths now is that I can get along with anyone in my class; even if I don't like them. I can work with them". She actually wrote that. And at the beginning of the year she was one of those who were too shy to speak up for herself. But by the end of the year, she could sit with the most challenging student in the room and not have a conflict with them.

[*Authors' note*: At this point in the interview, the interviewer said: "That's amazing, you need to write it up!" To which Vera replied: "Well we are, aren't we?" Which is partly why we felt we must include her whole account here.]

Chapter summary

Equity and inclusion are becoming more obviously necessary – and possible – in the 21st century as global migration, interconnection, and communication increase. They are, of course, concerns that have not been well addressed throughout human history. But in our view the time and opportunity has come to deal with them much more decisively, and schooling can play a large role in this.

Equity and inclusion are terms that need to be understood very broadly, as covering issues of race, ethnicity, gender, socio-economic status, ability, LGBTQ identity, language, and so on. In the past, inclusion tended to be seen mainly as bringing students with "special needs" into the mainstream classroom and integrating them into learning and life in that setting. While this remains a major dimension of inclusive education, others are also extremely important; and the various areas of inclusion overlap and need to be addressed in an integrated way.

Equity and inclusion are deep moral issues. However, there is widespread evidence that focusing on moral duty alone is not very effective with students. If substantial progress is to be achieved, the moral message has to be supplemented with reference to personal interests, natural empathy, global and environmental identity, and other considerations. In particular, it is important for students to realize that their individual wellbeing is bound up to a very large extent with the wellbeing and inclusion of others.

Strategies for fostering equity and inclusion among students include: discussing the importance of equity and inclusion (in this broad sense) for oneself and others; modelling equity and inclusion by the teacher; integrating students with special needs in the mainstream classroom; mini-lessons, discussions, and assignments on past and current bias and discrimination; and creating ways for students to interact and get to know each other.

Questions for reflection and discussion

1 What are equity and inclusion? How broadly should we interpret them?
2 Why are equity and inclusion important in a community, society, and a personal way of life?
3 To what extent are their commonalities across sub-groups and differences within them?
4 How can teachers support student development in this area?

10 Principle 10: Promote political understanding and involvement

I feel that only half of my job is teaching the curriculum ... if I'm not teaching students how to be a good citizen in society and they leave me, I'm not doing my job.
— Lucy, a district coordinator in her seventh year,
previously a Grade 7/8 teacher

The Principle, its importance, and some challenges

Issues of equity and inclusion, as discussed in the previous chapter, often arise at the local level. We now move to the typically (though not always) larger arena of politics. Some people claim not to be interested in politics because it is too remote, or because they think nothing can be done anyway. But politics affects us all greatly, and staying away from it makes matters worse. Moreover, studying politics can be fascinating, serve to educate us about broader societal matters, and enable us to contribute to society.

With improved information and communication technology (ICT) in the 21st century, there is more potential than in the past for the general population to gain political knowledge and understanding and have a political impact. However, for this potential to be realized, people have to understand what politics is, learn to critique it effectively, and know how to use ICT and other means to influence it.

What is teaching for political understanding and involvement?

Politics has to do with power relationships at individual, institutional, societal, and international levels. Students need to understand these relationships and develop the skills to negotiate them. Teachers have to help student tease out principles of political action that apply in almost every social and institutional context, such as attempting to control others, taking advantage of existing situations, enlisting others to help one's cause, and characterizing situations in a certain way to serve one's ends.

In the past, education about systems of government and phenomena such as revolution, empire, and colonization was often done in a descriptive way, rather than as political manifestations that need to be understood and questioned.

Critical thinking, widely advocated by education systems today, should be applied much more fully to politics. It is obviously in the interests of most governments – and even some teachers – to leave the status quo more or less as it is, since they have benefited from it. However, what those in authority should realize is that the status quo usually has many defects, for a large proportion of the population and also for themselves. Many creative solutions may be available that would result in a better situation for possibly everyone concerned.

Not only do students need to learn how to participate in politics and influence it, they have to learn how to react to it, what attitudes to adopt towards it. While a degree of optimism must be maintained both for our wellbeing and to keep reform efforts going, there is usually a limit to the extent to which improved political arrangements can be achieved, by ourselves or others. Teachers and students have to work on ways to produce change, but also strategies to maintain our sanity when we have done as much as we can.

Schooling is widely portrayed as a key way to help young people become informed and contributing "citizens". Reference to "teaching for citizenship" occurs again and again in statements on the purposes of public education throughout the world, partly to justify the amount of public money spent on education (a good example of politics in action). The extensive study of history and social studies in schools, for example, is frequently justified on this basis.

However, the concept of "citizenship education" is often too narrow and, in particular, too exclusively focused on students doing their "civic duty", without enough attention to what individuals can or cannot gain from civic participation or to the many abuses of power that exist in societies. The understanding of citizenship needs to be extended greatly to include politics in the fullest sense, at both individual and group levels. Even the school classroom should be seen by students as strongly political; and teachers can take advantage of this aspect of classroom life to increase students' general political understanding and skills, as we will illustrate later in this chapter.

Why promote political understanding and involvement?

Understanding politics helps students at a personal level. It enables them to understand how the world works, rather than constantly wondering about it and experiencing disappointment and despair. It helps them make whatever changes they can at the various levels, and steer a middle course between being overly optimistic and unduly pessimistic.

Political understanding and competence also enable students to contribute usefully to the world around them, making it a better place now and in the future. Although we have questioned "good citizenship" as living and acting only for the good of society, attention to the wellbeing of others is a major moral virtue, often comes naturally to us, and in many ways can positively impact our own lives.

Political understanding and skill help students in their social relationships at family, friendship, and other levels. Many of the same concepts and principles apply. This is not to downgrade social relationships, just to be realistic. Overly romanticizing relationships can result in their demise and deep disappointment in the long run; it can also mean that we oversee opportunities to improve them.

Finally, political understanding can help with class community and classroom management. It can enable students to see how their needs have to be reconciled with those of others and be more realistic about achieving their personal goals. They can come to experience classroom rules and structures as interesting and important rather than arbitrarily imposed. To summarize:

> ### Reasons for promoting political understanding and involvement
>
> - It enables students to understand how the world works
> - It helps them improve their life and avoid extremes of romanticism and despair
> - It leads to students contributing usefully to the world around them
> - It helps students in personal relationships as well: many of the same principles apply
> - It can help with class community and classroom management

What are the challenges of teaching for political understanding and involvement?

Teaching for political understanding and involvement may not be seen as sufficiently relevant to academic learning and related standardized test preparation. There may be complaints from various quarters and reduced professional status and reward.

Politics is a controversial area, especially when approached in the critical way we have recommended. Teachers who go down this path have to do a lot of preparation to ensure they avoid the many pitfalls.

Many parents have strong views on politics and may object to teachers working in the area at all. It is difficult to find an approach that satisfies everyone. Teachers may be accused of pushing a "political" stance.

Most teachers were not extensively trained in teaching politics, except in the descriptive way mentioned. Once again, a lot of time and effort is required to teach in this area to a significant degree.

Theory/research basis for promoting political understanding and involvement

A widely stated aim of schooling in earlier times and still today is to prepare students for citizenship, and citizenship rightly understood has a strong political component. For example, the 2009 OECD report on education for the 21st century sees a major goal of such education as fostering "competences" students will need to be effective "citizens" (Ananiadou and Claro, 2009: 8). It maintains that, due in part to increased access to ICT, students in the 21st century are experiencing "new forms of socialisation and social capital acquisition [and so schooling] needs to provide them with social values and attitudes as well as with the constructive experiences that will allow them to benefit from these opportunities and contribute actively to these new spaces of social life" (p. 5).

Similarly, the UK Department for Education *Character Education: Framework Guidance* document states that schools should be "effective in making pupils civic-minded and ready to contribute to society" (2019: 5–6). And Pollard et al. stress citizenship education as one of the central aims of schooling, saying that "good relationships and 'citizenship' in the classroom can act as a model for responsible, active citizenship in later life" (2019: 160).

According to Emma Smith, a central purpose of education "is to enhance pupils' enjoyment of learning and their preparation for citizenship" (2012: 83). Citizenship education has "important implications for developing students' perceptions about what it is to be part of an equitable and democratic society" (p. 86). Clearly, this means that students need to explore the nature and importance of democratic citizenship, especially at a time when the value and legitimacy of democracy is under attack around the world.

Meier, Knoester, and D'Andrea have founded a school that is focused on preparing students for "democratic citizenship" (2015: 1). They argue that "the purpose of public education must be to provide students with the skills of democracy: the ability to deliberate, to listen to others' opinions, to search for new answers … to imagine a different future … be effective and powerful citizens in a democracy" (p. 4) and explore "the possible meanings of patriotism" (p. 11).

As Pollard et al. and others maintain, however, it is important to balance people's civic involvement with their personal needs. Along these lines, Gill and Thomson state that, although "education is unavoidably political, and has a social end … [w]e should not design children so that they fit into a particular vision of society" (2012: 14). "It is unacceptable that … young people leave school with very little idea of … what their life might be and what kind of person they are" (p. 16).

It is essential, then, that students' emerging political understanding be critical, complex, and creative, rather than geared to a simple, pre-set societal structure. As noted above, Meier et al. (2015) envisage students being encouraged to search for *new* answers and design *different* futures. According to VanSledright, however, political teaching in schools in the past was often little more than indoctrination (2011: 13).

To highlight the need for an alternative approach, VanSledright gives a detailed case study of two history teachers at the same high school who teach the same American history course using very different approaches. One "traffics largely in an inspiring, commemorative, heritage-infused approach" (2011: 12), with a lot of talk of Americans' "freedom birthright" but no attention to the question "why were indigenous Americans repeatedly denied this birthright?" (p. 13). The other's approach, by contrast, is "as much about teaching potent life capabilities as it is about teaching history" (p. 32); it enables students "to read their world and make sound, astute decisions about what to take from it" (p. 33). Her students still learn a considerable amount of history in the traditional sense and, indeed, usually do better than her colleague's students on the same standardized history tests. But she wonders how well this standardized learning, just on its own, prepares her students for the challenges and complexities of the 21st century.

Strategies for promoting political understanding and involvement

There is a national organization called CIVIX, a non-partisan group who create all the materials for what's called Student Vote. For every election they create parallel material so you can hold very realistic looking elections in the classroom ... And their whole objective is to have a more engaged and informed populace.
                                        – Serena, a Grade 5/6 teacher in her fifteenth year

Even though students are young and cannot vote, it is important (for the reasons given) that they develop a solid foundation of understanding about politics. Here are the strategies we recommend:

Strategies for promoting political understanding and involvement

1 Discussing politics and how to approach it
2 Rehearsing and talking about voting
3 Addressing political issues and processes at the classroom and school level

---

Discussing politics and how to approach it

As we have seen, there are many different views about the nature of politics and how to approach it, and some see it largely in terms of compliance with our civic duties. So it is important to explore the field with students and try to arrive at adequate understandings. Lucy, in her seventh year, a coordinator but who had previously taught Grade 7/8, commented: "I felt that only half of my job is teaching the curriculum. I read somewhere that in middle school something like 80% of everything students learn is social, so if I'm not teaching them how to be a good citizen in society and they leave me, I'm not doing my job".

Anita, a Grade 8 teacher in her thirteenth year, spoke at length about how she discusses overall societal and political matters with her students, helping them become both more critical and more hopeful:

Kids at this age (Grade 8) are starting to become more independent, self-reflect more, and think about their relationships and how they act in public, all of those things, And not all teachers feel comfortable dealing with these general life matters, but that's who I am as a person … And it's really important to get into things that happen in the world. Our kids now are very cognisant of world events and, just like with adults, it can often feel overwhelming, especially if they hear of too many negative things: they can feel so powerless.

So a lot of what I've done this year is look at what we can do with this information. We can't let it overwhelm us, so how do we go out and find hope in the world and in our lives? So I do a lot of work with them around that, whether it's reading articles or just having class discussions.

So this year after the election my students all came in depressed and I was depressed as well, and normally we don't show bias in the classroom for one party of another, we try to have very non-partisan dialogues. But so many of our students are minorities, and they were scared and confused about why this is happening. So I decided that in my class we were going to look at our values as people, and we made a huge list of them on the board, it was amazing. And then I said, "Okay, now (a) in our daily lives and then (b) in our lives as a society, how do we show those values?"

And they came up with the two lists and wrote a paragraph about leadership, what qualities should we expect good leaders to have. And sometimes during the weekend update on Monday mornings, instead of talking about our weekends, I'll ask them to share one way that they showed their values over the weekend. So just kind of reinforcing those ideas with them. And they've been really receptive to that, which is really lovely.

Rehearsing and talking about voting

Even though their own actual voting is well into the future, talking with students about the election process can help them understand important aspects of politics and prepare for when they will be able to vote. Serena, a Grade 5/6 teacher with 15 years' experience, discussed this aspect of her teaching:

There is a national organization called CIVIX, a non-partisan group who create all the materials for what's called Student Vote. For every election they create parallel material so you can hold very realistic looking elections in the classroom, and they collect all the results and share it and you can see, by polling station and constituency, who would win in your class. And their whole objective is to have a more engaged and informed populace.

So they start with elementary and run all the way through high school, thinking that if we don't get people in the practice of voting when they're in school they won't vote. And the organization gets its funding by being non-partisan, so they have to be very careful about that. And they've teamed up with some amazing people to look at media illiteracy, the role of editorials that deconstruct things, opinion versus fact, the impact of social media, how to verify sources: they've come out with quite a comprehensive curriculum.

And I have done Student Vote six times now, at all the jurisdictional levels. On the whole the parents at my school are very informed and engaged, so my students walk in when it's an election cycle with a lot of opinions, and we talk about how their views differ from their parents' and so on.

Addressing political issues and processes at the classroom and school level

To make politics more tangible for their students, teachers can draw attention to parallels between general politics and structures at the classroom and school level, exploring the nature of power relationships and decision-making and how they can be negotiated and improved. Mike, a teacher of Grade 1 with 12 years' experience said: "I spend a lot of time building relationships with my students, avoiding that hierarchy between teacher and pupil that actually undermines learning. Both you and your students learn more. So I have the kids call me by my first name, just as a small token of limiting the hierarchy: it's less deferential".

Similarly, Marisa, a Grade 1/2 teacher in her twelfth year talked about how she tries to model a fairly egalitarian relationship with her students, even though technically she is in charge:

The kids tend to see me almost in a motherly role as well as being their teacher, which is nice; they feel comfortable with me. And I try to show them that I make mistakes and we laugh about that, because then they feel they can make mistakes. I also bring humour into the classroom, through music and dance parties, and find other ways to show them that I'm at their level, I'm not this leader they can't get to and who is very detached.

Jeannie, a teacher of Grade 3 with 13 years' experience, related how she supported her students' participation in a decision-making process at her school:

This year the school did something on giving students a voice. We have an adventure playground with climbing equipment and so forth, and it was run this way: at morning recess this grade goes on it, at lunch time a different grade goes on it, and at afternoon recess another grade goes on it.

And some of the kids said to me: sometimes we want to go on the playground when it's not our turn and it's empty, and it seems silly that we can't. So I said to them, because it's a school rule I can't change it alone, but you should go and talk to the principal. So they ended up doing a survey, talking to the principal, and presenting at a staff meeting. They prepared this whole presentation: this is who is using the playground, this is when it is empty, and this is what various teachers have said.

And the school ended up changing it. The new rule was that if the playground is not busy, all grades can use it, but if it gets too busy, then only the assigned grade can use it. And basically it taught the students that if they see something they don't understand or don't agree with or don't think is working, then by doing some research, asking some questions, talking to different people and coming up with a proposal, they can create change.

Chapter summary

Political life occurs at local, societal, and international levels. In the 21st century, with improved information and communication, it is increasingly possible for people to gain political understanding and have political impact. Some people say they are "not interested in politics" and, anyway, they are powerless to influence it. However, everyone is engaged in and affected by political processes in some form, even in family and friendship relationships, and they have to learn how to negotiate them.

Schools need to support students in learning about political matters and developing the skills to address them. In earlier times, schools tended to take a descriptive approach to both historical and current political phenomena rather than encouraging students to adopt a stance and get involved. A more active approach is needed. In addition, students need to learn how to react to political phenomena, in particular, how to maintain their mental health in negative political situations over which they have little or no control.

The importance of "citizenship education" has long been a common theme in writing about schooling. However, the concept of citizenship education has often been too narrow and, in particular, too exclusively focused on students doing their "civic duty", without enough attention to critiquing the status quo and exploring what individuals can or cannot gain from civic participation and from understanding the political dimension of public and personal life.

Among the strategies teachers can use to promote political understanding and commitment are: discussing what politics is and how to approach it; discussing particular areas of political abuse and progress; rehearsing and talking about voting; and addressing political issues and processes at the classroom and school level.

Questions for reflection and discussion

1 What is politics and why it is important?
2 To what extent and in what ways can individuals and sub-groups influence politics?
3 In so far as we cannot influence politics, how can we maintain our mental health?
4 How can teachers support student development in this area?

11 Principle 11: Foster international outlooks and skills

In our community we have a number of refugees from war-torn countries, and there are a lot of concerns related to that ... So in class we have experiences where students are learning each other's names ... Getting to know the people in the room and feeling included in the school is important.
— Candice, teaching homeroom and integrated arts in her thirteenth year

The Principle, its importance, and some challenges

Schooling has traditionally focused largely on life at local, state, and national levels, and any political education of the kind discussed in the previous chapter has dealt mainly with jurisdictions within the nation to which students currently belong. However, international matters have also received some attention, for example in subjects such as history, geography, literature and science.

In the 21st century, we need to go further in an international direction, both because life is becoming more international and because the international is more important than we realized in the past. The experiences of nations around the world of colonization, independence, migration, and so on have strong implications for one's own nation and way of life in many areas, such as identity, inclusion, work, and the economy.

What is meant by fostering international outlooks and skills?

The past emphasis on the local and national in schooling was partly because funding for schooling usually came from local and national sources. Also, young people were viewed as needing to be educated mainly in local and national matters so they could participate at those levels. Creating good local neighbours and citizens was seen as a primary objective.

Focusing more on international outlooks and skills, then, involves a shift in thinking about school goals, based on the idea that the international context is more important than we previously thought, impacting life at all levels. However, we believe that exploring international matters can be combined with studying more traditional subjects – such as history, science, literature, and even local citizenship – where the international has become more relevant.

It is important to recognize, however, that the international also impacts the individual. Accordingly, we are not just proposing an international perspective. Rather, we are talking of an approach to teaching at all levels that takes account of the increasing connections between nations across the world, the movement of peoples between nations, and the growing mixture of national backgrounds within a given country and local community.

Why foster international outlooks and skills?

Promoting international outlooks and skills helps prepare students for the workplace and other settings where it will be necessary to know about many countries, how to communicate with them, and how to utilize their technologies and other ways of doing things.

An emphasis on the international in the classroom helps build class community and mutual understanding and respect, which in turn facilitate small-group and whole-class learning. Brief contact with people of different national backgrounds can trigger or reinforce prejudice, whereas deeper and more sustained inquiry into other national groups can help reduce bias.

Study of the people and customs of many nations helps us become aware of our common humanity and the fact that differences between people tend to be at an individual level rather than running along national or ethnic lines. This helps reduce stereotyping, which is the main basis of prejudice and discrimination.

Encouraging an international outlook and way of operating facilitates international trade, migration, and exchange of various kinds. It is being increasingly documented by economists and others that migration is a major source of increased prosperity in wealthier countries, quite apart from the reduction in suffering of many of those who migrate.

Increased contact with different national groups can make life more interesting as we are exposed to varied phenomena and different points of view. This is precisely why many people engage in international travel, which increasingly can be done virtually in the school classroom. As noted, however, it is not just the differences that are interesting but also the discovery of similarities within the differences and coming to understand humans more fully. In summary:

Advantages of addressing the international dimension

- Many skills relevant to the workplace and other settings are acquired
- Class community is enhanced and shared learning strengthened
- Students become more aware of our common humanity
- International trade, migration, and exchange are facilitated
- Life becomes more interesting and enjoyable

What are the challenges of teaching for international outlooks and skills?

The knowledge teachers should ideally have to facilitate international learning is vast. Fortunately, internet resources in this area are growing rapidly. However, teachers still have to master these and the overarching concepts and principles needed to integrate them. Also, the technology required to make these resources available to students is often inadequate in public schools.

Adopting a strongly international perspective is often controversial. Parents, school officials, and others may see teachers who go down this path as promoting a particular political point of view.

Parents may view teaching in the area of culture, ethnicity, and so on as their domain, as part of normal parental upbringing. Teachers have to engage in a great deal of preparation and discussion to have a chance of winning over such parents and the politicians who support them.

A thorough international education goes well beyond most official curricula, requiring much time and effort on the teacher's part to find ways to teach adequately in this area while also fulfilling content teaching requirements.

Theory/research basis for fostering international outlooks and skills

Florian, Black-Hawkins, and Rouse note that schools are going increasingly in an international and global direction: "[T]here is an increasing recognition that the forces of globalization have changed the demographics of schooling. As the citizens of Europe exercise their freedom of mobility, and an increasing number of refugees seek asylum … elsewhere, schools become more diverse and multicultural in terms of ethnicity, language and religion" (2017: 13). Swartz says we need to open up the topic of the immigrant and refugee experience: "This world, where war, natural disaster, or acts of terrorism drive families out of their home countries, is much broader in scope than in past decades" (2020: 41). He proposes using the teaching of literature "to bring authenticity, humanity, and story power to learning about the immigrant and refugee experience" (p. 41).

According to Banks, "[m]odern education systems were established … to build social cohesion through homogenization and maintain social control" (2016: 29). However, such "assimilationist" approaches are becoming less and less effective and appropriate. A new approach to citizenship education is needed that helps students see "not only how migrant groups are changed by the host society and nation, but also how the host society and nation are changed in significant ways by the cultures of migrants and marginalized groups" (p. 30).

Shirley maintains that greater "internationalization" is needed in arriving at national educational policies and practices. In the past, "an insular imperative has characterized many nations" in educational matters (2017: 99). We are now in a position of "greater complexity than ever before", with economies increasingly international. Despite this, however, educators still try to "socialize students into national identities [even though] students' subjective life experiences increasingly are transnational, with their family members and friends drawn from many countries" (p. 104).

Strategies for fostering international outlooks and skills

There is a unit on contemporary art that I started last year and really love. And a lot of it is about identity and nationality. I showed different examples of contemporary art and got the students to interact with them in exciting ways.
— Nancy, a Grade 7/8 art teacher in her fifteenth year

As the world becomes more interconnected and people increasingly move between nations, it is important to deepen students' understanding of the international sphere and help them become more capable of negotiating it. Here are the strategies we propose:

Strategies for fostering international outlooks and skills

- Discussing international perspectives with students
- Studying international matters within school subjects
- Teaching international skills
- Drawing on family members

Discussing international perspectives with students

Explicit discussion of international matters helps students become more aware of the broader context in which we live and the growing links between different parts of the world. Anna, in her thirteenth year and teaching Kindergarten and Grade 1 said:

I now spend a lot more time talking about the surrounding world, outside our four walls, and bringing the outside in; for example, reminding students how lucky they are. Because they sometimes play with food and throw it around; and that gives an opportunity to talk about children who are trying to escape countries where water and flour are rationed, and how the food they are throwing around could help feed a family. And because I have a background in that I talk with them about it.

Similarly, Candice, teaching both homeroom and Grade 2/5 integrated arts (13 years' experience) reported:

> In our community we have a number of refugees from war-torn countries, and there are a lot of concerns related to that. They're moving to a new country and having to make new friends. So in class we have experiences where students are learning each other's names, like music name-games, and social interaction, like games where you shake each other's hands on the fourth beat. Getting to know the people in the room and feeling included in the school is important.

Studying international matters within school subjects

Exploration of international perspectives can occur in the context of studying academic subjects. Deirdre, a Kindergarten teacher in her seventh year observed:

> The new Common Core State Standards and assessments (in New York) have made it very difficult. Previously within fiction writing, a kid could write about an environmental matter and even a particular animal, but that is hard to do now. But then I decided, I'm just going to go full on and tell them to get really excited and try their best.
>
> So we started a unit on fiction writing and they loved it. They picked up on the excitement and wrote these amazing books on fictional characters with their problems and solutions. And they brought in things we learned from science, on deforestation and protecting rain forests, and also some of what we did around Earth Day like recycling. They brought that into their stories.

Paul, a Grade 8 teacher in his fourteenth year, talked about how he teaches world religions:

> World religions is something I really enjoy, and the kids don't know much about it. They hear little things at school, like "Oh these kids have gone for this holiday, or now it's Christmas, now it's Chanukah, now it's Diwali". But they don't really know much about it. And last year in my school there were some incidents of racism and Islam-phobia and anti-immigrant sentiments, which kind of shocked me. And public schools are secular of course, but I still think it's important to teach about religion as a subject so they understand. But many teachers are afraid of offending people by talking about it, and also they don't think there's enough time.
>
> So I offered world religions as a topic for inquiry and got a group together who were interested enough to run it; and we decided to incorporate religious celebrations as part of it, and food – which kids are so interested in. So we talked about all the different religions and watched videos, had debates and did announcements; and the students loved it.

Nancy, a Grade 7/8 art teacher in her fifteenth year, described how she teaches about art from around the world:

> There is a unit on contemporary art that I started last year and really love. And a lot of it is about identity and nationality. I showed different examples of contemporary art and got the students to interact with them in exciting ways. I took examples from across the globe as well as across sexual preferences, gender identities, ages, so it was very, very inclusive. And for the assignment they had to choose what part of their identity they want to express through the art.
>
> And you know, I have two beautiful books of the most famous contemporary artists but every page is about white males. So I say to my students, "One of the reasons I wanted to do contemporary art was to get away from the impressionists, who are all white males". I looked through those two books, thinking there would be representation of a multiple, global, inclusive, variety of people but there wasn't. For example, Frida Kahlo wasn't there.
>
> So I start the unit by talking about how important it is to see variety and see how different cultures express variety through their art, and it's important to see themselves in the artists and what they're expressing. And I think it was the best unit I've ever made, after my Graffiti unit.

Teaching international skills

A particular area of international teaching is making students aware of the growing number of skills that are used all around the world and helping them develop at least some of them. Serena, with 15 years' teaching experience and a teacher of Grades 5/6, spoke about her activity in this area:

> In my school district, global competency is increasingly being talked about. And they suddenly started using the term as if there had been professional development in which the meaning of the term was explained, but in fact there had been very little. In essence what they're asking for are things like creativity and communication and real-world application of learning, so it's a lot of what people are already doing. These are universal competencies that students will need in the future.
>
> So the school district is recognizing that we have to prepare students to function in a world the nature of which is still uncertain: creativity, collaboration, communication skills, universal skills that transfer across disciplines, problem-solving. It hasn't actually changed my teaching much because it largely matched what I was doing. But one application of it would be to think outside of your own small community to what's happening in business and other settings internationally.

Drawing on family members

In school districts where people of varied national backgrounds are living, an important way to help develop international perspectives is to invite family members into the classroom to talk about other countries or interact with students in some other role. Marisa, a Grade 1/2 teacher in her fifteenth year spoke about how she uses this strategy:

> I invite parents into the classroom as much as possible. Some I know have the time to volunteer, and that's a great way to bring families into the classroom and show respect for families with different traditions. And some have brought their distinctive expertise. Like one parent came to teach the kids henna designs, and talking about those designs became just a natural part of our everyday conversations. Building relationships with the students is very important to me, and I try to be very open and welcoming with the families as well.

Chapter summary

In the 21st century, teaching needs to go further in an international direction, both because life is becoming more international and because the international is more important than we previously realized. In the past, schooling focused mainly on local, state, and national matters, partly because of the way it was funded.

Studying people and customs of many nations makes students more aware of our common humanity and that differences between people are often at an individual level rather than running along national lines. This helps reduce stereotyping, which is a major basis of prejudice and discrimination. In addition, studying problems in other countries (e.g. extreme poverty, lack of clean water) makes privileged students more aware of their advantages and also provides a basis for seeing inequities in their own country and community.

Fostering international outlooks and skills helps build a populace who accept and can react appropriately to international migration and exchange of various kinds. Economists and others are increasingly documenting that welcoming immigrants from poorer countries is a major source of cultural enrichment and increased prosperity in wealthier ones, apart from the reduction of suffering among many of those who migrate.

An emphasis on the international in the classroom can help build a class community characterized by mutual understanding and respect, which in turn facilitates small-group and whole-class learning. Brief contact with people of different national backgrounds can trigger or reinforce prejudice, whereas deeper and more sustained inquiry into other national groups tends to help reduce bias.

Strategies for fostering international outlooks and skills in students include: discussing international perspectives with students; studying international matters within school subjects; teaching international skills; and drawing on family members to provide information, facilitate discussion, and illustrate commonalities between people of different national backgrounds.

Questions for reflection and discussion

1 Why is an international outlook important?
2 How do international exchange and migration help everyone?
3 What are some of the commonalities between people of different national backgrounds and individual differences within such groups?
4 What are some of the problems in poorer countries that have their counterpart – in an acute but smaller scale – in wealthier countries?
5 How can teachers support student development in international outlooks and skills?

12 Principle 12: Teach for overall global/ environmental awareness

The world is changing at such a fast pace now that you absolutely have to teach about the change. You could have talked about it probably twenty years ago … because things were also changing then, but it was not at the same rapid speed. And because we're all so connected globally today we have to get into it more.
— Maria, a Grade 4/5 teacher in her thirteenth year

The Principle, its importance, and some challenges

An international outlook is important, as just discussed, but there is also increasing interest in a more "holistic" and "organic" perspective that we are calling here a "global/environmental" outlook, one that embraces all human and non-human life and reality. This perspective is necessary to provide an even broader framework for political and international thought and action, and to promote wellbeing and safety at individual, local, societal, global, and environmental levels.

Many education writers in the 21st century have advocated holistic, environmental, and global education. But some practitioners have resisted going very far in this direction on the ground that it is not feasible given the other demands of the education system. In this chapter, we clarify what a global/environmental approach is, why it is important, and how it can be made feasible despite the subject coverage expectations placed on teachers.

Of course, it is challenging to implement a global/environmental approach of this kind, not only because of the other expectations but also because funding and decision-making are still largely at a national level, and national philosophies of education still tend to be rather insular (Shirley, 2017). However, we believe it is important for teachers to go as far as possible in this direction, for the sake of their students and the wellbeing of the world in general.

What is teaching for overall global/environmental awareness and commitment?

The type of education we are talking about goes beyond international education in several respects. It still stresses the importance of international structures and connections, but it considers the general setting within which these phenomena occur. That setting continues to include the personal, cultural, national, and international but includes other dimensions of reality.

Global/environmental education addresses basic human values and what life is ultimately about. We have already considered this topic at the personal level, but a global/environmental perspective attends to issues of life in general and the world as a whole, wrestling with connections between the individual and the global community, and between humans and the rest of nature. It explores origins, directions, and change at a global level.

Why teach for overall global/environmental awareness?

Promoting a global/environmental perspective provides a foundation for a more equitable and inclusive approach to other people. The common humanity of all people is emphasized along with their common connection to the world as a whole. Natural empathy and care for others and the earth are explored and utilized.

A global, holistic approach takes account of the wide range of factors that must be attended to if people are to attain their goals. Too often in education, social science, politics, and so on, just a few aspects of a situation are attended to. This is sometimes defended on the ground that we must be precise and scientific, but in fact it is unscientific because key components are omitted. Being holistic is more challenging in a way because so many things must be considered at once. However, simply leaving out certain elements creates challenges in that the "solutions" arrived at may simply be ineffective.

Apart from leading to more effective action, a global, holistic approach provides a more comprehensive and coherent worldview, bringing greater meaning and inspiration to life. Many authors maintain that a sense of meaning is essential for human happiness and wellbeing. But this sense of meaning has to span the different contexts of life and bring them together, otherwise it may be unsatisfying and short-lived.

A global/environmental perspective also provides a basis for joint action, with individuals, nations, organizations, and so on pulling together. Just as all relevant factors in a situation have to be considered, so connecting all the people implicated in an action together is necessary if the action is to be successful. To summarize:

Reasons for teaching for global/environmental awareness

- A global/environmental approach provides a basis for equity and inclusion
- Such an approach leads to more effective action by attending to a wider range of factors
- A global/environmental view of the world and life is more meaningful and inspiring
- It also provides a solid basis for joint action

What are the challenges of teaching for global/environmental awareness?

A global/environmental outlook takes teachers into areas previously thought to be the province of religion. While religions are changing rapidly in relevant areas, teachers need to be aware of this possible complication.

Parental and community beliefs may be questioned. Teachers need to consider how far they can go on sensitive issues, weighing the benefits for their students, society, and the world against the dangers of offending some parents and community members.

Within the same classroom there may be students of very different backgrounds. This can be very helpful for exploring global issues but again teachers have to tread carefully.

A global, holistic, environmental approach is highly interdisciplinary. Teachers must constantly go beyond their discipline (e.g. literature, physics) in addressing such issues. This places considerable demands on them in terms of preparing for and facilitating the classroom discussion.

Once again, the time required for a global/environmental approach often makes full curriculum coverage difficult, at least until ways are found to cover a considerable proportion of required content in the context of exploring global/environmental issues.

Theory/research basis for teaching for overall global/environmental awareness

An international approach, as discussed in Chapter 11, still differentiates between nations to a considerable extent. Moving to the global/environmental perspective explored in this chapter means we place less stress on national differentiation and more on a "systems" approach, which is still international but in a more integrated way.

A systems approach is proposed by Goleman and Senge, who emphasize "connections between understanding self, understanding other, and understanding the larger systems to which we all belong" (2014: 65). Combining these understandings gives us "the constructs and tools for better interpersonal decision-making" (p. 65). It also provides a basis for caring for one another. The research on which these authors draw shows that systems thinking leads students to "express their innate predisposition to care at a larger and larger scale", both for other people and the environment (p. 66). Moreover, going in this direction does not get in the way of teaching subject content and skills but rather results in "more effective strategies" for achieving educational goals (p. 72).

Collins makes a similar point. He is critical of the way science is often taught in schools: "most of what students learn in these school subjects is not very helpful for making wise policy or personal decisions" (2017: 81). He believes that if we integrated various scientific fields – including social science – around key issues we could still teach a great deal of science but in a more useful and engaging way. Learning science is very important: "Many different societal issues require scientific understanding, such as how to feed a growing population and how to reduce the cost of treating the diseases of an overweight population" (p. 82). Through science we can explore pollution (p. 74), climate change (p. 75), and species extinction (p. 75). But addressing these types of issues requires a more comprehensive, integrated approach to science than has often been adopted in the past.

An emphasis on environmental education is endorsed by Pollard et al. In their view, a major aspect of what "an education system should be designed to do" (2019: 542) is promote "environmental sustainability" (p. 546). "Global warming develops inexorably and appears to be having significant effects on weather, sea levels, flora and fauna", which in turn is significantly impacting human life and society. Environmental education is required "so that the next generation can be better prepared for the future" (p. 546).

Global/environmental understanding and commitment involves adopting what is often called a "holistic" approach (from the classical Greek word *holos* or "whole"). According to Miller, "Holistic education attempts to bring education into alignment with the fundamental realities of nature. Nature at its core is interrelated and dynamic" (2019: 5). In education, we have tended to "divide knowledge into subjects, units, and lessons [so] students often cannot see the relationship between these subjects … or the relevance of the subject to life" (p. 6). It is time to replace this approach with a holistic one that fosters "global connectedness" (p. 6).

Dolby connects a global approach in education to a multicultural one. She says our goal in the multicultural education of millennials is deep transformation of individuals and institutions; but "there is no evidence to suggest that we have been successful on a broad scale" (2012: 123). In order to be successful, "empathy for all living things must be the cornerstone of our pedagogy" (p. 127). Yes, we must teach systematically about past and current social injustices – our empathy must be "informed". But we need a "whole game" approach. With such an approach, "students can be bridged slowly from their positions of sympathy, to empathy, to informed empathy, to justice" (p. 130).

Strategies for teaching overall global/environmental awareness

In the first term all the Grade 8s do a language-based geography project where they have to redesign an abandoned or underused space anywhere in the world to serve the community in a sustainable way … looking into the science and geography of it. And when they've finished … they present it to parents.

– Anita, a Grade 8 teacher in her twelfth year

As we have said, teaching for an overall global/environmental perspective is challenging given past traditions of schooling and current expectations for curriculum coverage. Here are the strategies we recommend for teaching in this area:

Strategies for teaching for overall global/environmental awareness

1 General discussion of global/environmental perspectives
2 Thematic study of global/environmental matters within and across subjects
3 Specific study of environmental matters

General discussion of global/environmental perspectives

Because of curriculum requirements, there is a limit to how much teachers can discuss global matters with their students. However, discussion at the beginning or end of the day, at the beginning or end of a lesson, or on some other special occasion is possible. As we saw in Chapter 4, teachers are sometimes willing to set the curriculum aside to address key life issues. Carrie, now a school administrator and previously a middle-school teacher, talked in her thirteenth year about how teachers in her school discuss global human rights with their students:

> We did a big piece with all our classes around human rights. For several weeks every classroom had the same two-period interactive class on what equity means; and some classes looked at the human rights declaration and identified specific issues, for example the language kids sometimes use on Instagram that may not only offend their peers but other people they don't even know.

And Maria, the Grade 4/5 we met earlier, spoke of the need to talk with students about how the world is changing:

> The world is changing at such a fast pace now that you absolutely have to teach about the change. You could have talked about it probably twenty years ago when we were kids because things were also changing then, but it was not at the same rapid speed. And because we're all so connected globally today we have to get into it more. Also kids' attention spans seem shorter, and in fact we're all so impatient: we don't want to wait a second to get information.
>
> So we have to teach about what is happening, like the need to learn science, technology, and mathematics because that's where the future is. And human rights too: before things were hidden or not talked about, but now you can't not talk about these things because kids will find out on the internet ... And when there's a holiday coming up, that's the perfect time to look at something happening in the rest of the world.

Thematic study of global/environmental matters within and across subjects

Apart from general discussion as time permits, global understanding and commitment can be fostered within teaching subjects, notably history, geography, social studies, literature, and health and physical education. Maria again spoke of how she integrates global study into subject teaching with her Grade 4/5 students:

> I like to watch what's happening in the world; and I look it up, find an article, and then have the class read it and talk about it the next day. For example, we discussed the Mac and Cheese problem and that fit completely into my health class. I heard about it on the news, went and looked it up, printed off an article, and we all read it and started discussing right away. That motivates me and I think it motivates them. One of my girls went home and put it on her fridge and said, "Mom, no more Mac and Cheese".

> Another thing I do is bring what's relevant into my non-fiction literacy programme. That's the perfect time to read about what's happening in the world and the various social issues ... So I find a way to weave it into my programming.

In the same way, Serena, a Grade 5/6 teacher of thirteen years, described how she teaches about global matters in a subject context:

> One of the best things about living in a digital age is you can connect to people immediately: you're not restricted to the information in a textbook that was published eight years ago and may be no longer relevant. Like this year for government in Grade 5 and international relations in Grade 6 we did a unit on climate change – which my kids understandably are very disturbed about.

> We watched "Before the Flood", a National Geographic documentary that Leonardo DiCaprio narrates. And I had a very verbal class for the most part, and they were very into "rants" by TV personalities. So they did some research on climate change and then wrote rants very much like on TV, we were able to find a bunch of them online. And with their rants, the only stipulation was that a government had to be mentioned in some way, which covered us off on the subject connection.

> Can my students name all three levels of government? I'm pretty sure they can. Can they hit all the subject expectations? Probably not all of them, but that's okay with me. Because the overall expectations are what you want them to walk away with and hold.

Specific study of environmental matters

The environment is a major area of global understanding and action today, especially in relation to climate change and environmental protection. Deirdre, teaching Kindergarten in her seventh year, talked about the need to engage students on broader issues such as the environment:

> I have a student who is autistic and has social-emotional issues, but he became engaged when I read them a book in our deforestation lesson about how Willy the Whale and his mother were endangered by an oil spill. Previously he would just say one word – yes, no – and never be able to share feelings, but with that story he became very emotionally involved. He actually said that Willy the Whale was really sad, and kept going over to look at a book I have on oil spills. When you get into higher-order topics like that with the kids, it is amazing to see them bloom. It is like they are doing their own inquiry.

Again, Serena in her thirteenth year described how she addressed general environmental concerns in science with her Grade 5/6 students, often giving these issues priority over specific content:

> Half my class at this point have phones on them at all times, so if you need to know a particular fact you can Google it. Like if you need to know what metamorphic rock is, you can find a definition of it. More important than such specific knowledge are general understandings, like the impact of mining on an indigenous community. That's going to stay a lot longer with them. And anyway there are too many specifics for you to cover them all.

Anita, a Grade 8 teacher in her twelfth year, talked about a project at her school on environmental sustainability:

> In the first term all the Grade 8s do a language-based geography project where they have to redesign an abandoned or underused space anywhere in the world to serve the community in a sustainable way. They have to do research on the demographics of the area they choose and look at global examples of places that have been rehabilitated or made sustainable, looking into the science and geography of it. And when they've finished redesigning the space they present it to parents. It could be an abandoned house in their neighbourhood, or a historic building in the city that is already being changed into something else: an old entertainment park, an abandoned factory, some malting silos or something else. And it doesn't necessarily hit all the curriculum expectations, but that's okay.

Chapter summary

A global/environmental outlook takes us beyond the international to the overall context in which international life and exchange occur. As we have said often, a well-lived life is enormously complex and requires a comprehensive and integrated approach. Adopting a "holistic" approach of this kind is important for the world as a whole.

Promoting global/environmental awareness and commitment provides a foundation for more equitable and inclusive relationships between people. The commonalities among people (as well as the differences) are revealed along with common connections to the world as a whole, and empathy and care for others and the earth are explored and enhanced. This approach promises to enlist the support of students, who at present are often resistant to a more equitable and inclusive way of life.

Adopting such an approach to teaching presents challenges for teachers because most were educated and trained in specialized subject areas rather than in a global, holistic outlook. Just finding the time to develop the necessary knowledge and connections is difficult, especially when most school systems continue to emphasize narrow subject teaching and test preparation. However, we believe moving in this direction will be interesting and enriching for teachers, quite apart from the many benefits to students.

Some of the strategies teachers can use in promoting global/environmental awareness and commitment in students are: general discussion of a global/environmental perspective and its importance; thematic study of global/environmental matters within and across subjects; and study specifically of environmental matters, including growing ecological threats.

Questions for reflection and discussion

1 What is a global/ecological outlook? How does it go beyond an international outlook?
2 Why is such an outlook and set of practices important?
3 What are some of the challenges to the world ecosphere today?
4 How can these challenges be met at national and international levels?
5 How can teachers support student development in this area?

Part 4

Direction IV: Teaching for Digital Knowledge and Skills

The educational direction most often associated with the 21st century is increased use of technology by teachers and students alike, including in the classroom setting. Although there are other important areas of what we are calling 21st-century teaching, this is certainly a major one; and it is the focus of Part 4 of the book, that is Chapters 13–16.

We begin in Chapter 13 with a general exploration of IT use in the classroom by teachers and students. Then in Chapters 14–16 we discuss particular aspects of the topic: technology as a tool rather than just an end in itself; its use in individual learning; and its use to support collaboration. IT can be extremely helpful in education but we have to ensure that it is used in the service of the overall goals of 21st-century teaching.

The aspects of 21st-century teaching we focus on in Part 4 are:

Aspects of teaching for digital knowledge and skills

Chapter 13: Model and foster use of technology
Chapter 14: Promote use of technology as a means, not just an end
Chapter 15: Foster use of technology to individualize learning
Chapter 16: Foster use of technology for collaboration

13 Principle 13: Model and foster use of technology

My use of IT has increased a great deal in recent years. For example, in art I let kids search for things online to look at and use as resources and references; and they work on Google Docs and submit online assignments like logs and so forth.
— Felicity, an art and music teacher of Grades 7/8
in her fifteenth year

The Principle, its importance, and some challenges

Information and communication technology (often referred to simply as IT) has the potential to increase greatly the effectiveness of schooling by raising the level of student engagement and enjoyment; facilitating dialogue between students and between students and teachers; and making knowledge more available to teachers and students alike. For example, the power of search engines such as Google to put relevant information at our fingertips makes an enormous contribution to learning. Teachers need to become more adept in IT themselves, model its use in the classroom, and support student learning about both its benefits and how to use it.

Of course, students have their own routes to IT learning, and indeed a challenge in the area is that students are frequently ahead of their teachers in certain respects! But the same is true of other areas of learning. This just means that teachers have to apply to IT the dialogical, constructivist approach discussed in earlier chapters, with teachers and students learning on their own *and* together, and the teacher often serving as chair and facilitator of learning rather than the sole source of knowledge.

What is modelling and fostering use of technology?

Given the importance of IT in the 21st century, teachers should strongly promote its use by their students. But this requires that they themselves are constantly using IT and growing in knowledge of it. They do not always have to know more than their students, and not all teachers will be equally talented or interested in using technology. But considerable mastery by teachers is important so they can foster its use, their students can see they are serious about its importance, and their students can see first-hand the benefits it brings.

In fostering IT use, teachers should permit and encourage students to use it often in researching assignments, giving presentations, and completing course requirements. For example, an IT presentation or video rather than a written paper may often be acceptable as the final submission for an assignment. However, students should be given some choice in the extent to which they use IT because they – like teachers – will vary in how much they wish to use it, how adept they are in doing so, and how large a place it is likely to have in their lives in the future. Extensive use of it should not become an absolute value in education, any more than requiring all students to go to very high levels in particular academic subjects.

For modelling and fostering IT use to be effective, however, a broad approach is necessary. We need to avoid the frequent narrowness of much past and present practice in the area. In both popular and educational contexts the emphasis is often almost exclusively on what is spectacular and entertaining (in education this has been called "edutainment"). And in education in particular, lengthy PowerPoint presentations are often used which differ little from the traditional top-down lecture. Once again, IT has to be adapted to support interactive and engaging pedagogy rather than becoming transmission teaching in a new guise.

Why model and foster IT use?

Being able to use IT is a key 21st-century skill in the classroom, the workplace, and elsewhere. Although as we have said students vary in how much they want and need to use technology, a substantial mastery today at least in some areas is important for success and wellbeing.

Technology can make classroom learning much more effective. Both teachers and students can access information on a need-to-know basis; students can achieve a considerable degree of independence in learning; material can become available to students in a more vivid, detailed, and understandable form; and more up-to-date information is at everyone's fingertips.

IT can make learning and life more interesting and enjoyable, for teachers and students alike. Pleasing graphic material can be constantly available, connections to family and friends can be enhanced, access to news and the arts can be facilitated, and so on.

Students can get to know each other better and the class community can be enhanced. This is especially obvious with synchronous online teaching, on Zoom for example, where being able to see as well as hear each other makes a great difference. But even in face-to-face contexts, use of IT can add many new ways to learn about and interact with each other.

Connections to family by both teacher and students can be enhanced. Parents can easily submit queries and requests, teachers can quickly send home information about the programme and individual students, and students can post and receive messages.

> **Reasons for modelling and fostering IT use**
>
> - Being able to use IT is a key 21st-century skill in education, the workplace, and elsewhere
> - IT can make classroom learning much more effective
> - IT can make learning and life more interesting and enjoyable, for teachers and students alike
> - Students can get to know each other better and the class community can be enhanced
> - Connections to family by both teacher and students can be enhanced

What are the challenges of teaching in this area?

Some of the more interesting and valuable uses of IT are not seen by others as supporting traditional top-down teaching. Parents, school administrators, and others may view broad and extensive use of technology as undermining subject teaching and exam preparation. Much time and effort on the part of teachers is required to work out how to "do both" as much as possible, and also how to explain the value of their use of technology in teaching.

Teachers and students have to learn to use IT for educational purposes rather than primarily for entertainment. Promoting understanding in this respect and mastering more meaningful uses of technology takes considerable time and effort, and is something teachers will have to do largely on their own given the shortage of professional development these days. And it cannot be done "once for all" in teacher preparation or elsewhere as technology keeps changing.

Students vary in their interest and talent in IT use. Teachers have to learn to assess whether reluctant students are genuinely not interested or talented, or simply lack confidence and experience; and they have to work out when to push students in the area and when to work with them in developing a somewhat different style of learning and living.

Teachers' own interest and talent in IT use is often limited. Teachers have to push themselves to some extent in the area, but also sometimes learn to live with being behind many of their students in certain areas and needing to draw on their expertise.

Online teaching, in particular, is challenging and draining for teachers and students. Many new strategies have to be developed to address this problem, while also working out how to adapt effective approaches from face-to-face teaching to this new setting.

There are safety issues in relation to the use of IT. Teachers need to identify these and develop ways to address them. Sometimes restrictions on IT use in the classroom have to be implemented that do not fit with student wishes or with optimal learning.

Students usually do not have equal access to IT devices and home support. Again, this requires not only making devices and support available to students as much as possible, but also making tough decisions about limiting use of technology to some extent.

Theory/research basis for modelling and fostering use of technology

According to a 2012 OECD Special Report, "Digital media have the potential to transform learning environments and empower learners to become active in shaping their own education" (Schleicher, 2012: 43). Similarly, Bellanca maintains that "[t]echnology tools can contribute greatly to the enrichment of students' learning in projects ... helping students to learn, think, and collaborate more skillfully" (2010: 39). He outlines the tools that, in his view (in 2010), "are most valuable for transforming project learning into an enriched learning experience that dramatically improves student achievement, as well as their 21st century skills" (p. 42). The e-tools cited are: blogs, podcasts, whiteboards, tags, Twitter, e-portfolios, social networks, Moodle, and Web 2.0 (p. 44).

Collins and Halverson present two major arguments for increased use of IT in schools: "[T]he world is changing [so] we need to adapt schooling to prepare students for the changing world that they are entering [and] technology gives us enhanced capabilities for educating learners" (2018: 9). And Trilling and Fadel state that "our 21st century students need to acquire the skills to appropriately access, evaluate, use, manage, and add to the wealth of information and media they now have at their thumbs and fingertips ... [They] will have unprecedented power to amplify their ability to think, learn, communicate, collaborate, and create" (2009: 64).

Collins points out that, whereas "[c]hildren are spending increasing amounts of time communicating in different ways using new digital technologies" (2017: 17), schools by contrast "have been slow to incorporate these approaches into their teaching" (p. 22). Much more needs to be done. "Schools need to find ways to harness these new technologies not just for the elites ... but for all children, whatever their background" (pp. 32–33).

Goleman and Senge say we have to be careful with technology because it "can remove the person from the process", getting in the way of social and emotional learning (2014: 37). They believe that with careful planning, "technology and SEL can fit together in ways that make coherent sense ... [Y]ou can reinvent the classroom" (pp. 37–38). But their caution needs to be taken seriously. As we will see in the next chapter, teachers have to work hard to keep "the person in the process" and avoid largely technocratic uses of IT. They have to find ways to ensure that, when using IT, they still apply the holistic, child-centred pedagogy discussed in earlier chapters.

Like Goleman and Senge, VanSledright (2011) believes the internet can indeed help make progressive approaches to teaching more feasible. In history courses, both teachers and students can use the internet to implement an inquiry approach to learning that works from original documents: "digitized, Internet-based archival source materials have proliferated in recent years, making access to them easier for history teachers and therefore their use in classrooms more common" (2011: 18). He advocates an "ambitious" approach to history teaching that uses IT to facilitate inquiry learning, by contrast with the traditional "obsession with coverage" of history texts (p. 19).

Strategies for modelling and fostering use of technology

That is my ladybug right there, in red and black; it is basically a projector but we call it the ladybug and the children get so excited. I feed into it and it goes right onto the smart board, which we use every day for all sorts of things.
— Kira, a Kindergarten teacher in her seventh year

Despite the great potential of technology to enhance learning and life, its use in schooling is generally well below that found in many real-world settings. Strategies for increasing IT usage in the classroom in productive ways include the following:

Strategies for fostering use of IT

1 Using IT extensively in classroom presentations and learning activities
2 Supporting student IT use in class presentations, assignments, self-documentation, etc.
3 Increasing your own IT knowledge and skill
4 Modelling effective online teaching so students can learn how to participate in online classes
5 Modelling accessing information in class, with students helping
6 Modelling and teaching responsible use of IT devices
7 Using IT to keep in touch with families

Using IT extensively in classroom presentations and learning activities

Use of IT in classroom teaching is not only valuable in itself, it helps students see the benefits of technology and how to use it themselves. Jessica, in her twelfth year and teaching several primary/junior grades, described how she uses her laptop and phone to feed into the classroom screen:

I use my laptop a lot for drama, singing, dancing, and story-telling: I take it from room to room and just log in. I'm able to do much of my lesson that way, especially with younger students because they like the stories, songs, and so on; and sometimes I use my phone if the laptop can't connect.

Anita, a Grade 8 teacher in her fifteenth year noted: "I show quite a few videos or YouTube clips about something that's educational and that the kids are really interested in". And Kira, a Kindergarten teacher with 7 years' experience reported:

> That is my ladybug right there, in red and black; it is basically a projector but we call it the ladybug and the children get so excited. I feed into it and it goes right onto the smart board, which we use every day for all sorts of things. For example, there is a website called starfall.com to teach letters of the alphabet; when I introduce a new letter we click on the letter together and it gives all the different words beginning with that letter: like "v" for volcano, vacuum, and so on.

> Also for our morning messages from the office: the students go up and they're video-taped and we can watch that on the smart board. I put poems up there for poetry. I've done Prezis, like talking about shapes and vertices, and they did a great job with that. We did a whole unit on Mo Willems, the author of *Don't Let the Pigeon Drive the Bus*. There is a wonderful clip of him sharing how he makes his books, and that inspires our students to be an author just like Mo Willems.

> Before in teaching writing I would have to hold up a page and say, "you are going to write here, not the second line, the first line, right here". But now I can just put it under the ladybug and they can see it on the smart board. It just makes it so much easier. And in reading books to them I used to sit in my chair and read, and it was hard for the kids at the back to see the pictures. But now I just put them under the ladybug and it is up there on the smart board.

Supporting student IT use in class presentations, assignments, self-documentation, etc.

In addition to participating in the teacher's IT use, students should also be encouraged to use it in their own classroom activities. Felicity, an art and music teacher of Grades 7/8 and in her fifteenth year, spoke about this aspect of student learning:

> My use of IT has increased a great deal in recent years. For example, in art I let kids search for things online to look at and use as resources and references; and they work on Google Docs and submit online assignments like logs and so forth. And a lot of the kids write so much better with technology.

Sophia, also in her fifteenth year and teaching Kindergarten reported:

> One thing I do is make videos of the kids, like I capture them using a certain strategy and talking about it, and we attach a QR code to it; so when they go

up to present with a tablet, they can put it up there and we can see that strategy being utilized. Or on curriculum night, parents can use their phone at the various centres to make an image pop up of one of the children working at that centre, so they can see, "Oh, this is what children do here". So I really like using technology to document what the kids are doing and have the children document themselves. They can decide what they're going to put into their digital portfolios.

Increasing your own IT knowledge and skill

Although in many aspects of technology it is difficult for teachers to keep up with all their students, the more teachers know about IT the better they will be able to facilitate general class work and growth in the area. Again Sophia spoke of her continued IT development:

I try to stay aware of what's happening and what the latest apps are, for example. I speak with other teachers, especially those who are on the Technology Committee, who will often share ideas about what's coming down the pipeline. So it's just keeping my eyes and ears open and using various resources; like on Pinterest you'll see a cool idea and ask yourself, "Oh, how did that happen?" and start delving into how to do it.

Similarly, Kendra, a Grade 8 teacher in her twelfth year said:

[To increase my own learning in IT] I surf the net a lot and also look for workshops to go to. And my principal knows that I really love tech, so whenever there's a workshop that looks interesting she asks me, "Do you want to go to this?" There's another teacher in Grade 7 who is also a little bit of a geek, and we often seem to get first dibs to go; and the more we say yes, the more she offers them.

Modelling effective online teaching so students can learn how to participate in online classes

To the extent that schooling has to be online, teachers can support their students in learning how to participate in this type of IT use. The teachers in our study had not done online teaching and so did not speak about it. However, based on our own experience teaching on Zoom during the Covid-19 pandemic, we suggest modelling strategies such as the following:

Online Zoom-based teaching
- Build community by maximizing student talk
- Chat with students as they arrive, during the break, and after class

- Keep teacher presentations brief
- Make just a couple of brief but inviting readings available in Dropbox beforehand
- Use brief but inviting videos
- Have brief, colourful PowerPoint (PPT) slides available in Dropbox beforehand
- Go back and forth often between the PPT and the class checkerboard so everyone can see each other
- Randomly create small groups of no more than five, and visit each group during discussion
- Have reporting back to the whole class by all members of groups, again chosen randomly
- Have brief (3–4 minute) presentations by 2–4 students towards the end of each class, with 3–4 respondents per presentation

Modelling accessing information in class, with students helping

A key feature of modern IT is that knowledge can be retrieved almost any-where and anytime, and it is important to help students develop skills and hab-its of taking advantage of this. Anita, with 15 years' experience and a Grade 8 teacher, spoke about this:

> I get access to information as I teach, whether it's putting an article on the screen or, if we need to look up a word, looking it up or asking a student to look it up. We rarely use actual dictionaries anymore. Or if we get curious about something – it can be quite spontaneous, which is nice – I just say let's look that up, and we do.

Modelling and teaching responsible use of IT devices

Learning to use IT devices responsibly is important both for the effective run-ning of the class and for general life learning. Serena, another teacher with 15 years' experience and a teacher of Grades 5/6, talked about the need for "digital citizenship":

> Depending on the cohort, we sometimes have a problem of students spend-ing too much time on their devices. Two years ago we had a group who always wanted their phones out, and it got to the point where I had to call a class meeting and just say, "This isn't working because I'm spending too much of my time trying to manage you. It comes down to self-regulation and you're not, so now I have to". And usually that's enough for them to say, "Okay, we agree".
>
> So the rule is that either they keep their devices in their bag or have them on them but not use them. When they need to use them they'll ask, like often they use them as calculators, which is okay. But they can't be texting or

taking photos. And I do a big unit at the beginning of the year on digital citizenship and I put it out there, not rules *per se* but understanding how to operate a digital device, like you can't be taking pictures without people's consent or during work or in the middle of a meeting. And for them to come to those kinds of understandings along the way is huge.

Using IT to keep in touch with families

Using IT to connect with families is important both for good family relations and to help students see the value of technology and how to use it. As we saw earlier, Sophia and her students created videos of students performing certain learning activities and made them available to parents, either by sending them home or using QR codes on curriculum nights. She said: "So then the parents are involved in what's happening, and I get feedback from them". Similarly, Kendra, a Grade 8 teacher in her twelfth year reported:

A lot of my IT use is for parent and family communication. I have a classroom Twitter account and sometimes I post pictures of students – I don't show their faces because I don't always remember who has a media release, so it's just of what they happen to be working on. Some teachers are good at putting happy faces on them, but showing their work or activities is more my thing. I also have my own website, and again it's mainly for parent communication and for kids to download things that perhaps they missed in school or lost, or to view readings they can't access.

Chapter summary

Information technology was already widely available at the end of the 20th century, but given its rapidly growing use and usefulness in the 21st century, it should be strongly promoted among students. It has the potential to greatly increase the enjoyment and effectiveness of schooling and prepare young people for work and life beyond the school.

IT use should be understood broadly, as covering a wide range of goals and activities. As we will explore more fully in later chapters, students need to learn how to use it responsibly and not just for entertainment. Teachers will not always be able to stay ahead of their students in IT skill in all areas, but they have an important role in ensuring that students' use of IT is balanced and appropriate.

Students should be given a great deal of opportunity to use IT to communicate with each other and the teacher, search the internet, make class presentations, and do assignments. Students – like teachers – will vary in their comfort and skill in IT use, but all should be encouraged and helped to grow in the area. Teachers themselves should continue to grow in their use of IT both personally and professionally so they can help their students more in the area and model the importance and rewards of technology.

In this pandemic age, online teaching is especially important. Teachers need to learn how to teach synchronously and in ways that preserve many of the principles that apply in good face-to-face teaching. Although the interviews with the teachers in our longitudinal study ended before the pandemic began, we ourselves have done a great deal of synchronous Zoom-based teaching and have shared some of our findings in this chapter.

Among the strategies teachers can use to promote IT knowledge and skills are the following: using IT extensively yourself in classroom presentations and learning activities; supporting and encouraging student IT use in class presentations, assignments, self-documentation, etc.; increasing your personal IT use and skill; modelling effective online teaching so students can learn how to participate in online classes; modelling accessing information in class, with students helping; modelling and teaching responsible use of IT devices; and using IT to keep in touch with families.

Questions for reflection and discussion

1   Why is it important to promote extensive IT use among students?
2   Should students be allowed to vary in how much they use IT?
3   Is it okay for teachers themselves to vary in how much they use IT?
4   How can teachers promote IT use among students?

14 Principle 14: Promote use of technology as a means, not just an end

My (Kindergarten) kids don't bring their own devices to class, and even with the school iPads I decide when they come out ... If they're learning about something new, or documenting their learning activities, then they can do a walk about with the technology ... But I want them engaged in real life, learning about art, doing inquiries and so on.

– Sophia, in her fifteenth year and highly proficient technologically because of her former career

The Principle, its importance, and some challenges

In the previous chapter we discussed the many advantages of IT use in teaching and the importance of promoting its use among students. However, IT is not an absolute good. We need to work out how much to use it and in what ways, and develop a corresponding approach to teaching it.

What does it mean to promote use of technology as a means, not just an end?

To some extent, IT use can be an end in itself, notably when it brings enjoyment and entertainment. However, even then we should look for additional goals to pursue while we are enjoying it so that we are optimizing our way of life. The point is that it should not be seen *just* as an end but much of the time as a means, a tool for achieving a wide range of educational and life goals.

As much as possible IT use should be *meaningful*, beyond the meaning that enjoyment brings and the enjoyment that meaning brings. Most of the time it should serve a purpose, such as collaborative learning, individual learning, problem-solving, social interaction, a musical and artistic experience, information retrieval, and so on.

The use of technology should also be *balanced*, not taking place all the time or in every setting, and not occurring to the neglect of other important goals and activities. Of course, so many activities today have at least a small IT component, such as listening to music while we exercise or using the computer as we write. Often, then, the issue of balance is within an activity or setting: making sure that the technology enhances or at least does not undermine other purposes.

Why promote use of technology as a means, not just an end?

Seeing IT largely as a tool enables us to keep our eyes on the full range of life goals. These of course include entertainment and enjoyment, and some authors believe (as we saw in Chapter 4) that enjoyment or happiness is ultimately what life is about. But even with this philosophy, we have to achieve many "proximate" goals, such as an income, good health, and good relationships, or our happiness will quickly evaporate.

Such a perspective can lead to valuable discussion with students of life purposes and the need for an overall way of life. In particular, talk of the purposes of IT can lead into discussion of career preparation and choice, and the use of technology within a career. Such a perspective gives a basis for placing restrictions on IT use, without appearing to be arbitrary and domineering.

It can also lead into discussion of the need for a broad range of IT uses and skills. The problem with technology use among young people is often that they focus on just a few IT activities and skills.

Talking of purposes can also help persuade students who initially are not keen on IT to spend more time on it and develop skills in the area. In summary:

Reasons for promoting use of IT as a means, not just an end

- This approach leads to discussion of the need for a wide range of goals in life
- It leads to consideration of career preparation and choice and the role of IT in a career
- It gives a rationale for placing restrictions on IT use in the classroom, and encouraging balanced use beyond the school
- It can lead to discussion of the need for a broad range of IT skills
- It can help in persuading some students to become more involved with technology

---

What are the challenges of teaching IT as a means, not just an end?

Important though it is to encourage students to adopt a meaningful, balanced approach to IT use, teachers face several challenges in doing so. We believe these challenges can largely be overcome, but they remain. They include:

Parents and others in the outside world often overuse IT, and in just a few areas. Accordingly, teachers' efforts to increase meaningful and balanced use may be undermined.

Other teachers may have different ideas and rules with regard to IT use, again undermining individual teachers' efforts to make it more meaningful and balanced.

IT use may be seen by students and parents as largely a personal matter that should not be the concern of teachers.

Controlling the use of IT in the classroom is often difficult. Some teachers simply ban personal devices from the classroom, which can result in missing out on valuable opportunities to learn. Others allow them while recognizing this will sometimes result in inappropriate use.

Teachers' own mastery of IT may be somewhat limited, in terms of both amount and range. They then have to find ways to encourage broad use without always practising it themselves.

Theory/research basis for promoting use of technology as a means, not just an end

Pollard et al., while accepting that "ICT resources ... are now integral to teaching and learning" (2019: 237) and that "there clearly are massive potential opportunities for the use of new technologies" (p. 240), nevertheless caution that "ICT can be used well, or badly" (p. 237). They say there is considerable evidence that digital technology can "enhance educational outcomes", but only when it supplements other teaching instead of replacing it. They reference research showing that "technology should be integrated into coherent, purposive programmes of work" (p. 237).

Similarly, Bulfin, Parr, and Bellis (2016), though strong supporters and users of technology in education, are emphatic that it should be used as a means to good pedagogical ends rather than for its own sake. They say that: "Global technology companies, international bodies like UNESCO and the OECD, national governments, and even educational researchers, continue to express great enthusiasm for the 'transforming impact [of ICT] on national education systems' (UNESCO, 2011)" (Bulfin et al., 2016: 119). But too often the use of IT in education around the world is linked to an unquestioning technologizing of teaching that in turn is tied to standardization of teaching, which research has shown is "contributing to the de-professionalizing of teachers" and having a "dampening effect ... on creativity in teachers' professional practice" (pp. 119–120).

In the view of Bulfin et al., not only is unquestioning belief in the value of IT resulting in de-professionalization and damaging standardization, it is leading to a return to top-down transmission teaching. The compartmentalization and packaging-up of knowledge and its standardized delivery to teachers through teacher education and from them to students is precisely what progressive and constructivist thinkers have argued against for the past century and a half. It goes strongly against the type of 21st-century teaching discussed in Parts 1–3 of this book.

Along the same lines, Collins and Halverson say that while growing pressures from inside and outside will inevitably mean that schools become more technologically rich, this will not necessarily mean a victory for those who have high expectations for such enrichment: "Even with the implementation of Khan Academy, MOOCs, and Wikipedia, educators and policy makers may continue to focus on teaching basic skills as the core mission of schooling ... We need strong leadership from innovative educators to make sure that this new system embodies our society's critical goals for education" (2018: 126–127).

Going beyond schooling to life in general, Dolan strongly advocates IT use but, again, cautions that it is not an unconditional good: "Recent technological advances have brought a range of benefits, including national income growth, lower consumer prices, and possibly even higher life satisfaction ... But modern technology has brought a few costs, too, the biggest of which is distraction" (2014: 157). He admits that technology can *also* be used to counter these negative effects, through various focusing and attention-setting programmes. But he says that such solutions require considerable training and personal effort, together with "ways of breaking free from the addiction of virtual interaction" (p. 165). In his view, we often have to take deliberate steps to distance ourselves from the internet.

Strategies for promoting use of technology as a means, not just an end

We should make suggestions to parents, like your child shouldn't be spending another three or four hours a day on a screen after school, instead of doing something else like reading a book or going outside to play.
– Wanda, a Grade 3 teacher in her fifteenth year

The literature just discussed suggests that teachers should not just be gung-ho about technology, promoting it unconditionally. They need to help students counter overly zealous outlooks while still supporting extensive use of IT as discussed in Chapter 13. Here are some strategies we recommend for doing this:

Strategies for promoting use of IT as a means, not just an end

1 Modelling and teaching *meaningful* use of IT
2 Modelling and teaching *balanced* use of IT
3 Talking to family members about meaningful and balanced use of IT

Modelling and teaching *meaningful* use of IT

As discussed before, in everyday life IT often serves as a means of distraction and entertainment rather than substantial learning and achievement. And even in the classroom it can be just an easy way to get students' attention or keep them occupied, instead of promoting important learning. In order to combat this, teachers need to model meaningful use of IT and discuss with students the importance of using technology for purposes beyond entertainment. Of course, enjoyment and entertainment can still be there, and in fact enhanced; the point is to make sure meaningfulness is not overlooked.

This approach was illustrated by Tanya in her tenth year when teaching Grade 2:

> We need to think carefully about how we use technology in the classroom. I'm trying to use the class iPads to have the students show their understanding of concepts, as opposed to just fun games with lower-level thinking skills. I want to use them in a way that stretches students' learning and has them reflect on their learning. For example, we've used the Thirty Hands app for a media project integrated with science, and also for a social studies culminating task. This app shows their knowledge and understanding of a topic.

Along the same lines, Serena, a Grade 2/3 teacher in her tenth year reported:

> In recent years I'm working to push really meaningful inquiry with my kids. For example, I've been trying to improve my media literacy in relation to technology because that's not a huge area of comfort for me and I know there's a wealth of things out there. I'm not a big believer in tech for tech's sake and I think that happens a lot in classrooms. We buy Promethean boards or smart boards for everybody and really they're used just like white boards and nothing has changed. So I'm trying to engage in meaningful tech activities.

Anna, in her fifteenth year and teaching Kindergarten, gave an example of how she uses IT to promote physical exercise in her class:

> I use GoNoodle to help students do different kinds of physical activities during indoor recess and DPA [daily physical activity]. And there are a lot of different activities, like Zoomba, or a science-based one where they're dancing to a rhyme but it's also teaching them something. Or they can do yoga, which is good for just calming down after lunchtime, and it tells them a story while they're doing it.

Modelling and teaching *balanced* use of IT

Apart from meaningful use of IT, it is important to model using technology in a balanced way and also talk explicitly with students about not *over*-using IT, whatever its merits and attractions. The teachers in our study varied somewhat on this issue, but all believed that a degree of moderation is necessary. Anita, a Grade 8 teacher in her fifteenth year said: "I don't place *too* much emphasis on technology in the classroom, because there are so many other pressing issues and learning goals, and anyway it is such a pain when computers don't work or students can't log on or whatever". And Sophia, also in her fifteenth year and highly proficient technologically (as needed in her former career) commented:

> My (Kindergarten) kids don't bring their own devices to class, and even with the school iPads I decide when they come out; and they don't come out too often. If they're learning about something new, or documenting their learning

activities, then they can do a walk about with the technology. Or if they need it for assistive or accommodation reasons, that's fine. But to be honest, there's so much use of technology today that I want to give them a break.

Technology can be an easy solution, it's easy to sit the child down in front of a Tablet and have them do some number-sense activity. But I want them engaged in real life, learning about art, doing inquiries, and so on.

While herself teaching Kindergarten, Anna in her fifteenth year described the approach to IT use in higher grades at her school:

At my school, even in Grade 8, the teachers have basically said to the students: "We know you have your phones, but you can only use them in here for a purpose". They're not supposed to have them out even during recess, because they could be taking videos and posting things; there are very clear guidelines on that.

Of course, if the class are all going on Twitter to talk about a project they're doing, or videotaping different drama and dance skits, or doing research of some kind, they are free to do that; but we definitely don't have children on their phones all the time. They have them in their bags and only bring them out if there's an actual need; which happens, because sometimes they'll do online math tutorials on their phones or on the school laptops or iPads.

Paul, a middle school teacher with 15 years' experience – and, like Sophia, highly IT proficient because of his former profession – talked about his recent shift to a more balanced approach to technology:

There was a time when I felt, well, if they're really into screens maybe we should use screens more. And I still think there's a big place for technology. But there are teachers I know who get kids to bring their phones to class and use them for trivia things, little quizzes and multiple-choice tests; and from what I can see kids feel like, well, school should just be a game.

And I've swung back to looking for a way to do something that's very valuable but presented in a way that hooks them: they are really fascinated but also get a lot out of it. I'm trying to get them to have deeper motivation than, hey, this is fun for 10 minutes. So a deeper motivation, like what are you expecting out of your life, and wouldn't it be amazing to learn such and such, to be this kind of skilled person, or have this ability – as well as using technology.

Talking to family members about meaningful and balanced use of IT

It is important to involve families in helping students develop a balanced approach to technology, although this presents some challenges. Wanda, a Grade 3 teacher in her fifteenth year, spoke about this:

We should make suggestions to parents, like your child shouldn't be spending another three or four hours a day on a screen after school, instead of doing something else like reading a book or going outside to play. But it's hard, because with many parents, when they come in for interviews or curriculum night, they've got their phone on all the time. And many people out there are saying, well, that's the way of the world, we have to adjust.

But it's sad when you see teenagers sitting side-by-side and communicating by texting each other, when they're right there. Of course, they have to use IT to find out about assignments and access other information; but we have to help them find a different way to approach it. And some parents don't want their kids to be on technology all the time, any more than we do.

Chapter summary

As discussed in the previous chapter, IT use today is extremely important and should be encouraged. However, it should not be seen *just* as an end in itself: it has to further the basic goals and processes of 21st-century education rather than undermining them. It can undermine them in at least two ways: by being used mainly as a source of entertainment, and by serving as an instrument of standardization of teaching and learning.

True, IT is partly an end in itself in that it often brings immediate enjoyment. As we saw in Chapter 4, enjoyment and satisfaction are a large part of what life is about. But teachers should work to ensure that IT use – in the classroom and beyond – serves other ends as well. As for standardization of teaching, this simply takes schooling back to earlier times.

There are many challenges to using IT in purposeful, balanced, safe ways. Parents and others in the outside world often overuse it and in just a narrow range of areas; peer groups often pressure students to use it inappropriately; and the prevailing culture of celebrity and "the spectacular" tends to impact students.

Strategies teachers can use to promote purposeful, balanced, safe use of IT include: modelling and explicit discussion of such use of IT, and talking to parents about the need for this approach to IT use.

Questions for reflection and discussion

1 What is the range of purposes to which IT can be put in schools?
2 What are some of the goals and processes of schooling that IT can undermine?
3 What are some examples of inappropriate use of IT by teachers and students?
4 How can teachers support student development of purposeful, balanced, safe use of IT?

15 Principle 15: Foster use of technology to individualize learning

When I taught Grades 4–8, I had them research their own projects a great deal. But I had to teach them how to decipher what's really important in the content.
— Anna, a Kindergarten teacher in her fifteenth year

The Principle, its importance, and some challenges

We tend to think of IT mainly in terms of communicating with others, but in fact it offers great possibilities for people to individualize their learning. Individuals can gain access to a vast array of ideas and information and use it to develop ways of thinking and life directions that reflect their particular needs, talents, and circumstances.

Of course, individuals should also attend to the larger community and societal context and be aware of how important it is to them personally. However, the ideas they get via the Internet have been developed by others and bear the marks of their point of view. Individuals should assess them and adapt them in part to their own situation rather than just absorb them.

What does it mean to foster technology use for individualized learning?

Individualization (or differentiation, personalization) of learning is an educational approach widely recommended today. We discussed it in Chapter 1 as having many advantages. It enables students to take account of their distinctive needs and circumstances as they develop their ideas, in line with the "constructivist" approach to learning also often advocated. And they can contribute to the knowledge development of others based on their special insights and experiences.

In terms of process, individualized inquiry supports a degree of independence and so increases student autonomy. As also noted in Chapter 1, autonomy is a quality greatly needed in the 21st century as people in the workplace and other life settings are increasingly expected to have input rather than just following directions. However, autonomy must always be balanced, since individuals need to fit in with others to a considerable degree and they have commitments and ethical obligations towards others.

Technology obviously has a great deal to contribute in this complex scenario. Because IT enables us to reach out to other people, near and far, it facilitates drawing on the ideas of others and helping other people. But also, because it can be used for multiple private reflections on widely available data, it can help greatly at the individual level too. It is this individual use of IT, and the ways to foster it in students, that we focus on in this chapter

Why use technology to support individualized learning?

Individualized learning takes account of the learner's distinctive needs and circumstances. Too often teaching – including IT-based teaching – is used to try to impose a uniform outlook and set of ideas and values on students. Broad IT literacy that goes well beyond sending and receiving messages can help make student learning more relevant though still strongly information-based.

Emphasis on the individual in teaching also makes the insights of individuals more available to others. This assumes, of course, a willingness on the part of those involved to listen to each other and continually modify their position, which is something that needs to be stressed by teachers even as they work to foster individual construction. A major purpose of developing individual ideas is to share them with others and get feedback, as part of an ongoing dialogue.

Technology can greatly speed up the process of individualized knowledge development through ease of access to ideas and information. Private work can be done against a backdrop of ready access to a vast store of shared views and information. Individual knowledge-building can also occur more quickly because of IT-enhanced document development processes.

Individualized IT-based learning can be more engaging and enjoyable to students, allowing them to follow their interests and needs with a strong sense of purpose and control. To summarize:

Reasons for fostering use of technology to individualize learning

- Individualized learning takes account of the learner's individual needs and circumstances
- It also takes advantage of the individual insights people have to offer each other
- Individualized learning supports autonomy development
- Technology can greatly speed up individualized knowledge development
- Individualized IT-based learning can be more engaging and enjoyable

---

What are the challenges of fostering IT-based individualized learning?

IT-based individualized pedagogy is innovative in two ways: its emphasis on the individual and its heavy use of technology. This may give rise to a number of challenges, including the following:

Students vary in their access to devices. This may result in some individual activities and projects having to be less ambitious, which in turn has implications for assessment and student self-image.

Students with special needs sometimes feel embarrassed that they have to use special devices. Teachers have to work with the students so they feel more at ease and the class community to build understanding and acceptance.

Teachers sometimes have difficulty keeping up with individual student IT uses. This takes humility on teachers' part and a willingness to accept assignments they do not fully understand.

Teachers are often expected to deliver more standard, controlled learning. This may result in some disapproval of their pedagogy. It also requires teachers to take steps to try to explain the approach.

There are safety issues with students going on the Internet on their own. Teachers need to guard against these risks while not curtailing student initiative too much.

Theory/research basis for promoting technology for individualized learning

We noted in Chapter 1 that Trilling and Fadel (2009) view autonomy as a key 21st-century skill. Now we see that they emphasize an individualized use of IT in part because it enables such autonomy. "[H]elping students become more self-reliant and independent as learners has always been a challenge. Technology is helping, though, providing a wealth of always-on self-service tools for researching and learning online" (2009: 78). They report that in a major learning project (SARS) involving individualized IT use, teachers "were amazed at the level of self-direction, motivation, and independence their students demonstrated" (p. 78).

As we saw earlier, Collins (2017) sees the need for a "new literacy", one that is heavily IT-based. This is necessary because young people today are deeply immersed in technology and will become increasingly so. Among other things, IT literacy and use carries great advantages in terms of enabling students to "develop self-sufficiency" and move towards "more independent living and working" (2017: 34–35). He documents schools that have gone in this direction, what he calls "passion schools" (pp. 104–120). These are characterized by a high level of IT use, employing problem-based learning and learning-by-design, which embed the traditional school subjects in projects and tasks that students work on largely by themselves.

Collins and Halverson stress the need for "customization" in learning. They say that "[o]ne of the major effects of technology proliferation has been the ability to cater to individual preferences" 2018: 15), and education should take full advantage of this. Adults and young people alike are "becoming less and less willing to learn what somebody else thinks is best" (p. 16). Given these cultural changes as well as the advances in technology, they foresee schools being increasingly "pressured to embrace the technologies that make learner control possible" (p. 17). They believe we should go strongly in this direction.

Strategies for fostering use of technology for individualized learning

> *A good use of technology is when you have somebody who has difficulty encoding, and so instead of writing words down they can speak into a device and it types for them.*
>
> – Mike, a lower primary teacher in his twelfth year

As we have said throughout the book, the individual perspective is very important so that individuals' needs can be met and because individuals have distinctive insights. Also, if individuals are having their needs met they are often in a stronger position to support other people. While IT is clearly of great value in connecting people, it also has enormous potential to help people inquire and plan individually. Here are some strategies we propose for fostering individual use of IT:

Strategies for fostering IT use for students' individualized learning

1 Encouraging students to do individualized IT-based assignments and presentations
2 Supporting students in using IT-based learning programmes on their own
3 Supporting IT use by students with special needs

Encouraging students to do individualized IT-based assignments and presentations

If students use IT a lot in individual assignments and presentations, they will learn more about why and how to use technology in learning and life. Anna, in her fifteenth year said: "When I taught Grades 4–8, I had them research their own projects a great deal. But I had to teach them how to decipher what's actually important in the content they access. Like, you can't just print things off and stick them on a piece of paper and say that's it".

Tanya, a Grade 2 teacher in her tenth year, talked about how she supports her students in doing IT-based assignments and presentations:

> Having students show their learning through IT is my favourite use of technology ... Like for their social studies assignment on traditions and celebrations, they have to interview a family member about a family tradition or celebration, and perhaps bring artifacts from home to help teach others about it. And where they don't have an artifact to show, they make an illustration to support their answer. Then they use a class iPad to take a picture of their artifacts or illustrations and those become slides; and finally they record an audio explanation to match each of their pictures.

Carrie, now a principal after 15 years but having previously taught upper primary and middle-school reported:

> Our use of IT at the school has increased quite a bit recently, especially with teachers using Google Classroom effectively. Before there was a lot of technology but I don't think it was being used for a very focused purpose; it was like, it's Friday so we're going to show a video using a data projector. Now they're using Google Classroom to build the skill right into what they're doing, instead of just a scheduled visit to the computer lab to learn a computer skill.
>
> And one thing a teacher did this year that I liked was have the students use QR codes to open up book talks. The kids videoed themselves talking about books they had read and then created their own poster with a QR code in it. So you can take your iPad or your cell phone up to it and click on it and up comes the video of the kid talking about the book and why they liked it or why they didn't. That piece was really valuable because it got the kids talking without having to be in front of a live audience, which some of them aren't yet comfortable with. It also appealed to them in terms of just being able to do something like that. And I think shifting teachers' thinking towards building on students' interest in technology to drive the learning has really been powerful.

Supporting students in using IT-based learning programmes on their own

Despite the growing emphasis on inquiry learning and open-ended projects, much of the learning students need to do is mastery of subject content and skills. This still involves some adjustment to individuals, but much of what is involved is clear teaching of basic concepts and skills. Along these lines, Sandra, who taught Kindergarten in her twelfth year, spoke of helping her students learn how to use an IT-based encyclopaedia:

> We have iPads in Kindergarten classes, one for every two students. And my favourite use for senior Kindergarten is the website PebbleGo, which is a sort of encyclopaedia for kids. And it requires a lot of frontloading, but the kids come to learn how to work out what they want to know and then pose their questions to the website.

Paul, a Grade 5/6 teacher in his tenth year, talked about how he introduced his students to the Kahn Academy website (kahnacademy.org):

> Basically it offers a huge collection of instructional videos combined with online activities that are really well designed. The kids get a free account and watch the videos and do the lessons; and I have a coach account and can track every student and what they're doing. And one great thing is that if they are working on a certain topic, they can't move on until they have done a certain number of the questions correctly.

They can also use it for homework, and if they have time and their parents want them to do lots of work, they can sit online. And if they get stuck it can give you a hint how to get started again, or two hints to give you a solution if you can't get it yourself so that you can move on. It's not for everyone, but for lots of kids it's really useful.

Four years later and now teaching Grades 7/8, Paul again talked about helping students work individually with IT to acquire knowledge, understanding, and skills in particular subject areas:

For math this year I've given my students access to videos that go over the concepts they have to learn, and when they use it they do much better on the tests. On YouTube there's this site called Math Antics; and it's just a guy talking about the math and explaining stuff, using little animations and funny sounds and so forth. The kids like it and some watch it over and over, which they wouldn't with me. They can also watch it from home, and luckily this year everyone in my class had Internet access at home.

And there's another site called Gizmos, where in learning about fractions for example they can manipulate something and see it changing, like when they change the denominator to twice as much the pieces become half the size. And again they can also use it at home. So it's basically just for online manipulation, but it's well designed and logically thought out, and they learn a lot.

Supporting IT use by students with special needs

IT use is very important for students with learning disabilities who cannot learn or perform easily in the usual ways. Sandra, teaching Kindergarten in her twelfth year commented:

Something that's really great for young kids with fine motor difficulties is Handwriting Without Tears, which now I think is called Learning Without Tears. It was created by an occupational therapist for children who have a hard time with their fine motor skills, can't hold a pencil, and so forth.

Similarly, Mike in his twelfth year and teaching lower primary said: "A good use of technology is when you have somebody who has difficulty encoding, and so instead of them writing words down they can speak into a device and it types for them. Those kids can get a laptop and learn how to use it to express their ideas".

Felicity, however, noted in her fifteenth year that she had encountered difficulties getting students to use voice-to-text technology. "I think some of them are embarrassed that kids hear them talking out what others are typing". Obviously teachers need to find ways to overcome this impediment to the greatest extent possible, such as by making the use of such technology less obvious or by getting other students to understand and accept it.

Serena, in her fifteenth year, spoke of the special case of so-called "gifted" children who have difficulty writing. "My kids are classified as gifted but often have a learning disability that impacts writing, so I encourage them to dictate their work on a voice-to-text device so they get down something that's reflective of their ideas as opposed to their writing ability, which is at such a lower level". And Jeannie, a Grade 3 teacher in her thirteenth year, described the somewhat similar situation of ESL students, who may have remarkable talents but be barely able to express themselves in English:

Using technology can definitely be helpful in enabling ESL students to show their thinking in different ways. One of the students I taught this year was a very recent immigrant from Syria. He was super bright, great at problem-solving, and his math skills you wouldn't believe. But his language skills in English were very limited, though he still had lots to contribute and experiences that were different but very relevant. So it was really important to give him opportunities to show his ideas so students could understand him and he could feel part of what was going on.

Chapter summary

Information technology has enormous potential to help individualization of learning in the way required for students to achieve autonomy (as discussed in Chapter 1) and develop an approach to learning and life suited to their distinctive needs, talents, and circumstances. Students should be constantly reminded of the importance and possibility of this kind of development and the extensive role IT can play in furthering it.

If teachers are to promote individualization of learning through IT, they need to introduce students to a broad range of IT practices to which individuals have access. These include frequent use of many kinds of search and retrieval tools; use of social media not only for enjoyment but also to gain feedback on a variety of topics; and use of a diversity of streaming services for individual enrichment – cultural, artistic, and so on.

The challenges in this area that teachers need to address include: students vary in their access to devices; students with special needs sometimes feel embarrassed that they have to use special devices; teachers sometimes have difficulty keeping up with individual student IT use; teachers are often expected to deliver more standard, controlled learning; and there are safety issues when students go on the Internet on their own.

Among the strategies for fostering individualized learning using IT are: encouraging students to do individualized IT-based assignments and presentations; supporting students in using IT-based learning techniques on their own; and supporting IT use by students with special needs.

Questions for reflection and discussion

1 How can IT use help with individualization of learning? What are the specific IT practices involved?
2 What are some of the challenges in this area and how can they be overcome?
3 How can teachers support student development of individual IT-based learning?

16 Principle 16: Foster use of technology for collaborative learning

I really like Google Docs because it makes student collaboration easy. They can embed their planning ideas for a project or presentation, along with videos or pictures, and then work in slightly different spaces but see each other's work and edit it in real-time.

– Serena, a Grade 5/6 teacher in her fifteenth year

The Principle, its importance, and some challenges

Technology can help greatly with collaboration, and this is not surprising. The term "internet" points to connections between people; Wikipedia and other information sites rely on collaboration; and central to social media is the sharing of information and opinions.

However, students need to see more fully the key role of IT in collaboration and be helped to master the skills for using it in this way. We saw in the previous chapter the importance of using technology for individual searches and inquiries. Its use for collaborative inquiry also needs to be emphasized.

What is meant by fostering IT-based collaborative learning?

Using IT in collaborative activities requires seeing collaboration as important in the first place. This was a topic discussed in Chapter 6 of this book: the notion that people working together in teams can often achieve more than if they work alone. This occurs for at least two reasons. First, different people have different insights to contribute. And second, solutions to inquiries have to take into account the distinctive needs and circumstances of the various parties involved.

In fostering IT-based collaboration in their students, teachers have to help them see the complexity of knowledge. Students must recognize that learning is not simply a matter of experts sharing "established facts", but involves everyone participating in the "construction" of knowledge, as discussed in Chapter 2. Students have to acquire confidence in their own ideas, and learn to draw on an array of other people – both experts and non-experts.

Again, given the complexity of knowledge and the range of sources that have to be drawn on, a broad approach to IT is required. Students need to learn to routinely consult search engines, course texts, podcasts, news items, the views of their teachers and fellow students, and so on. In order to support this broad use of IT, students should be encouraged to use a wide range of sources in preparing class presentations and completing assignments.

Of course, encouraging group IT assignments is a key way to support collaboration in learning. But the assignments need to be carefully designed if authentic collaboration is to occur. Each member in the group should have a say in the topic chosen, the aspect of the topic they are responsible for, and the mode of presenting it. There is not a sharp separation between individualization and collaboration.

Why foster IT-based collaborative learning?

Teaching students how to collaborate using IT helps underscore the importance of collaboration. In all the various whole-class discussions and small group collaborative projects, students will see the efficacy and satisfaction of a collaborative approach to life and learning.

Another advantage of collaboration is that students' IT skills are broadened. Students find that in order to tap into the ideas and contributions of others they have to employ many inquiry methods. And they learn different ways of doing so from the varying IT practices of those they are collaborating with.

Students get to know each other better. A condition of taking account of other people's needs, talents, and circumstances is becoming more familiar with them. This knowledge they get directly by working with them.

Community in the classroom is strengthened. Meaningful IT communication between members of the class increases greatly through collaboration, both in whole-class and small group activities and discussions.

Collaboration leads to greater use of IT for meaningful purposes rather than just entertainment. Students are introduced to a whole new set of important technology tools.

Students learn more about how to use IT safely. Because the collaborative activities occur largely in the school setting and under the broad supervision of the teacher, certain protocols and teaching are in place to ensure safety and students learn from these. To summarize:

Reasons for fostering IT use for collaboration

- The importance of collaboration is underscored
- The range of IT skills is broadened
- Students get to know each other better
- Community in the classroom is strengthened
- IT is used for meaningful reasons rather than just entertainment
- Students learn how to use IT safely

What are the challenges of fostering IT-based collaborative learning?

Fostering IT-based collaboration takes time. As with collaborative learning generally, teaching and learning how to do it with IT takes time. This leaves less time to "cover" the set curriculum and prepare students for standardized tests. There is great payoff, however, because students are acquiring IT and collaboration skills on top of their subject content learning.

Such an approach makes it more difficult to teach a uniform curriculum, which is widely expected of teachers. The kind of choice that is essential in this approach, along with adjustment to individual ideas and needs and differing uses of IT, leads to a dynamic the teacher cannot fully control.

Teachers are not used to – or trained in – this approach to teaching, one that combines heavy IT use with collaboration. At a system level, technology is increasingly used today to try to transmit a pre-set curriculum rather than facilitate an open-ended collaborative inquiry process, and the former is what teachers have largely experienced and been trained in.

Students have differing levels of IT skill and access to devices, making IT-based collaboration difficult. Teachers have to work hard to make more school-based devices available and adapt the collaboration to ensure that no students are left out.

Use of IT for collaborative purposes requires a level of communication that may raise safety issues. Again, teachers have to find a balance between maximizing social exchange and exposing students to unsafe situations.

Theory/research basis for fostering IT-based collaborative learning

As we have seen, while Pollard et al. advocate extensive use of IT in classroom settings, they say that students have to be supported in learning to do it appropriately: "simply having ICT in the classroom does not determine its effective use for pupils' learning" (2019: 237). In particular, they say teachers should adopt technology that "enables new processes of teaching and learning" that are "dialogic" and place communication at the centre of learning (pp. 237–238). They give the example of a primary teacher and a secondary history teacher using the interactive whiteboard "to stimulate discussion, set the scene for collaborative group work or enable their pupils to 'take over' the use of the board in whole-class or group work" (p. 238).

Bellanca advises teachers to adopt IT-based collaboration methods used in the workplace, noting that "many of the same e-tools used in the modern workplace can enrich ... students' learning experiences" in the classroom (2010: 123). "Technology-supported cooperative learning tends to increase achievement, positive attitudes toward technology and cooperation, cognitive development, learning control, social competencies, positive relationship with team members ... and innovation in groupware and hardware" (p. 124). And by drawing on such methods, not only is learning in the classroom enhanced but students acquire IT-based collaboration skills essential for the 21st-century workplace.

Similarly, Collins states: "Work is becoming more collaborative as our society grows more complex. Teams are the critical unit in the workplace of the future. Working with others is being recognized as a sine qua non for success in the modern world" (2017: 67). Accordingly, teaching IT knowledge and skills must be combined with fostering collaboration. Educators have to ensure that students are ready for "the highly technological yet collaborative workplaces they will be entering" (p. 69).

Related to collaborative use of IT, advice given by Collins and Halverson to parents – but that teachers can equally apply – is to "encourage their children to join online communities that share their interests ... For example, children might pursue a passion for coding through an interest in something like *Episode*, a phone app [that] allows users to create their own interactive narratives ... [This] can create a powerful bridge toward 21st century literacies" (2018: 122–123).

Finally, according to Trilling and Fadel, young people of the internet generation increasingly see "[c]ollaboration and relationships to be a vital part of all they do" (2009: 30). They remark: "Both face-to-face and virtual collaborations online have been shown to increase learning motivation, create better and more innovative results, and develop social and cross-cultural skills" (p. 34). Moreover, modern technologies are "freeing up time to focus on the 21st century skills" such as collaboration and communication (p. 40).

Strategies for fostering use of technology for collaborative learning

[W]e use the smart board on a daily basis. It's a great way to get students engaged and involved in the learning experience, coming up to the board and manipulating things.

– Mary, in her twelfth year and teaching mainly at the lower primary level

As we have said, technology is a very important means of collaboration in the classroom, the workplace, and other settings. The following are some strategies for fostering the use of IT for collaboration:

Strategies for fostering use of IT for collaboration

1 Whole-class IT-based activities, including online classes
2 Project work in pairs and small groups
3 Modelling and discussing how to use IT collaboratively but safely

Whole-class IT-based activities, including online classes

Students can develop IT-based collaboration skills by participating in whole-class activities where the teacher and students use technology to search for ideas and information and discuss the issues. Such activities include online classes – on Zoom, for example – where everyone appears at once on the class "checkerboard" and takes part in presentations and discussions. The teachers in our study had not been involved with online teaching by our last interview, but some strategies for collaboration in that context were mentioned in Chapter 13 (p. 119–120).

Regarding whole-class IT-based activities in general, Serena, a teacher of Grades 5/6 in her fifteenth year commented:

> We often bring real-life examples into the classroom by watching recent or historic news items. For example, we use the novel *Refugee* with three narrators speaking about their experiences over time. We also do video calls with experts, scientists for example; which is great because often you can't get people to come into your classroom but they are willing to give you twenty minutes online and respond to questions. And that way, students are getting an experience of talking to a true expert in their field, without the logistical concerns of bringing in a visiting speaker.

Mary, in her twelfth year, described her approach to using IT in the classroom, mainly at the lower primary level:

> Over the past few years, more resources have been allocated to technology at my school. Each classroom now has their own iPads and laptops and we have a smart board that can be connected to these devices. And we use the smart board on a daily basis. It's a great way to get students engaged and involved in the learning experience, coming up to the board and manipulating things.

Project work in pairs and small groups

Learning how to collaborate using IT can also be helped greatly by having students do projects and assignments in pairs or small groups. Anita, a teacher of Grade 8 in her twelfth year noted:

> In this school we have a lot of laptops and iPads, a functioning computer lab, and computers all over the school, and the kids use them in all their subjects. We use Google Docs regularly with the kids, so there is a lot of sharing that way. Google Docs is a cloud-based system where you can have two people working together on a task, logged onto their own computers or sharing one, depending on availability. You can be half-way across the world but both be seeing the same document and working on it in real time. And for their inquiry projects I have them working together, three or four kids to a group. Sometimes for science I will have them work in pairs, depending on how many computers we have.

Carrie, now in her fifteenth year and a principal but with a lot of experience as a middle school teacher, spoke about how students who previously had difficulty with projects often do well with a shared approach:

> Some students really thrive using a Chromebook to write up everything. Many kids who struggled with written output from a fine motor point of view get work done more quickly when suddenly they can use a computer. They're often the ones who are the most responsible in group work, shifting to being a little bit of a group leader: 'I'll type, you give me the information', or 'I'm only good at finding information, you type". So I think it's been a very important piece because that's vital for the workplace now, knowing how to approach this sort of group work.

Kendra, a Grade 8 teacher in her fifteenth year reported:

> Sometimes I set up their assignments as a partnered activity, but other times I let them choose whether to work alone or with one, two, or three partners. And they know that if the group is larger the product will have to be more extensive, whereas if they're working alone or with just one person it will probably be shorter and I will grade it accordingly.

And Serena, a Grade 5/6 teacher with 15 years' experience said:

> I really like Google Docs because it makes student collaboration easy. They can embed their planning ideas for a project or presentation, along with videos or pictures, and then work in slightly different spaces but see each other's work and edit it in real time. My goal for group size is three or four, but sometimes we have groups of six depending on the assignment; but then they need multiple devices. It is good because it allows them to do research on slightly different things but put it together in the same place. The collaborative nature of it is a big advantage.

Modelling and discussing how to use IT collaboratively but safely

The advantages of collaboration using technology are many, but there are also some safety concerns because of the sharing. This is especially obvious with respect to social media. Felicity, a middle school teacher specializing in music and the arts and in her fifteenth year reported:

> We had an issue this year with kids going online and bullying and making really inappropriate comments: we even had to get the police involved. It's a really scary time for kids because Grade 7 and 8 kids are so impulsive, they don't always think about the consequences. So we need to constantly educate them. This year we had someone come in to talk with them about online pornography, trafficking, and things like that."

Along the same lines, Kendra, a Grade 8 teacher of science and maths in her twelfth year observed:

> There have been some instances of students posting ridiculous things about each other on Instagram or Snapchat; although the kids have actually been pretty good about letting me know when they see something inappropriate, knowing that I won't rat them out for having told me. And I usually deal with it pretty quietly unless it's in the realm of cyber bullying, when it has to go to the office. It's like with any kind of disclosure, if you tell me something and I need to go to somebody else, I will – I let them know that.

Another area where students have to be careful is what personal information they include in their portfolios or resumes. Kelly, who taught Grade 5 in her tenth year, talked about this issue:

> This year my students were working on their portfolios about their strengths, learning styles, goals, family, and so on, preparing their Google slides. And we talked about it, and also had a speaker come in to talk about how everything kids put on the internet is really important; because when they are Googled in the future or visited on Instagram, what they've included about when they were in Grade 2 or Grade 3 or 5 or 8 is going to pop up. So they have to make sure that what they have there shows their best side.

Chapter summary

We saw in Chapter 15 the potential of IT to help individualize learning. Here we focus on its usefulness in facilitating collaborative learning. These two purposes are not as separate as they might seem. A major benefit of collaborative learning is that as they work together, students are exposed to alternative ideas and life approaches that they can use in developing their individual way of life.

IT helps with collaboration by enabling students to quickly share material of many different kinds, whether or not they are in the same physical space. It also means that emerging documents can be easily modified in agreed ways. It is important, however, that the individual component be maintained throughout, with all participants given a chance to have input on joint reports and retain their own interpretations and applications of the ideas included. As well as the usual advantages of collaborative learning (as discussed in Chapter 6), using IT for this purpose allows students to hone their IT skills as they collaborate: they are doing two things at once.

Some strategies for fostering use of technology for collaboration are: initiating whole-class IT-based activities, including online classes with a highly interactive quality; teaching students a range of IT-based collaborative techniques; encouraging students to do project work in pairs and small groups; and modelling and discussing how to use IT safely.

Questions for reflection and discussion

1 Why is fostering IT-based collaborative learning important?
2 What are some IT programs and techniques that enable collaborative learning?
3 How can teachers support students in developing IT-based collaborative learning?

Part 5

Direction V: Enhanced Teacher Identity, Professionalism, and Wellbeing

So far in the book we have focused mainly on new directions in *teaching* – where it should be going in the 21st century and the specific approaches and strategies involved. In Part 5, we move to qualities of *teachers*: the outlook, attitudes, and self-concept they need to go in 21st-century directions. But much of what we advocate in Part 5 follows from the ideas discussed in Parts 1–4. Going in 21st-century directions in teaching requires teachers who see the profession and themselves in a certain way. Accordingly, we will often refer back to the ideas of the earlier chapters. The aspects covered in Part 5 are:

> **Aspects of enhanced teacher identity, professionalism, and wellbeing**
>
> Chapter 17: Take a stand on what and how to teach
> Chapter 18: Develop a 21st-century pedagogy
> Chapter 19: Continue to enquire and grow as a teacher
> Chapter 20: Promote your own wellbeing
> Chapter 21: Connect teaching to life

In Chapter 17, we argue that in order to teach in the way needed in the 21st century – relevant, flexible, dialogical, caring, inclusive, etc. – teachers have to largely take charge of their teaching, making judgements and *taking a stand on what and how to teach*. They should not just follow orders. Teaching is too complex and challenging to be controlled from outside by people often unfamiliar with it, or with very narrow expertise.

In Chapter 18, we outline the distinctive *pedagogy* required for the 21st century, one involving teaching for knowledge *and* relevance; learning from and with students; building community in the classroom; getting to know students; giving students choice; and so on. All these aspects of 21st-century pedagogy have been advocated in earlier chapters, especially in the strategy sections. Here we bring them together in an integrated picture of 21st-century pedagogy.

In Chapter 19, we discuss how the breadth, complexity, and changing nature of teaching in the 21st century demands that teachers *continue to enquire and grow* throughout their career: they can never fully "master" it.

In Chapter 20, we explore how in order to teach in the manner needed – and with energy and enthusiasm throughout their career – teachers have to be experiencing *wellbeing in their own life*.

Finally, in Chapter 21, we bring together ideas from throughout the book to show the many ways in which *teaching and life have to be connected* to each other and have similar characteristics, if effective teaching/learning and overall wellbeing are to be achieved by teachers and students alike.

17 Principle 17: Take a stand on what and how to teach

I sometimes modify the curriculum and even leave out topics, but every year is different ... I do always address high priority areas; for example, number sense in my view is the most important strand in math ... But with some of the other strands it depends partly on the students' interests.
          – Karen, a Kindergarten teacher in her fourteenth year

The Principle, its importance, and some challenges

To go in the directions discussed in earlier chapters, teachers have to take a stand on what and how to teach. This is necessary because the 21st-century directions proposed are not widely understood or accepted by politicians, members of the public, or parents; so going in these directions depends a great deal on teacher initiative. Moreover, teachers are in a strong position to make decisions about what and how to teach, given their knowledge of their students and their extensive experience in classrooms over the years.

Taking charge in this way is often referred to in terms of "professionalism". Teachers should be seen – and see themselves – as professionals who make decisions rather than mere technicians who transmit a pre-set package of subject content. Unfortunately, many recent school reform efforts have tended to undermine teachers' professionalism by trying to "script" their actions and push them in a narrowly subject-centred direction. Our view is that, given the complexity of teaching and the expertise they have, teachers need to "resist" these pressures to a considerable extent.

What is meant by taking a stand on what and how to teach?

Decision-making of the kind we are advocating is central to good teaching. As discussed in earlier chapters, teachers need to be flexible, constantly making judgements about what, when, and how to teach, taking advantage of "teachable moments" in whole-class settings, and responding to the needs and interests of individual students. Some of the decisions have to be made well in advance, while others are made just before a lesson or on the spur of the moment during the lesson. Given this essential role of teacher judgement, it is inappropriate for outsiders to try to control teacher behaviour.

As mentioned, making decisions in this way requires teachers to "resist" attempts to determine fully what and how they teach. Perhaps resist on its own is too strong a word: a recent book on this topic edited by Santoro and Cain (2018) uses the term "principled resistance" rather than simply resistance. But something of the kind is needed. Teachers should certainly take note of what authorities and experts say; and there are some matters (e.g. health protection during a pandemic) on which they clearly have to follow the rules. However, much of the time they should make the final decision on what and how to teach.

As mentioned above, taking charge in this way is often referred to as being "professional". It should be noted, however, that the word professional is not being used here in the sense of staying distant from students. While a degree of detachment is necessary (e.g. teachers should keep self-interest in check in the classroom and not show favouritism towards certain students), the personal dimension is very important. Indeed, up to a point a personal connection is essential to teacher professionalism. The strong teacher–student relationship advocated in earlier chapters – with teachers getting to know their students, enjoying interacting with them, and caring about them – is necessary if teachers are to establish rapport with their students and make sound pedagogical decisions.

Why take a stand on what and how to teach?

Teachers taking charge of their teaching has many advantages. For one thing, they can do a better job. Classes vary from one to another, and students within a class are diverse in their needs and learning styles. If teachers take account of these differences in the topics they emphasize and how students study them, students will be more engaged and their learning deeper and more relevant.

In addition, seeing themselves as ultimately in charge of their teaching gives teachers a greater sense of dignity and self-respect. And this enhanced self-awareness is not just an indulgence, it is solidly based in a sound view of teachers' ability to study their teaching and refine their expertise. This in turn inspires and enables them to continue to learn more over the years. They can focus on their learning and problem-solving rather than constantly waiting for instructions from others.

For similar reasons, a professional approach makes teaching more interesting and fulfilling. When teachers understand intimately what they are doing and why, it becomes more meaningful. And as their students learn more and have their needs met, teachers can take satisfaction in how they are helping them develop.

Finally, this approach to teaching results in increased teacher resilience and retention. Recent government and school-district initiatives aimed at closely controlling teacher practice and directing it towards standardized outcomes have lowered teacher morale and led to an exodus from the profession. If teachers resist these pressures – to the extent possible – it can help to counter these trends. In summary,

> **Reasons why teachers should take charge**
>
> - Increased teacher effectiveness
> - Enhanced teacher dignity and self-regard
> - Teaching is more interesting and fulfilling
> - Increased teacher resilience and retention

What are the challenges of taking a stand on what and how to teach?

Though more effective and fulfilling, taking charge of teaching makes it more demanding. More thought, time, and effort are involved, and if we make a mistake we cannot blame it on the system. Of course, such an approach can actually make teaching more natural and meaningful, resulting in the kind of "flow" discussed in Chapter 4. However, achieving natural flow of this kind in turn requires a great deal of attention.

Many current trends at a system level are in the opposite direction, towards teacher conformity. This means that teachers who take personal responsibility for their teaching are in danger of being looked down on by their administration, colleagues, parents, and even some students. There may be some penalties in terms of promotion and teaching placements. We would argue that, if well implemented and explained, a more reflective approach to teaching can in fact result in professional recognition and advancement, due to the increased teaching effectiveness. But to secure such an outcome again takes considerable time and effort.

Teachers on the whole have not been prepared for this approach to teaching. For many, substantial modification of their view of teaching and pedagogical practices is required. This in turn involves extensive changes in preservice preparation and ongoing teacher development.

Theory/research basis for taking a stand on what and how to teach

According to Pollard et al., being professional as a teacher includes having "civic responsibility," "moral purpose", and "commitment to quality" (2019: 538). In their view, teachers' unions have not always placed enough emphasis on these aspects of professionalism, attending mainly to the interests of teachers themselves. The civic/moral emphasis has often had to come from other organizations – for example, in England the General Teaching Council (p. 540). In the authors' view, an "extended professionalism" is needed that goes beyond narrow effectiveness to pursuing "overall educational purposes" and a reflective, collaborative teaching approach where teachers' judgement is respected. Governments need to value and trust teachers more. "Teachers really do matter.

Extended professionalism ... is the foundation of high quality education in the modern world" (p. 542)

"De-professionalization" occurs when teachers are not respected and are subjected to detailed, top-down control. When they are prevented in this way from exercising judgement, the effectiveness of their teaching is greatly reduced (Noddings, 2013). According to Bransford, Darling-Hammond, and LePage, teachers should be seen (and should see themselves) as "adaptive experts" (2005: 3) who "exercise trustworthy judgment based on a strong base of knowledge" (p. 2). Teachers have intimate knowledge of their students and the unfolding situation in their classroom, enabling them to individualize student learning and take advantage of teachable moments as they occur.

Along the same lines, Cochran-Smith and Lytle point to the absurdity of a situation where teachers, throughout their career, "are expected to learn about their own profession not by studying their own experiences but by studying the findings of those who are not themselves school-based teachers" (1993: 1). In a later work, these authors state:

> [P]ractitioners are deliberative intellectuals who constantly theorize practice as part of practice itself ... [T]he goal of teacher learning initiatives is the joint construction of local knowledge, the questioning of common assumptions, and thoughtful critique of the usefulness of the research generated by others both inside and outside contexts of practice. (Cochran-Smith and Lytle, 2009: 2)

As noted earlier, some authors maintain that when governments and school systems attempt complete top-down control of teachers, thus de-professionalizing them, it is teachers' responsibility to "resist" at least some of what they are being told to do, for the good of their students and society generally. Santoro and Cain, who as we saw earlier call this type of teacher action "principled resistance", state that public school teachers "face myriad demands for compliance from an array of powerful actors: school leaders, politicians, highly paid consultants, and textbook publishers, just to name a few. Within this context teachers' resistance is often interpreted simply as insubordination and recalcitrance" (2018: 1). In fact, appropriate teacher resistance is solidly founded on at least three types of consideration: pedagogical, professional, and democratic (pp. 2–4). It is based on teachers' understanding of "the fundamental responsibilities of teachers and the teaching profession" (p. 7).

Strategies for taking a stand on what and how to teach

I feel that so much of the curriculum can be integrated. And for me last year a big thing was bringing writing into math, because students have to be able to explain how they think in order to show evidence for their work ... We try to work it so we are keeping to our program but still satisfying Common Core demands.
— Linda, teaching lower elementary in her seventh year

Despite the repeated attempts, it is rare that teachers are completely controlled by outside directives. They care deeply about their students, have their needs visibly before them daily, and have a degree of privacy in the classroom that enables them to adapt to the needs of their students. However, as Yandell says, although teachers do have such leeway, government policy "has its effects" (2016: 39). Accordingly, ways must be found for teachers to take a stand on what and how to teach. Here are some strategies for taking a stand on what and how to teach:

Strategies for taking charge of what and how to teach

1 Getting to know your students and the curriculum so you are in a position to decide what and how to teach
2 Explaining to parents, colleagues, and others the importance of what you are doing
3 Finding ways to do *both*: achieve relevant goals *and* teach curriculum content
4 Explaining to parents, colleagues, and others how you are doing both

---

Getting to know your students and the curriculum so you are in a position to decide what and how to teach

Two key justifications for taking a stand on what and how to teach are that (1) in this way you are meeting the needs of your students more fully and, anyway, (2) you are still teaching the essence of the curriculum. Being able to use these justifications requires that teachers are actually doing these two things. Karen, a Kindergarten teacher in her fourteenth year, talked about how she adapts her teaching to her students to achieve both these ends:

> I sometimes modify the curriculum and even leave out topics, but every year it's different because I follow the children's lead. Like this year we spent a lot of time on addition whereas last year we didn't so much. It depends on what the kids are talking about and interested in. I do always address high priority areas; for example, number sense in my view is the most important strand in math, so I always cover it and talk about it. But with some of the other strands it depends partly on the students' interests.

Similarly, Anna, another Kindergarten teacher with 14 years' experience said:

> I have taught very difficult classes [in former schools] where some things were very hard for them to grasp. So when things were busy and report cards were coming up, you would think: what will be the most important things for the students to learn? Like I've had groups who can't skip-count by 2's, so we focused on counting by 10's or 5's. It doesn't mean we never did counting by 2's, but not so much and I didn't test them on that.

And John, a teacher of K-6 in his fourteenth year commented: "At the end of the day, what is important is the group of students you have (I'm thinking especially social studies and health). Kids all have different learning styles and interests, and tapping into those sometimes means some sacrifices in the topics we cover".

With respect to the teacher's knowledge of the curriculum, Wanda, a teacher of Grades 2–4 also in her fourteenth year, talked about how she analyses the curriculum to see how she can meet the broad expectations while also making decisions about what and how to teach:

> In the curriculum there are overall expectations and specific expectations. And if you're trying to accomplish the overall expectations, there are lots of ways you can do that while modifying the specific expectations. You can't possibly cover all 150 specific expectations in a year, so you choose some of the main ones that will enable you to achieve the overall expectations. And among the specific expectations you choose ones you think you're going to be able to achieve, given the time constraints, the prior knowledge of your students, the extent of your own knowledge, and the available resources: it's a combination of things.

Explaining to parents, colleagues, and others the importance of what you are doing

Having made sure they are indeed teaching valuable things and in ways that are effective both generally and for their students, teachers should as far as possible explain this to parents, colleagues, and others. David, again in his fourteenth year, talked about how, as a principal, he respects the right of teachers to make decisions about their teaching, so long as they can justify it:

> I think teachers must often modify curriculum expectations, because if that's not happening they're ignoring the learner. And I empower my teachers, saying to them: "I'm not the curriculum police, I won't be banging down your door because you didn't cover expectation 5d/64. But what I will do, if there's ever an issue that comes to my attention, is ask: How do you professionally justify what you have been doing in the classroom?" And if they can give me a sound answer that is rooted in student need, who am I to judge?

Nancy, a teacher of 14 years' experience who teaches art and music across middle school, spoke about how she justifies her approach to teaching visual arts:

> The kids find going systematically through the principles and elements of art really boring. So I will mention the principles and elements set out in the curriculum at the beginning of the year and keep mentioning them, but they're largely in the background. I used to keep talking about them but now I find it's too much and not interesting enough. So I'm trying to make the course more current and exciting for them, and more accessible so they can build skills.

Finding ways to do *both*: achieve relevant goals *and* teach curriculum content

As discussed in earlier chapters, a major way for teachers to satisfy critics of 21st-century teaching is to do much of what the system wants in terms of subject coverage while *also* doing other things they think important. Linda, a teacher of lower elementary students in her seventh year spoke about how she does this:

> I feel that so much of the curriculum can be integrated. And for me last year a big thing was bringing writing into math, because students have to be able to explain how they think in order to show evidence for their work. So if the kids were making a pattern, I had them describe it verbally and then write about it; and that would combine math and writing.

> The new Common Core curriculum is making things difficult by adding more and more content, but the way we're getting around that as kindergarten teachers is, for example, if we are studying plants and "going green" we pick a non-fiction book that is about, say, "from fields to flowers" or something like that. And that is still within our social studies requirement of studying plants and going green, but it also satisfies studying non-fiction texts. We try to work it so we are keeping to our programme but still satisfying Common Core demands.

Explaining to parents, colleagues, and others how you are doing both

It is not enough to "do both", teachers also have to explain to people how they are succeeding in this. Nina, a Grade 2 teacher in her fourteenth year, described how parents can in fact be very supportive of teacher initiatives if you have a good relationship with them and they see that what you are doing is not only covering the curriculum but also providing their children with an enriched education.

> In science I often interpret the curriculum in my own way but I get appreciative comments from parents, like it seems as if their kids are in a "gifted" programme. For example, we are studying butterflies now and the kids are really interested; and I thought if the kids are so interested, why not use some scientific words? So they were asking how caterpillars breathe, and I said, see those holes in their sides, that's how they breathe and they are actually called spiracles. And you can call them holes in their sides or spiracles, it's up to you. And parents like their kids being exposed to that sort of thing.

Chapter summary

Schooling today is in many ways still rooted in the past. To go in the 21st-century directions discussed in earlier chapters, teachers have to adopt a new identity: as able professionals who take a stand on many aspects of what and how to teach.

It is legitimate for teachers to adopt this identity and stance because they care deeply about their students and also have a great many opportunities to assess their students' needs and observe the effectiveness of different teaching approaches. Because of their extensive classroom experience, year in and year out, teachers are experts on teaching. Education theorists and researchers also have considerable expertise, but it tends to be in specialized areas and they typically do not have the same opportunities for classroom observation and experimentation.

By taking a stand on what and how to teach, teachers face several challenges. Teachers on the whole did not experience this approach in their own schooling and it is something they are still learning. And this way of teaching is more demanding – initially at least – than simply transmitting prescribed subject content. Furthermore, such an approach is often not approved by system and school administrators, parents, or the general public. However, we believe that in the long run it is a more effective, fulfilling, and enjoyable way to teach.

Strategies for taking a stand on what and how to teach include: getting to know your students and the curriculum so you are in a position to work out how to modify the programme; explaining to parents, colleagues, and others the importance of what you are doing; finding ways to do *both* – achieve relevant goals and teach required content; and explaining to parents, colleagues, and others how you are doing both.

Questions for reflection and discussion

1 Why is it important for teachers to take a stand on what and how to teach?
2 How far should they go in this direction?
3 How can teachers justify this stance? Are they *really* experts on teaching?
4 What does it mean to be a professional? Are teachers professionals?
5 How can teachers adopt this stance and continue to maintain respect and keep their employment?

18 Principle 18: Develop a 21st-century pedagogy

The internet helps with individualizing teaching, because I can give different tasks and more support to the ones who need it just by checking their names off differently. Also I can make available tools that read and write for students as required. There are just so many ways you can differentiate.

– Laura, teaching library and rotary science in her twelfth year

The Principle, its importance, and some challenges

To go in 21st-century directions, teachers need a 21st-century pedagogy, one that is part of their personal and professional identity, makes their teaching more effective, and enhances their wellbeing. Developing such a pedagogy is not easy, since it often differs from what teachers experienced in their own schooling and moreover is not viewed as sound by some people.

This type of pedagogy is already implicit in previous parts of the book. In particular, the strategy sections in each chapter contain general ideas and practical suggestions about pedagogy. In this chapter, we bring many of these ideas and suggestions together, laying out an overall, integrated pedagogy. We call it a 21st-century pedagogy because, even though it would have been useful in previous centuries, it is especially necessary in the present one.

The format of this chapter is rather different from earlier ones. We begin with the same general sections (though in shortened form), but by far the largest section of the chapter addresses in turn ten key components of 21st-century pedagogy. And instead of having separate sections on theory/research and teacher examples, we include brief summaries of these under each of the ten pedagogy components.

What is 21st-century pedagogy?

The main components of what we are calling 21st-century pedagogy are the following:

Components of 21st-century pedagogy

Component 1: Teach for *both* subject knowledge *and* relevance ("Do both")
Component 2: Learn with *and* from your students
Component 3: Build community and inclusion in the classroom
Component 4: Get to know your students

Component 5: Give students choice
Component 6: Individualize learning
Component 7: Plan *and* be flexible
Component 8: Set up routines and recurring activities
Component 9: Model what you teach
Component 10: Teach collaboratively

Why develop a 21st-century pedagogy?

For teachers to go in 21st-century directions, it is not enough just to decide to do so. They have to have a different approach to teaching from the one commonly used in the past. For example, they have to teach *both* for subject knowledge *and* relevance (Component 1) if they are to foster students' personal development while *also* teaching the subject knowledge the school system demands and students need. And they have to work out how to learn with *and* from their students (Component 2) if students are to develop the problem-solving, inquiry approach they need in the 21st century.

In addition, a new pedagogy is necessary if teachers are to model the approach to work and life they are recommending to their students. For example, if students are to achieve overall social development, it is important to see this embodied in the pedagogy of their teachers. And if students are to experience mental health, teachers have to set up routines and recurring activities in the classroom that exemplify a way of life characterized by attention to wellbeing.

Furthermore, of course, the proposed pedagogy is beneficial to teachers themselves, enabling them to understand their work and life approach better, survive and thrive in the profession, and have the energy and enthusiasm necessary to support their students. To summarize:

Reasons for developing 21st-century pedagogy

- Such a pedagogy is needed if teachers are to be successful in going in 21st-century directions
- Teaching in a 21st-century way models for students the approach to life and learning they are being encouraged to adopt
- Such modelling helps teachers themselves understand what they are recommending to their students
- 21st-century pedagogy is more enjoyable and satisfying for teachers and students alike

What are the challenges of developing and adopting a 21st-century pedagogy?

It is not easy to develop and implement such a pedagogy, and teachers need to be aware of this and realize they are in it for the long haul – but also that every advance they make will be worthwhile for them and their students. The challenges include:

Teachers were not themselves taught in this way.

Given the shortage of professional development in school systems today, teachers have to develop the pedagogy to a considerable extent on their own.

This kind of pedagogy is often not accepted by politicians, school authorities, parents, and even some students. Adopting it may result in disapproval and even professional sanctions.

Given its novelty and complexity, teaching in this way takes more time and effort initially. In our view, the investment is well worth it, but a long road of learning is ahead.

Major components of 21st-century pedagogy

In this main part of the chapter, we review in turn key dimensions of the overall pedagogical approach we see as needed for the 21st century. Though we deal with them separately, the various components are closely connected: they make up an integrated whole. As mentioned, this section will form the bulk of the chapter and include theory/research and teacher examples briefly in each sub-section rather than in separate sections.

Component 1: Teach for *both* subject knowledge *and* relevance ("Do both")

We have mentioned this aspect of 21st-century pedagogy often throughout the book because it is so crucial. Addressing *at the same time* both subject content and broader life relevance is essential if teachers are to satisfy school system demands while also helping students develop in the ways needed for 21st-century living. Without "doing both" in this way, it would largely be impossible to go in the directions we are proposing.

As noted in earlier chapters, many theorists maintain it is indeed possible to combine teaching for subject knowledge and relevance. For example, Bellanca states that teachers can integrate "standards-aligned content with 21st century skills" (2010: 1). And Boaler argues that effective teaching materials can be created using existing curriculum and resources, providing a basis for "new, enhanced learning experiences" (2016: 77). Teachers often do not have to develop new materials: the potential for "doing both" is largely at their fingertips, provided they understand the importance and possibility of doing so.

In previous chapters, we have given many examples of teachers in our longitudinal study teaching for both subject knowledge and relevance. Here we note the case of David, now a principal but previously a middle- and high-school teacher, who commented in his thirteenth year that it is feasible to teach for subject knowledge and relevance at the same time,

> ... with the caveat that certain subjects are more difficult than others in this respect. And I don't mean because these subjects are not relevant but because you have to find the relevance. A perfect example is the "when am I going to use this?" question students ask in math. I think we need to remind educators that it's not a bad question, and if you don't know the answer for now tell them that and work on finding out, on your own or with them.

Component 2: Learn with *and* from your students

Another aspect of 21st-century pedagogy is teachers talking less in class than in the past and giving their students more talk time, spread as evenly as possible across all students. This enables students to "construct" their knowledge and become aware of – and respected for – their ideas and abilities. In addition, it means teachers can learn from their students rather than just transmitting a pre-set package of knowledge. These outcomes are especially important in the 21st century, with the world changing rapidly and new information and ideas constantly disseminated through media – to which students as well as teachers have ready access.

In *Democracy and Education*, John Dewey argued that teachers and students should learn together, saying that learning should be a "shared activity" in which the teacher does not just "stand off and look on" but rather "the teacher is a learner and the learner ... a teacher" (1916: 188). Similarly, a century later, Gillies talks about the importance of "academically productive talk" in the classroom, where the teacher's contribution "often switches from providing authoritative knowledge ... to being more dialogic" (2016: 2).

Turning to the teachers in our study, Jessica, a Grade 1/2 teacher in her eleventh year said:

> I remember when I was in teacher education, and I was placed in a school, my host teacher always told me that having general knowledge about everything was very important. She said it's good "if you can just read a newspaper, listen to the news, have general knowledge about what's happening". And I've carried her suggestion throughout my teaching career ... And I find my students have benefitted from having a general understanding, general knowledge of different aspects of the world. And I always go and research it and come back and tell them, I don't just brush off the conversation. And they will come back and ask, did you find this out? And then we'll look it up together.

Component 3: Build community and inclusion in the classroom

Establishing a genuinely social and inclusive classroom community not only supports students' enjoyment and general wellbeing, as discussed elsewhere; it is also a key *pedagogical* link to various 21st-century teaching practices such as learning with students and modelling an approach to life. Students do not participate well in class if they feel inferior to other students or excluded by them, and they have difficulty learning to be inclusive themselves if they do not see it being modelled.

Among educational theorists and researchers, Roland Martin (2011) proposes thinking of the classroom as a "schoolhome", a place with an emphasis on teachers and students caring for each other and thereby learning how to have positive, caring relationships. And Tranter et al. recommend a "relationship-based approach" to schooling that results in students being "more eager to attend school and more willing to learn alongside their peers" (2018: 70).

Drawing on the teachers in our study, Kindergarten teacher Karen in her fifteenth year reported that she spends a great deal of time establishing community and inclusion in her classroom: "I feel like it's the most important thing. If they enjoy coming and they feel part of the community, that is half the battle because they feel good here; they want to do their best and help each other".

Candice, a teacher of integrated arts across Grades 1–6 and in her fourteenth year said: "Fostering the social side I see as my most important role as a teacher ... With technology we're losing skills for social interaction in some ways, and I see my role as a music teacher as making social connections for kids".

And Jessica, teaching library and elementary support and special education in her twelfth year stated:

> I like to start off the year with different books that focus on certain expectations or values, for example respect – respecting each other and respecting staff. And I follow the school district's list of character traits and focus on them. And students are really engaged in it, they love the conversation and using their own personal experiences to connect to a book, whether it's narrative or non-fiction.

Component 4: Get to know your students

With a class community and a lot of student talk teachers get to know their students better, and this can be strengthened further by chatting individually with them as opportunities arise. Getting to know their students enables teachers to support their learning better, further strengthens the class community, and models to the students a caring, social way of being.

According to Pollard et al., "teacher–pupil classroom relationships underpin" effective learning (2019: 115). Meier et al. endorse an approach where everyone in the class gets to know each other, "focusing on what [each] child [is] good at, what he or she like[s] to do, or other characteristics" (2015: 55). And Goleman and Senge say that we need to establish a classroom in which "the teacher embodies and models kindness and concern for her students" (2014: 32).

Among the study participants, Grades 1/2 teacher Mary in her twelfth year said that she spends a great deal of time building a relationship with her students, because

> if students feel the teacher likes them and they like the teacher, so much more learning is going to happen. They need to know that I care about them, that I see them. So every day I touch base with every single one of them, whether just asking them a simple question, greeting them at the door as they come in, or chit-chatting with them when I'm on recess duty ... having fun with them, joking around, talking to them about things going on in their lives.

And Laura in her twelfth year reported spending a lot of her time

> ... having those relationships or talking sports with them and letting them know that we're human too and not just there to deliver the curriculum. They can have open relationships with us and talk about different things. I think that also helps with the mental wellness piece ... And at the beginning of the year we do an "All About Me" type project so I can get to know some of their likes and dislikes, which helps me in my side discussions with them in the hallway or during recess, which are so beneficial.

Component 5: Give students choice

Letting students have choice results in them being more engaged, becoming more autonomous, learning more about their own interests and abilities, and developing their personal set of skills. And as with student talk it means the teacher and other students can get to know them, and also learn from the way they approach things.

Among theorists and researchers, student choice is often emphasized. For example, Trilling and Fadel maintain that students need to acquire "initiative and self-direction", given that we live in a world where managers have less time "for mentoring and guiding employees" (2009: 28). Meier is critical of the lack of provision for student initiative in traditional schooling, where students learn "largely passively": this is not like "real life" (2002: 12). And Tranter et al. argue that students need to "develop a stronger sense of who they truly are" (2018: 117).

Turning to the study participants, Candice, teaching Grades 1–6 integrated arts when in her twelfth year, spoke of how she uses a student-driven approach, in which students ask questions based in part on what they already know and then try to answer them:

> [B]ecause it's student-driven it's real-life learning, it can be modified in real time by new information, and it takes students from where they are to knowing something more. So it is definitely a case of giving students power in their learning, [and my role as a teacher is to] create situations that help them learn. For example, in music I do a lot of improvisation with students,

like I give them a few rhythm patterns or notes and they make a larger piece of music, so it's kind of music inquiry.

Similarly, Karen teaching Kindergarten in her fourteenth year reported that she gives students choice by

... [setting up] open-ended centres for activity time, where they're allowed to choose the centre they go to and the activity they want [with the teacher as far as possible] providing the materials they need ... because different kids enjoy different activities. And it's interesting because some will come back and revisit the same activity over and over again, adding more details and learning how to balance the things; and they create these amazing things and show so much pride and growth. But there are some things that they are required to do, so they're not just sitting building with blocks every day all day. It's not completely their choice, I definitely balance it with some guided writing and reading and math lessons, where they're in a small group and work together. So, it's a balance.

Component 6: Individualize learning

Individualization of learning is connected closely to allowing students to talk and make choices, as discussed above. Individualization of teaching and learning has often been proposed by theorists but it is not extensively practised. It is essential if students are to be optimally engaged and arrive at the autonomy and sense of self they need in today's world, as discussed in earlier chapters.

Many theorists and researchers emphasize individualization, notably O'Meara (2010), Peterson and Hittie (2003), Tomlinson (2001), Waring and Evans (2015), and West-Burnham and Coates (2005). According to Waring and Evans, other terms may be used such as "personalization" and "differentiation," but in most situations we prefer "individualization" because it makes the emphasis on the individual student clearer. This clarity is in some ways a disadvantage in the current climate in which standardization of teaching and learning is often demanded. However, many writers maintain that teachers should resist this pressure to the greatest extent possible (Santoro and Cain, 2018).

As for the participants in our study, Nora – teaching middle-school in her fifth year – spoke of the need to individualize learning, noting that the internet enables students to discover things much more quickly. And she maintains that "ideas and information make much more sense [to students] when they are looking them up instead of flipping through books or being lectured at". Similarly, Laura, a teacher of library and Grades 1–6 rotary science in her twelfth year, stressed the importance of individualization and the advantages of the internet in this respect:

IT helps with individualizing teaching, because I can give different tasks and more support to the ones who need it just by checking their names off differently. Also I can make available tools that read and write for students as required. There are just so many ways you can differentiate.

Component 7: Plan *and* be flexible

Some beginning teachers emphasize having detailed lesson plans while others favour being highly creative and responsive in the moment. But no matter how they started out, most of the teachers in our study moved rather quickly to a middle position where they develop plans but *also* are open to modifying their plans substantially, depending on the individual and group needs of their students.

A middle position of this kind is favoured by many writers. For example, Pollard et al. advocate what they call "extended professionalism" that has due regard for the "overall educational purposes" of the school system but supports teachers taking strong initiative on many matters (2019: 542). Similarly, Bransford et al. (2005) stress the need for teachers to identify as "adaptive experts" who often make decisions based on their professional expertise. Cochran-Smith and Lytle maintain that teachers are "deliberative intellectuals" who should constantly exercise judgement about what and how to teach (2009: 2).

Among the study participants, Vera, a Grade 3 teacher in her thirteenth year said:

> Some days, I have this great lesson planned but half an hour after we've started we're still answering questions ... And by the time the standardized test rolls around at the end of the year I am like, oh gosh, I should not have spent so long on this, but that is the way it goes ... If you don't answer their questions they won't focus on the lesson.

Nancy, a middle-school rotary art teacher in her fifteenth year, said a key piece of advice to give a beginning teacher is: "Don't let your boss control how you do your job. Make sure you're self-motivated and go with your own interests. Be confident in how you teach and be self-reflective and accountable for what you teach". And Miranda, teaching kindergarten in her twelfth year said:

> We were always told in teachers college how important it was to plan, and I do think that is important; but the part they didn't always say was that we should be open to changing things. And sometimes when you change your plan and go with what the kids need or want, sometimes those are your best lessons.

Component 8: Set up routines and recurring activities

Closely related to combining planning with flexibility, as just discussed, is establishing routines and recurring activities in the classroom. This is a form of planning but one that allows for considerable modification along the way. Routines are valuable because they give students a sense of security and familiarity and can make learning more enjoyable. They also – once established – reduce a teacher's workload, leaving more time for other aspects of teaching or for enhancing their work/life balance.

Enjoyable and effective routines and activities give rise to a state of "flow", as advocated by social psychologist Mihaly Csikszentmihalyi (1990). Having things just "flow along" in this way optimizes productivity and wellbeing. Smith and Wilhelm (2002) propose applying this approach to teaching, with particular reference to the education of male high school students of working-class background. However, they have found in their research that the original concept of flow needs to be modified in ways not mentioned by Csikszentmihalyi. Routine and intense engagement alone are not sufficient: the boys studied said that a strong social component is needed, along with a sense of meaning and accomplishment.

Many of the teachers in our study talked about the importance of classroom routines. Mary, in her twelfth year and teaching Grades 1/2, reported that every Thursday she has a "Think Outside the Box" activity, where students come into the classroom and there is a piece of paper on the desk with a partly-drawn shape that they have to complete in any way they want. And apart from supporting creativity and affirming students with unusual talents, it has become an enjoyable routine for the students and also takes some pressure off her as the teacher to deliver yet another lesson.

Dina, a Kindergarten teacher in her eleventh year, described how she has set up her room with centres and regular activities to facilitate student choice.

[The centres] have become a routine for them so they now know how to use the materials, which gives them more freedom and choice. There are separate tables, so they know this is the space for art, and this is for the writing, and so on. And there are stations for the materials which can be brought to the table and then put back at a shelf area ... So it's not just a teacher-directed thing with me going in and setting everything up. They know where things belong and can take them out and bring them back.

Component 9: Model what you teach

We have justified several pedagogical components so far partly on the ground that they model the approach to learning and life we are recommending for the 21st century. But modelling what is being advocated is an important pedagogical strategy in itself. It saves time, shows students that teachers really mean what they say because they practise it themselves, helps teachers refine their message as they try to implement it, and shows students what is being proposed right there in the classroom.

Dewey rejected the notion that "education is a process of preparation or getting ready" for the future rather than experiencing in the present an approach to life (1916: 63). He saw education as "leading into the future" (p. 65), but argued that unless students experience the approach to life in the present they will not understand it or learn how to practise it. Accordingly, what teachers are recommending to students should as much as possible be modelled in the present in the classroom. Along similar lines, Meier maintains that the "habits of mind" schooling that should be fostering in students must be embodied in the pedagogical processes and general life of the school itself, including the assessment methods and the attitudes and behaviour of teachers (2015: 13–14).

As for the teachers in our study, Tanya – a Grade 2 teacher in her tenth year – talked about how she builds happiness into classroom life: "I try to model the sense of happiness and enjoyment that can come from your daily experiences". While Jessica, in her twelfth year and responsible for library, special education, and general support, said that a major part of building community and inclusion is modelling it:

> Making sure everybody's voice is heard is a big thing. If a child does not feel safe to speak or to advocate for him or herself that changes the dynamic for that student with peers and with the teacher. I always come from a place of trying to be as equitable and diverse as possible in the different things I do. And it's not just character-related or socially-related, it's also how I teach.

And Vera, teaching Grades 3/4 in her fifteenth year said:

> I feel I model [inclusion] every day at every moment I possibly can. It's one of those community-building things: live out what you believe so people can see you are a person who respects everyone no matter what … Because while it is certainly necessary to call out discrimination and so forth, it can become just a token addressing of the issue, [whereas] actually building inclusion in the classroom shows how I am changing my own mind and heart about people and learning to understand my own biases and misconceptions.

Component 10: Teach collaboratively

Teaching collaboratively is not always feasible, given the typical "egg-crate" design of schools (Lortie, 1975); and sometimes it has been imposed on teachers in unfortunate ways. Nevertheless, it has great potential: it can make teaching more enjoyable because of the social element involved and can enable teachers to draw on each other's knowledge and talents rather than having to create everything on their own.

Many writers emphasize the need for collaborative learning among students (e.g. Ananiadou and Claro, 2009; Bellanca, 2010; Trilling and Fadell, 2009), but for students to learn how to collaborate it helps greatly if they see such behaviour modelled by their teachers. Pollard et al. state that "[r]eflective teaching, professional learning and personal fulfilment are enhanced through collaboration and dialogue with colleagues" (2019: 93). They give the example of Lesson Study, which "involves groups of teachers collaboratively planning, teaching, observing and analysing learning and teaching in specified lessons … looking in detail as something teachers want to try out in a lesson series (p. 95)."

Drawing on the teacher interviews from our study, Nancy, a middle-school art teacher in her fifteenth year talked about how she collaborates with subject specialists at her school, integrating art into their subject area. For example, in partnership with a Grade 7 English teacher, she does an activity where students create a poem by blacking out words on a photocopied page of a fiction book. And she and a Grade 8 science teacher work together to help students enhance their sketching techniques for doing microscope drawings.

Mary, a Grade 5 teacher in her ninth year, reported that she helps maintain her professional motivation and satisfaction by

> ... working with colleagues: meeting with them, planning with them, hearing what they do in their classrooms, and learning from them. Planning with like-minded teachers, like-minded in the sense of motivation. They don't necessarily teach exactly like me, but they are as motivated to try things as I am and motivated by big ideas as opposed to little specific curriculum expectations.

Chapter summary

If teachers are to go in the 21st-century directions discussed in earlier chapters, they need to develop a corresponding pedagogy, one that fosters personal and social development, commitment to equity and inclusion, global/environmental awareness, and other 21st-century goals. Such a pedagogy is broad and complex – like life itself – and to be feasible the various components have to be integrated.

A key component of 21st-century pedagogy is teaching for *both* subject knowledge *and* relevance ("doing both"). This is necessary because extensive subject learning will always be an expectation, so teachers have to learn how to do all the other things in addition. This is not easy, since it has not been common in the past and is not widely accepted even today. However, developing such a pedagogy can open up ways to make teaching not only more effective but also more enjoyable and enriching for teachers and students alike.

There are many other dimensions of 21st-century pedagogy. For example, teachers need to learn with *and* from their students, build community and inclusion in the classroom, and give students individual voice, choice, and attention so they are able to develop autonomy and confidence and grow in the many ways required for 21st-century living. This in turn demands flexibility in teaching in order to adapt to differing and changing student needs and talents.

Another crucial dimension of the pedagogy is modelling in the classroom the approach to life and learning teachers are proposing to their students. This helps teachers refine what they are recommending and enables students to see concretely what it means. In addition, it is a more enjoyable way to teach. Collaborating with other teachers in particular is an important way to model values such as teamwork, social life, and joint construction of knowledge.

Questions for reflection and discussion

1 Why is it important to have a pedagogy that matches the goals and directions of 21st-century learning?
2 What are the key components of 21st-century pedagogy?
3 What are some ways in which these components connect?
4 How can teachers move towards a pedagogy with these components?

Principle 19: Continue to enquire and grow as a teacher

A key piece of advice [I would give a new teacher] is: you'll get through it year after year and you'll get better year after year ... A lot of first-year teachers hear that you'll get through it, but they don't hear that you'll get better, you'll be able to look back and see what you improved upon. Certainly you'll know your mistakes, but you'll see how you got past those mistakes.
— David, a middle-school principal in his fifteenth year

The Principle, its importance, and some challenges

As we saw in Chapter 17, the complexity of teaching requires that teachers take charge of their practice: outsiders cannot tell them exactly what and how to teach. This same complexity, along with constant societal and global change, means that learning to teach is a never-ending task: teachers have to continue to enquire and grow throughout their career. They already know a great deal – which is why they should have considerable trust in their own judgement and decisions – but there is always more to learn.

What is meant by ongoing teacher enquiry and growth?

The ongoing development of teachers spans the whole of their work and life (as we will explore more fully in Chapter 21). The personal greatly affects the professional and vice versa, so development of both is needed. However, in this chapter we will focus mainly on teachers' professional learning and growth.

Much of teachers' ongoing learning has to occur on their initiative: it should not just be something done *to* them by outside experts. External input can be very valuable, but it should largely be provided dialogically, critically assessed by teachers, and viewed as one source of insight among many. This is clearly true of practical teaching strategies, but even in regard to subject content knowledge, teachers themselves have to continue to rework their understandings. Apart from reading and taking courses, discussing subject content with their students year after year provides teachers with a major opportunity to assess key disciplinary ideas.

As we have said before, ongoing educational enquiry or research is something teachers are in an excellent position to do. There has been a tendency to overlook teacher enquiry – or to view it as not *real* enquiry or research and as leading at most to "tacit" or "practical" knowledge. However, we reject this position. Teachers have a sizeable sample of students each year and can observe them closely, week after week for ten months. Most education academics would be very glad to have such research opportunities.

While maintaining that teachers can and do conduct important enquiry or research, however, we do not believe that it must be entirely of the traditional "research" type. It need not be "controlled" or "systematic" in the standard sense (though in some ways it is very systematic). Most teachers do not have the time or incentive to conduct enquiry with all the formal features: they are too busy with their teaching, and anyway are not rewarded for formal research and writing. But in our view, this in no way calls into question the great value and productivity of their enquiry, whatever name we choose to give it.

Why continue to enquire and grow as a teacher?

The most obvious reason for teachers to continue to learn and develop professionally is so their teaching becomes more effective and, as a result, more helpful to their students. While teachers do not have some of the same kinds of incentives as academics to conduct research, their strong commitment to the learning and general wellbeing of their students provides a powerful motivation.

Teacher enquiry can add significantly to the general knowledge base of others involved or interested in education. This may include a teacher's friends and colleagues. For this to occur, however, teachers and others have to become more aware of how much they have to contribute and ways found – both informal and formal – to share the knowledge. A method we recommend and have used extensively is for academics to interview teachers and publish and teach about their ideas and practices.

Teacher enquiry and growth makes day-to-day teaching more enjoyable and satisfying for teachers. Becoming better at teaching brings satisfaction in itself, and seeing their students learning and enjoying the process more is gratifying. Also, the process of teacher enquiry can be interesting and enjoyable.

Becoming more informed and able professionally can give teachers increased pride and a sense of moving forward rather than just doing the same things year after year. It can also enhance their identity as a professional, and is a basis for making the many decisions they have to make about what and how to teach. In summary:

Reasons for continuing to enquire and grow as a teacher

- It makes teachers' practice more effective and so more helpful to their students
- It can add to the knowledge of others involved in education
- It makes day-to-day teaching more enjoyable and satisfying
- It gives teachers a sense of pride and forward movement

What are the challenges of ongoing teacher enquiry and growth?

Teacher enquiry is often underrated by others and even by teachers themselves. Accordingly, it is often not recognized, and for teachers to pursue it strongly a preliminary step is needed of becoming aware of how much they can learn and grow.

Teacher learning and improvement usually takes longer than teachers might like. As with so many other things in life, teachers have to be satisfied with gradual change and set aside over-the-top messages about "sudden transformation".

There is a shortage of financial support for teacher enquiry and growth, to the extent this is needed.

Teacher enquiry often leads to conclusions and teaching approaches not endorsed by authorities or the public. To some extent, teachers have to live with the lack of recognition of and support for their discoveries.

Teacher enquiry and learning are not usually externally rewarded. Teachers largely have to pursue them for their own reasons.

Theory/research basis for ongoing teacher enquiry and growth

What is the status of the knowledge generated by practitioners? As noted above, many people (even teachers themselves) assume it has less authority than knowledge arrived at by academic researchers, and they look to the latter as providing the main directions for school improvement. It is often thought that practice-based knowledge cannot be generalized beyond a practitioner's specific situation, and the current press for "research-based" or "evidence-based" schooling suggests a lack of confidence in practice-based knowledge. However, Cochran-Smith and Lytle see an emphasis on evidence-based research of a kind that excludes teacher enquiry as having "devastating implications" for schooling (2009: 10). It results in a portrayal of good teachers as "wise consumers" of ideas and strategies generated by others (p. 11).

In line with Cochran-Smith and Lytle's position, many theorists maintain that informal practitioner knowledge has basically the same qualities as sound academic knowledge and deserves similar status. Dewey (1916, 1938), for example, argued that both theoretical and practical dimensions are essential to *all* genuine knowledge, and teacher-generated ideas about teaching have both. Dewey's position is largely supported by Schön, who rejects the "technical-rationalist" notion that teacher expertise comes primarily through "the application of scientific theory and technique" (1983: 21). Rather, when teachers see a student having difficulty learning, they "must do a piece of experimental research, then and there, in the classroom" (p. 66). On Schön's view, such research generates "theory" (p. 181), which provides "springboards for making sense of new situations" (p. 317).

In the same vein, Allen (1989) states that, contrary to Aristotle's view that practical knowledge (*phronesis*) is inferior to theoretical knowledge (*theoria*), practical knowledge is actually more basic since it integrates theory and practice. Allen sees the generation of "universal statements" associated with academic discourse as a kind of "distancing move" that has heuristic value but is a tool rather than the goal of inquiry. Like Dewey, he argues that reality is too complex and context-specific to be captured by universal statements; generalizations are only useful if they have implicit within them reference to the diverse concrete situations that give them their actual meaning.

Others take a similar position. For example, Zeichner (1995) is critical of the view that teacher research is just "a form of PD [professional development]" and does not result in legitimate knowledge. This leads to the unfortunate situation where university researchers ignore teachers' knowledge and teachers "ignore the researchers right back" (1995: 154). But because of the status differential, teachers have to endure top-down PD that "ignores what teachers already know and can do and relies primarily on the distribution of prepackaged and allegedly 'research-based' solutions to school problems" (p. 161). And Carr states that teachers have "extensive theoretical powers" and constantly use theory in "conceptualizing their own activities" (1995: 34–35). He says that academics must acknowledge teachers as theorists and work in tandem with them if they are to have a significant influence on the field.

Strategies for ongoing teacher enquiry and growth

We believe that teachers already continue to enquire and grow significantly over the years, and findings from our longitudinal study of teachers support this view. Part of the reason is that teachers have strong motivation to keep on learning, given that the benefits of improvements are daily right in front of them in students they care deeply about. Also, as noted, teachers have excellent opportunities to enquire, year after year, in their classrooms.

However, in the 21st century ongoing teacher learning is more important than ever before, and also more possible given advances in communication and social structures. Specific strategies for continued teacher enquiry and growth include the following:

Strategies for ongoing teacher enquiry and growth

1   Learning through experimentation and observation in your own classroom
2   Linking up with other teachers in your school
3   Linking up with teachers beyond your school
4   Taking courses, reading, visiting websites, etc.
5   Connecting to families
6   Enquiring and growing gradually

Learning through experimentation and observation in your own classroom

In our view, on-the-job learning in the classroom is by far the main source of ongoing teacher development since (as noted above) teachers spend so much of their professional life in the classroom, with abundant opportunities for experimentation and observation. This includes a type of "action research", but of an informal kind we have written about elsewhere (Beck, 2017). Formal data-gathering and subsequent presentation or publication need not occur.

Among the teachers in our study, Jody – an elementary teacher in her tenth year – reported that "over time" she had learned in her classroom that every student "is at a different place". Kelly, also in her tenth year, noted that she had discovered over the years that teaching students social skills "gets easier and the kids get better at it, and they start doing it without me". And Lucy, now in her seventh year, commented that when she first taught Grades 7/8, the students did not want to share their writing because of peer ridicule, but she found – through experience – that it is possible to build a classroom community in which every student can share safely, with the others listening and applauding.

Jessica's "classroom" for half the day in her twelfth year was the school library, and she reported learning – largely on her own – how to run a successful book fair. It was

> ... something new to me [and involved] a lot of planning and coordinating and trying to get the school excited ... setting up activities and games and having classes come in. But I drew on my previous position as a drama teacher and introduced some books that were going to be featured in the fair ... So you kind of got creative, and I do enjoy using creativity in some respects. But for the most part I had to work it out by myself.

Linking up with other teachers in your school

Beyond the classroom, teachers have many opportunities to get together regularly with colleagues in their school – teachers, administrators, and other staff. This provides important social support, but can also be a key context for finding out about various teaching ideas and methods. Among the many venues and types of school-based professional learning for teachers, a favourite is visiting each other's classrooms to watch or participate in teaching activities.

Many of our study participants mentioned that they had learned things from other teachers in their school, describing how it happened. Karen, teaching Kindergarten in her fifteenth year said:

> It's good to talk to other teachers and try different things ... When Full Day Kindergarten began six years ago, I suggested that we meet as a Kindergarten team once a month, just casually ... [W]e meet and talk about what's coming up, what's going on. And we've done that quite regularly over the past six years. And we also talk in the staff room or go out for lunch together, and have conversations about what's working and what we're doing at that point.

We actually go up to the staffroom fifteen minutes earlier than the rest of the teachers, so we get there and often sit together and have conversations. But also we just go popping into each other's rooms and see what they're doing and asking for ideas.

Mary, a Grade 1/2 teacher in her twelfth year commented:

[You can address the challenges of teaching by] asking a lot of questions, communicating with your colleagues, seeking out help and clarification and not trying to work it all out on your own. Because so much of the time we're in our own classroom doing our own thing, when there are so many other amazing things happening right next door or across the hall.

And Dina, a Kindergarten teacher with 11 years' experience reported:

I have a new teaching partner who teaches the other Kindergarten class. She just started when I was on maternity leave, and I have actually worked with her in other schools. Talking to her has opened a lot of discussion over, for example, where do we give students choice, and how can we give them more choice in art so it's not so crazy with materials on the floor and paint on the walls, but also so that they can play with their hands and get creative. We brainstormed around how we can facilitate smaller centres and with some teacher direction but also more freedom and choice.

Linking up with teachers beyond your school

Often the main professional "kindred spirits" are beyond a teacher's own school. Sometimes school boards provide funding and opportunities for teachers from different schools to get together, but this only happened to our teachers a couple of time in fifteen years. Increasingly, however, teachers are engaging in regular emailing, tweeting, etc., going beyond their school, school district, or even region or country.

Miranda, then in her twelfth year, reported how she had combined meeting with immediate colleagues with linking up with teachers from other schools. "I was involved in a principal math project that was fun. We had a group of teachers and two principals from two different schools who got together to talk about math and come up with questions and activities to do in people's classrooms, and then implemented it in each other's classrooms". She added: "I really don't like online learning with webcasts and things, for me it has to be one-on-one or face-to-face". (Obviously, she may have changed her views on this since the Covid-19 pandemic.)

Like Miranda, Laura – who was also in her twelfth year – said she enjoys meeting up with teachers from other schools. However, she is also very willing to meet online:

A friend of mine and I started a Twitter chat for educators to connect and grow a community. We talk once a month on the last Thursday of every month from 7:30 to 8:30pm, just on Twitter with a way to create questions that are relevant to various topics. We try to do stuff that's relevant in the moment, so people want to talk about it and get ideas and share. And we have a website where we share the archives of people who aren't online [live with us], so they can still get benefit from the resources and ideas by looking at the archive.

And Karen, a Kindergarten teacher in her fifteenth year observed:

It's funny because even though I've been teaching for a long time, I feel I'm always learning, I'm always trying new things and changing things up every year, and that makes teaching continue to be fun and interesting. One thing that's changed for me is that I was always reluctant to be on Facebook or anything like that, but I've actually developed a community of Kindergarten teachers on Facebook and I really enjoy it. It has given me lots of new ideas and also affirmed some of my ideas about how to teach.

Taking courses, reading, visiting websites, etc.

Apart from learning from other teachers – in one's own school or beyond – teachers can continue to enquire and grow by taking courses and doing workshops (online or face-to-face), reading books and articles, and visiting websites, etc. Of course, the online option has been especially valuable during the Covid-19 pandemic. Taking courses can be expensive but has the advantage that it gives teachers a formal qualification. It also allows a degree of choice based on personal preference and the reputation of the programme, by contrast with compulsory school and school system workshops.

Mary, a teacher of 12 years commented:

When I was feeling the challenge of diving deeper into the inquiry process in a primary classroom, and struggling with it because I wasn't quite sure how to go about it, one of the ways that helped me most was to be on Twitter and check out a lot of the Grade 1 and 2 classrooms that I follow and some of the amazing things that have been done. And that triggered some ideas for me to test out in my classroom.

And Laura, also in her twelfth year and in charge of elementary IT support remarked (regarding professional learning activities):

I like the conference style. We've had a couple of conferences each year where you have a choice of what workshops you want to go to, what your needs are. So it's not the type of PD where someone comes in and just sits in front of you and talks at you, telling you what you need to know or maybe you already know. So I like the freedom of being able to choose what I'm going to be learning. And they usually offer a wide range from beginner all the way to expert, and there are different action points for people to come in on. But I also like the advantages of using technology, like doing a webinar.

So you're sitting there listening, but at the same time performing the duties of a busy mom with a little boy. If I miss it initially I can go and catch up on a recorded webinar and get the learning while sitting at home.

Dina, a Kindergarten teacher with 12 years' experience, said that she uses both IT sources and traditional professional reading:

[In recent years I've participated in professional learning] a fair amount, but not the standard kind, like going to a PD seminar or registering for an online course. I join a lot of teacher blogs, Instagram accounts, Facebook, guidance groups with teachers, Kindergarten teachers, Reggio-based schools. I feel the opening up of social media has provided an opportunity to reach other people in the profession and learn from each other, online or through private messaging, talking to them about how they accomplished something I'm trying to accomplish ... I feel like we're sharing more ideas that way and that in turn makes me grow or motivates me to do what somebody else is doing when I see it happening and there's a visual sharing. But I also read books, I'm an old school person. I'll buy a class-room management book and read sections on what I'm specifically seeking.

Connecting to families

Educators often talk about the need to maintain contact with families, but largely in order to keep them informed and on board. Connecting to families, however, can also be an important means of ongoing teacher learning – about what is happening in the community, relationships between young people and their families, and so on.

Among the teachers in our study, Miranda, a Grade 5 teacher in her tenth year reported:

At our school we have a school improvement plan and we involve parents in developing it both in the first month of school during the meet-the-teacher event and through a parent survey and an informational game that happens throughout the school. So they started at the library for instance and then it said you have these questions, then you had to go to the next station. So trying to get them to go throughout the whole school rather than just the one classroom and then leave ... And there were quite a few parents who com-pleted the survey, and I know they will be willing to talk more about it in September when we discuss the new school improvement plan.

And Mary, a Grade 1/2 teacher with 12 year's experience, talked about how she is communicating with parents more, and learning through the interaction:

[In terms of] on-the-job learning, one thing I learned was through communi-cating with parents. I had been focused mainly on telling them about the lessons we do, the expectations in the curriculum, and the activities we use to cover the curriculum; and I communicated a lot of that through weekly emails and multiple Twitter posts each day. But what I think parents also need, and what I need to work on, is communicating more on the personal level with parents about their children. Because I think that's what they care about more than the math lesson we're doing. They want to know what we're doing in math but also how their child is responding. How are they doing? Are they struggling? Are they happy?

And I saw that last year when I came to first term report cards and had one little girl who had been struggling in math, and decided to call her parents to give them a little heads-up ... And they were really upset because they had not heard about this earlier. And I realized that while I assumed they were doing the job at home, asking their child if they really understand things and coming to me if there's a problem, they're not; and they may not understand all the teacher jargon I throw at them through my emails.

Enquire and grow gradually

Finally, something we wish to stress is the need for teachers to enquire and grow gradually. As Kennedy (2010) and others have said, we tend to have an obsession today with school "transformation" and the total reform of teaching based on "expert knowledge" and government initiatives that are over-sold for political reasons. But in fact virtually all improvement takes place gradually, and pressuring teachers to improve suddenly does more harm than good. There is a link here to the need for realism in teaching, which we will discuss in Chapter 20 when talking about teacher wellbeing.

Along these lines, David, in his fifteenth year and now a middle-school principal commented:

A key piece of advice [I would give a new teacher] is: you'll get through it year after year and you'll get better year after year. And I think the second part of that is more important than the first. A lot of first-year teachers hear that you'll get through it, but they don't hear that you'll get better, you'll be able to look back and see what you improved upon. Certainly you'll know your mistakes, but you'll see how you got past those mistakes.

And Miranda, a Grade 4/5 teacher with 7 years' experience observed: "I wouldn't say teaching has gotten easier but you get the flow. Like with any job, you become better at it. With anything you become better at it if you practise it all the time. So I've practised teaching now for seven years and I find I'm able to bring in more things".

Chapter summary

In order to take their teaching in the directions needed for the 21st century, teachers have to continue to enquire and grow. This is necessary both because the world is changing ever more rapidly and because teaching and life are so complex that there is no end to the professional learning and improvement that can occur.

In our view, by far the greatest amount of teacher learning happens informally in the classroom. This is because teachers spend most of their professional lives in the classroom, with abundant opportunities to observe what is needed and what works, week in and week out for most of the year. However, there are many other ways to enquire and grow, a key one being through informal interaction with other teachers in one's own school and beyond. Connecting to families can also be a valuable means of teacher learning. And apart from in-print reading, an increasingly powerful source of insight is IT-based communication with teachers, education academics, and others.

A major challenge in this area is that informal teacher learning, especially in the classroom, has been greatly underrated by governments, school systems, and even teachers themselves. This has to change for many reasons: (a) so teachers look for even more opportunities to learn on-the-job; (b) so they have a better self-concept and greater awareness of their expertise, hence the ability to make decisions about what and how to teach (as discussed in Chapter 17); (c) so governments and school systems are less inclined to exercise complete top-down control of teachers; and (d) so professional development providers adopt a dialogical relationship with teachers rather than just telling them what they should be doing.

Questions for reflection and discussion

1 Why is ongoing teacher enquiry and growth necessary?
2 What are the main ways in which ongoing teacher enquiry and growth occurs?
3 What are the ways in which you will try to enquire and grow?

20 Principle 20: Promote your own wellbeing

One thing I'm doing is reducing my marking time by having check-ins with students in class and using checklists and templates to write things on, and by preparing questions ahead of time that I can ask them in class.

– Mary, a Grade 5 teacher in her ninth year

The Principle, its importance, and some challenges

All the ideas discussed earlier about student mental health and overall wellbeing apply equally to teachers. Teachers should see themselves as human beings, legitimately striving for a good life, not just "helping professionals" whose sole concern is caring for others.

Only if they are seeking – and to a significant degree achieving – self-regard and wellbeing can teachers be learning how to promote wellbeing in their students, relating to their students and colleagues in natural and productive ways, and maintaining the energy and enthusiasm they need to help their students and survive in a challenging profession.

What is promoting your own wellbeing?

Wellbeing for teachers means just what it does for students: having a full good life, one characterized by considerable enjoyment, satisfaction, positivity, and "happiness", to the extent this is possible for humans. Just as with students, pursuing a good life of this kind should be a major activity of teachers. And achieving it is essential for being an effective 21st-century teacher, since teachers cannot do much to facilitate their students' general life development if they themselves do not know what wellbeing is and how to pursue it.

As discussed before, it is sometimes suggested that people should not consciously pursue enjoyment, satisfaction, and so on, since this is an unworthy "hedonism" and furthermore is self-defeating because "if you pursue happiness it will elude you". Rather, it is said, we should aim to live a "good" or "meaningful" life, with happiness coming as a by-product. In our view, however, while living morally and meaningfully is certainly important, seeking wellbeing or enjoyment/satisfaction is fundamental to human nature and essential for sound living.

Why promote your own wellbeing as a teacher?

Promoting our own wellbeing is basic to human nature, and denying this has many harmful effects. If teachers try to suppress this natural urge they will become resentful – at least unconsciously – and the tendency will re-emerge in unfortunate ways (Freud's "return of the repressed"), for example in an authoritarian teaching approach.

Promoting their own wellbeing increases teachers' energy and motivation, enabling them to survive, thrive, and continue to be there for their students.

Pursuing wellbeing themselves gives teachers greater understanding of what they are trying to teach their students about mental health, wellbeing, and a sound overall way of life, along with knowledge of concrete strategies for achieving these ends. Only if they pursue wellbeing themselves can teachers model this pursuit for their students, in everyday interactions and in the way they teach and run the classroom. In summary:

Reasons for teachers to promote their own wellbeing

- Promoting your own wellbeing is basic to human nature, and trying to deny it has many harmful effects
- Teachers promoting their own wellbeing increases their energy and motivation
- It gives teachers more insight into what they are trying to teach their students
- It means teachers are in a better position to model what they are advocating

---

What are the challenges of promoting your own wellbeing?

It goes against what many people see as appropriate teacher behaviour. As a result, it can lead to disapproval and even professional disadvantage.

Such an approach goes against how most teachers have been raised and trained. The idea of teaching as a self-denying "helping profession" is widespread. The same is true for health professionals, as events during the Covid-19 pandemic have shown.

Teachers promoting their own wellbeing takes time, something that is a scarce commodity given the continuing pressure to teach a vast curriculum in great detail.

Finding ways to pursue one's own wellbeing while also meeting system expectations requires a very complex approach to life and teaching. We believe it is possible to a considerable degree, but a great deal of work is required.

Theory/research basis for promoting your own wellbeing as a teacher

Renowned psychologist Mihaly Csikszentmihalyi (1990) emphasized the need for happiness or "positivity" in life; and he focused especially on achieving this in the workplace through a state of "flow", where we become so absorbed in the processes, goals, and satisfactions of our work that our lives just flow along in a productive and satisfying way. Smith and Wilhelm (2002), as we saw in an earlier chapter, advocate application of the concept of flow to teaching but see Csikszentmihalyi's formulation of it as a little too austere: in their view, certain additional elements need to be built in, notably social relationships. Gabriele Oettingen, in her book *Rethinking Positive Thinking* (2014), suggests another amendment to the flow approach: namely, to include "mental contrasting", whereby we avoid *too* much emphasis on happiness – which can in fact lead to *un*happiness – by constantly attending to the negatives in our situation along with the positives. While agreeing with these modifications, however, we believe the basic concept of flow is very valuable, in the workplace and other life contexts.

According to Chapman and West-Burnham, happiness "unlocks creativity, enables flexibility of thought, allows openness to new information and makes learning meaningful" (2010: 89); and obviously this applies as much to teachers as to students. Burnett and Evans' book, *Designing Your Life: How to Build a Well-Lived, Joyful Life* (2016), is concerned centrally with the workplace, but stresses the need to develop a joyful overall way of life if we are to be truly productive in our work. In the first chapter, the authors say that in the book they'll "be focusing mostly on work [which is their academic field] but you won't be able to understand how to design your work until you understand how it fits into the rest of your life" (2016: 14).

In *Happiness by Design* (2014), Paul Dolan also emphasizes wellbeing or happiness in the workplace and beyond, but questions the common assumption that it can be achieved just by adopting certain mental outlooks (important though these often are). He stresses the need to gradually develop the overall environment of our lives so the "context" we have built "nudges" us (Thaler and Sunstein, 2009) in sound directions without superhuman and unhappy exertion on our part (Dolan, 2014: 153). This applies well to the situation of teachers, who can build a class atmosphere and community that supports their own wellbeing while also promoting the learning and enjoyment of their students.

Strategies for promoting your own wellbeing as a teacher

Strategies for promoting teachers' wellbeing while also enhancing the wellbeing and learning of their students include the following:

Strategies for promoting your own wellbeing as a teacher

1 Pursuing work/life balance
2 Teaching more efficiently

3 Making your teaching more enjoyable
4 Developing a good relationship with your students
5 Collaborating with other teachers
6 Continuing to grow professionally
7 Trying new things
8 Being realistic
9 Looking at the positives
10 Practising mindfulness, cognitive-behavioural techniques, and other well-being strategies

Pursuing work/life balance

Work/life balance is as important for teachers as for students. It enables teachers to understand more fully what a balanced life is so they can talk about it with their students, and it makes teachers more reasonable in the demands they place on their students: if they are too hard on themselves, they will tend to be too hard on their students.

Miranda, a Grade 4/5 teacher in her seventh year said: "I always work hard, I get bored if I'm not doing something. But you have to make sure there is time for your family as well". While Vera, a Grade 1 teacher in her tenth year commented:

> Ever since I got married, my partner and I have been trying to manage [work/life balance] together, and it has gotten better. I try to be home a little earlier because we have a dog and it's cruel to leave a dog for so many hours. And I now just appreciate that the work will still be there, or I can take it with me if I really, really need to. But because I'm teaching Grade 1 again, the marking has calmed down.

Yvonne, middle school teacher with 7 years' experience, talked about the better work/life balance in the school to which she had just moved:

> [I'm doing well] because the teachers here are in the same chapter of life as me: they have children and some of them have children who are teenagers like mine, whereas at my old school everyone was young and either single or married without children. And there seems to be an expectation here that when you go home you focus largely on your family. In my previous school there was a different expectation about how much your work carried into the rest of your life ... But actually I learned some of this when I first started teaching. I would work the entire weekend and when I came in on Monday morning I would be burnt out. The same with the summer, I spent the whole summer working. And I had to learn that it was actually more responsible to carve out some sacred time for self-care in order to be more productive at my job. And I'm still learning about that.

Teaching more efficiently

Achieving work/life balance is more feasible if teachers find ways to do much the same things but more quickly. This enables them to satisfy most of the demands placed on them while also attending to other parts of their life. For example, lesson plans can be less detailed; regular learning activities can be set up that largely run themselves; and some student assessment can be done in class rather than after school or on weekends.

Candice, a teacher of Grades 1–6 integrated arts and in her fifteenth year commented: "A key piece of advice I would give to new teachers is to set attainable goals. Because teaching can be an all-consuming 24/7 job if you let it". Mary, the Grade 5 teacher we met earlier reported: "One thing I'm doing is reducing my marking time by having check-ins with students in class and using checklists and templates to write things on, and by preparing questions ahead of time that I can ask them in class". And Miranda in her seventh year said: "[To make teaching feasible] I am always talking to other teachers, sharing ideas so that way I'm not just reinventing things all the time. And another thing is the internet: the internet has everything, and is much faster: you don't always have to go and look things up in books.

Making your teaching more enjoyable

Another way for teachers to enhance their wellbeing is to make their teaching more enjoyable. Becoming more efficient as discussed in the previous section helps with this: marking, for example, can shift from a chore to a somewhat pleasant process of learning about students if you find a way to do it more quickly. Other strategies include developing new approaches to subject areas and choosing teaching methods that fit more with your personality. These changes may seem somewhat self-serving, but students often enjoy themselves more and learn more when teachers are invested in their teaching and drawing on their distinctive knowledge and talents.

Candice, who we met in the previous sub-section, talked about the importance of teaching in such a way that "students have fun in class [and] want to be there", adding that their pleasure and satisfaction "is definitely motivating for me". And Jessica, in her twelfth year and on maternity leave said:

> … even though I've now been in teaching twelve years, I'm constantly in new roles so it always feels new and fresh and challenging … [Moving to half-time librarian] has been a good learning curve and I'm looking forward to going back to that role next year. Actually, I did a lot of career exploration during my maternity leave because I thought maybe I had exhausted my time as a classroom teacher and could do something else. [But] it always came back in bright neon colours that I like being an educator.

Developing a good relationship with your students

We have talked before about how students benefit when teachers get to know them and have a good relationship with them. This can also enhance teachers'

wellbeing by making their teaching more effective and enjoyable and helping them learn about human nature and life in general: a class of students
bring with them a vast array of personality characteristics and background
experiences.

Nora, a middle-school teacher in her fifth year, talked about how much she
values her relationship with her students and described how she strengthens
the relationship by not being too authoritarian with them. And Jody, while
teaching Grade 1 in her ninth year said:

> [The thing I enjoy most is] my relationships with the children. I think without
> your relationships you can't teach them really. Like the autistic boy in my
> class last week said, "Oh I hate teachers" and I looked at him and said "You
> hate teachers?" And he said, "Oh, not you Ms". Like I hope not, I've done
> summersaults over backward for this kid.

Collaborating with other teachers

Collaboration with other teachers can promote wellbeing by making teaching
more effective and hence more satisfying, as discussed in Chapter 19; and the
social aspect of collaboration can deepen friendships and increase the enjoyment of teaching.

One of the teachers in our study, Serena – a teacher of Grade 5/6 gifted students in her fifteenth year – said she greatly values her collaboration with a
colleague teaching next door and it has lasted several years. Yvonne, now in
her fifth year, worked at a school where co-teaching was expected, and spoke
of the advantages and disadvantages. Her co-teacher that year was very strong
in classroom management and helped greatly in that respect; she was also very
organized and taught her how to be more efficient. However, the previous year
"my co-teacher and I were too much alike and weren't complementing each
other". Some teachers stressed the need to allow individual teachers – in the
end – to decide how to teach, criticizing recent system initiatives of "forced
collaboration" where teams of teachers at a given grade level were required to
teach the same things in exactly the same way.

Continuing to grow professionally

Ongoing teacher learning and growth, as discussed in Chapter 19, can be a
major factor in teacher wellbeing. Such learning can be enjoyable in itself, lead
to a better relationship with students, parents, and colleagues, and increase the
satisfaction that arises from seeing students learning and enjoying their studies.

As mentioned in the previous chapter, many of the teachers in our study
spoke of their continued learning and the enjoyment and satisfaction they
gained from it. Here we note other examples. Margaret, who was teaching elementary pupils in her fifth year said that a teacher "has to be willing to learn".
When she first started teaching she was very disappointed that she wasn't giving her students a good enough education, but as her practice improved she

"felt much better about it". And Karen, a Kindergarten teacher with 15 years' experience commented:

> I feel better now because I can see the bigger picture, whereas before I was always just responding to demands from different places. Now I'm okay, I'm working on what I need to work on to make myself a better teacher, as opposed to what the present government or school board policies are. I'll listen to them and learn from them, but I'm not going to flip out about them.

Vera, in her fifteenth year, reported a half-day event at her school where the teachers held discussions in groups, and while she had some reservations about it, "one of the groups was actually good because we developed our own Google classroom inquiry and taught ourselves to use Google Suite things, so I learned how to use Google forms and how better to use Google classroom for assignments and we shared information with each other".

Trying new things

For many teachers (though not all), their wellbeing as teachers depends to a considerable extent on changing what they do from time to time – e.g. teaching a different grade level, focusing on different topics, moving to a new school – to give them new challenges and a change of scene.

Louise spoke in her fifth year of her need to keep moving on to new challenges. Her move from high school to middle school teaching at the end of her fourth year boosted her motivation a considerable amount. She said she is "the kind of person who needs to be doing something different", like teaching new units and using new texts and other resources. Candice, with 12 years' experience reported: "Changing into music has totally changed what teaching is for me, I'm definitely happier doing that … And I've sometimes thought about switching to another profession, but … is that really what I want to do? I don't think so, even with a higher income. I think I would stick with teaching".

And Laura, now in her eleventh year, spoke of how much she was enjoying teaching because of her recent move to being the K-8 librarian and IT person:

> I love it. Media and digital literacy is the stuff I just love, being able to do that every day with the kids and create global projects with them and other things. And even getting started with the little ones in Grade 2 – I loved it. This is why I wanted to move towards making it more of a full-time thing with the library, because then I can just concentrate on that and actually do the whole school instead of just Grade 2 and up. I'm so excited about it.

Being realistic

As in life in general (as noted in Chapter 4), teachers' wellbeing can be undermined if they expect too much. It is important for them to recognize that teaching is a challenging, demanding, even "draining" profession. If they do not "name" this reality, they will be caught off-guard by it and end up less satisfied than they might otherwise be.

Turning to the teachers, Lucy, a consultant in her fifth year but previously a teacher of Grades 7/8, talked about how her experiences in the classroom and also having children of her own helped her see how important it is not to expect too much: it ends up having the opposite effect. "So my overall demeanour has changed. Whereas I used to be so stressed about everything we have to do, now it's just: take everything as it comes".

Laura, responsible for library and Grades 1–6 science teaching and teacher support in her twelfth year, said that a key piece of advice she would give to a beginning teacher is:

> [Fail] forward, learn from your mistakes, not everything is going to work ... I remember in my first few years of teaching being so upset when something didn't work out, or the kids weren't listening to me enough, or the perfect lesson I had planned completely flopped. So now my attitude is, like everything you do in life you learn from it, so take from it whatever you want and just move on.

Dina, a Kindergarten teacher in her twelfth year said:

> I value an administrator or co-worker who recognizes that teaching is a tough job, and when they see it in your face they come up and say something like, "It's okay, you're going to get through it" ... Because let's face it, I'm with 28 little people and constantly the only adult. Even the kids will say sometimes, "Miss, I see you're tired, are you okay?" And it's nice to know that you're valued as a person, because this is a challenging job.

Looking at the positives

While acknowledging the hard realities of teaching, it is also necessary to recognize the positives and that for a great many teachers these outweigh the negatives. As well as being aware of the positives, it is important to deliberately *dwell* on them, calling them to mind from time to time in order to maintain emotional wellbeing.

Jody, in her tenth year and having just moved from Kindergarten to Grade 1, said it had been a difficult year because of a lack of admin support and an unusually large number of students with behavioural difficulties. She added, however, that there were some major positives: "Because I had followed these kids from Kindergarten to Grade 1, it was amazing to see how they came from low skill levels to being readers and writers. It was really cool, really fascinating from that point of view". Another highlight was that she had "a really good team teacher who taught next door, and our whole division worked as a team".

Miranda, a Kindergarten teacher in her twelfth year said: "Honestly, I love the notes that I get from families and kids at the end of the year telling me how much they have loved their year. I keep those and if it was a tiring final month

I open them up and read them; and I think that's why you do it, because it's fun". And Vera, teaching Grades 3/4 in her fifteenth year observed:

> [The highlight of teaching for me is] the little things, the small successes; like when a kid who didn't know how to get along with people does, or when my little ones who I taught in Grade 1 come back as adults and I don't even recognize them but they remember me and say I taught them how to tie their shoelaces in Grade 1. And I say, "thank you so much, you made my day". Or like one day there was a note on my desk from two of my girls who I taught in Grade 1 and now were in Grade 9 or 10, and it said they just came back to see me but I had already left. So they left me a note, "from your favourite little peanuts". And I still have that note, because this is what makes it all worthwhile. You're forever part of someone's history, and it is an honour to be viewed as a positive force in someone's life forever.

Practising mindfulness, cognitive-behavioural techniques, and other wellbeing strategies

There are many strategies for mental health – in a broad sense – that teachers often advocate to students (as discussed in Chapter 3) that they need to apply to themselves in order to optimize their wellbeing. Mindfulness is often mentioned along with cognitive-behavioural techniques (CBT) such as focusing, mental contrasting (Oettingen), nudging (Thaler), context-building (Dolan), and so on. Actually, recognizing the realities of teaching but often dwelling on the positives, as discussed in the previous two sub-sections, are good examples of focusing and mental contrasting.

One of the teachers in our study, Vera – who was teaching Grade 3 in her fifteenth year – talked about her practice of mindfulness. "My mindfulness training was life-changing, because if I hadn't done that I wouldn't have had the mindset and skills I needed to manage this past year. It was very timely, teaching me a great deal about who I am and what I value and how to pass that on to my students".

Finally, Karen, a Kindergarten teacher in her fifteenth year said:

> I try to get a lot of sleep and take care of myself, because I find that with Kindergarten there's less prep outside the school day but it's more intense during the day. I also make sure to take off some days when I need to rest, because if I am here and not 100% it's hard to be patient, to be present with the kids and empathetic. So I try to keep in tune with my own mental, emotional, and physical health so I can be present with the kids and responsive to them.

Chapter summary

Too often teaching is seen by teachers and others as a "helping profession" in which teachers should care for their students without much thought for their

Classroom Teaching in the 21st Century

own wellbeing. This, however, is not only life-denying for teachers, it is self-defeating from a professional point of view, since teachers must have a certain level of wellbeing to provide the energy and motivation they need to support their students and survive in the profession.

Another consideration is that pursuing their own wellbeing gives teachers a deeper understanding of approaches to life and learning that they should be discussing with their students. It also means they can model a sound approach to life in their relationships with students and the way they run the classroom, so students can see what building a way of life is and that the teacher really believes it is important.

It is sometimes suggested that thinking about and deliberately pursuing wellbeing in fact undermines wellbeing: enjoyment, "happiness", and so on should come as a by-product of other endeavours, such as giving students a solid education. However, as discussed in Chapters 3 and 4, this is not an optimal life approach for students and the same is true for teachers. There are many explicit strategies that teachers can adopt that will increase their wellbeing, so long as they do not focus on it *too* much.

Questions for reflection and discussion

1 Why should teachers attend to their own wellbeing?
2 Why is this important for their students as well as themselves?
3 What are some key strategies teachers can adopt to optimize their wellbeing while also meeting the needs of their students?

21 Principle 21: Connect teaching to life

One of my general life values is seeing the positive side of things, choosing to be happy; and I try to present that in the classroom. We celebrate the little things, we get enjoyment from going outside for daily physical activity, learning about new topics, reading books.

– Tanya, a Grade 2 teacher in her tenth year

The Principle, its importance, and some challenges

Throughout the book, we have seen many connections between teaching and an overall way of life; for example, the importance in both contexts of autonomy, mental health, and community. In this final chapter, we further explain and illustrate the principle that teaching and life should be connected. It is a 21st-century principle, both because it is essential in today's interconnected world and because it goes beyond earlier centuries when teaching focused almost entirely on transmitting a narrow band of academic knowledge.

Like Chapter 18, this chapter is different from others in that the main and by far the longest section addresses in turn a number of areas of connection between life and teaching; and there are not separate sections on theory/research and teaching strategies – these are noted (briefly) under each area of life/teaching connection. This is a fitting concluding chapter to the book because it brings together many key themes and provides an overview of the comprehensive life/teaching approach we have been proposing for the 21st century.

What is connecting teaching to life?

Obviously, teachers' work *is* different from their personal life in certain ways, and the two have to be kept somewhat separate. For example, teachers look after the needs of their close relatives and friends in ways they usually cannot for their students; and their choice of online content for watching at home reflects their personal preferences more than it should in the classroom.

However, there can also be a great many similarities and overlaps between life and teaching. To take the same examples, teachers' intimate knowledge of their family and friends can help them better understand and attend to the needs of their students; and their personal online viewing can give them many ideas about what to introduce – perhaps in a modified form – to their students.

Connecting life and teaching requires the adoption of a much broader approach to teaching (as discussed in earlier chapters), but again this is beneficial to everyone. The areas of overlap are multiplied and as a result the two domains reinforce each other in major ways. By contrast, if we think of teaching in the traditional manner as limited to a few subject areas approached in a rather academic way, both teaching and life suffer.

The seven areas of connection and overlap between life and teaching we will focus on in the main section of the chapter are:

Some areas of connection between life and teaching

1 Enjoyment and satisfaction
2 Realism
3 Complexity
4 Routines
5 Self-care
6 Relationships with and caring for others
7 Inclusion

We believe these are of great importance in both life and teaching, and developing and emphasizing them in one arena helps teachers implement them in the other.

Why connect teaching to life?

Many new teachers are shocked at how time-consuming teaching is and initially choose to focus mainly on their teaching, to the neglect of their personal life. Connecting the two is a more adequate way to resolve the dilemma. Teachers save time by doing two things at once: they prepare for teaching as they live their life and enhance their life directly and indirectly by teaching in certain ways.

A frequent crisis point for younger teachers comes when they start to have children of their own and find that keeping up their previous time commitment to school work is simply impossible, given their at least equal obligation to their own children. In keeping with the general principle we are discussing, many of these teachers discover a win-win approach where having children of their own enables them to see more deeply the needs of their students and the insights gained from teaching help with their child-rearing. Many of the teachers in our study reported this phenomenon.

Connecting life and teaching not only saves time as teachers do two things at once, it also increases the depth and pleasure of their experiences and activities in both contexts. For example, teachers who for recreation read many of the same novels as their students understand and enjoy their reading more as a result of class discussions, and in turn they have a more enjoyable experience during class discussions as a result of having read the novels.

Increasing the life/teaching connection also places teachers in a better position to model in the classroom the interests and activities they are trying to introduce their students to, something we discussed earlier as important. In addition, it enables teachers to engage in the kind of dialogue with students we have previously advocated. To summarize:

Reasons for connecting life and teaching

- A lot of time is saved
- Conflicts between working as a teacher and having children of one's own are alleviated
- The depth and pleasure of experiences in both life and teaching are increased
- Connecting the two places teachers in a better position to model in the classroom the approach to life they are recommending to their students

---

What are the challenges of connecting life and teaching?

A common assumption is that in order to be "professional", teachers have to keep their life and teaching separate. Accordingly, teachers who connect the two may be frowned upon by colleagues, administrators, and others.

Broadening teaching in the way required to connect it with life is not easy in the current climate, where a narrowly academic approach to teaching is still largely expected.

It is not always easy to make the modifications of life and teaching needed to bring them together. It sometimes seems easier to keep them separate (though we believe that in the long run, it is not).

Most teachers did not experience – and were not prepared for – this approach to teaching. Again, a lot of time and effort is needed to go in this direction,

Key connections between life and teaching

In this main section of the chapter, we explore seven key areas of connection between life and teaching. Of course, many other areas could have been included but these help clarify the general principle, show why it is important, and provide strategies for implementing the general approach.

Enjoyment and satisfaction

In both life and teaching it is important to emphasize enjoyment, satisfaction, and other "positive" emotions, often referred to as "wellbeing" or "happiness". In the past, the focus in schools and other settings was largely on doing your duty, being a good citizen, and helping others. These are crucial, of course, but as noted in Chapter 4, having positive emotions is a large part of what motivates humans and makes life seem worthwhile; we need to highlight it more for students and teachers alike. We agree with Dolan (2014) and Burnett and Evans (2016) that people should deliberately "design" a life with substantial happiness in it.

In life, the importance of positivity is widely emphasized by psychologists, most notably Mihaly Csikszentmihalyi and Martin Seligman. According to Seligman, in the latter half of the 20th century psychologists were "consumed with a single topic only – mental illness", and the time "has finally arrived for a science that seeks to … provide guideposts for finding what Aristotle called the 'good life'" (2002: ix). The good life he identifies largely with "pursuit of happiness", going on to say that while there are limits to happiness, positive psychology shows how we can "live in the upper reaches of [our] set range of happiness" (pp. ix–x).

In teaching, teachers should work to promote their own happiness, so they can survive and thrive in the profession and understand enough about the pursuit of happiness to help their students in this area. They should try to maintain a work/life balance, in part for their own wellbeing but also so they can model for their students a well-rounded life. If teachers are too hard on themselves, they will lose their enthusiasm for their work and in turn be too hard on their students.

Also, of course, teachers should foster in their students a sense of the importance of happiness and help them learn how to pursue it effectively. A key strategy for doing this is to have frequent class discussions of what different students enjoy in their everyday life and how their enjoyment and satisfaction could be increased. Tanya, teaching Grade 2 in her tenth year, talked about how she emphasizes happiness in her class:

> One of my general life values is seeing the positive side of things, choosing to be happy; and I try to present that in the classroom. We celebrate the little things, we get enjoyment from going outside for daily physical activity, learning about new topics, reading books. I try to model the sense of happiness and enjoyment that can come from your daily experiences.

Obviously, much subject content also has to be taught, but this too can be made enjoyable by prioritizing the more interesting and meaningful topics, building class community, and creating a generally positive classroom atmosphere.

One advantage of promoting enjoyment and satisfaction in the classroom is that it can increase students' willingness to come to school and their engagement when they are there. Miranda, a Kindergarten teacher with 12 years' experience said:

> I think it's so important that the kids come to school wanting to come to school, loving school. That's important because then they are so much more open to learning, and they are not always even thinking they are learning but rather just coming to school with the activities and areas in the classroom that we have planned, just engaged in what's going on and willing to give it a try.

Realism

In life. While pursuing positivity, we need to be realistic about how successful we will be in achieving it. Oettingen (2014) advocates the strategy of "mental contrasting" whereby we think about both the positives and negatives in situations. People are often told to "think positively" or "look on the bright side"; but while this is useful to a degree, if we expect *too* much we will often be disappointed and end up less happy than if we had lower expectations. We need a balanced approach where we recognize that there will always be some negatives, so a very high level of happiness across a life-time is probably impossible. This is a sobering thought, but accepting it can increase our happiness overall.

But is a balance of optimism and realism sufficient for us? Is it enough to keep us going? Apparently for most people it is. Most people do keep going (the survival of the human race shows that); and some studies suggest that people on average become happier in late middle-age, even though they are more aware of the limitations of life and have abandoned many of their earlier hopes. It seems that, in line with Oettingen's "mental contrasting" and Seligman's "limited range of happiness" notions, settling for being "quite happy" works for most people.

In teaching. In the school classroom, specifically, it is important to be realistic. For example, we should largely avoid embracing sudden reform initiatives (Kennedy, 2010) and seeing the "super-teacher" as the norm (Kosnik, 1999). Obviously teaching like any profession can be improved and we should seek such improvement. But often politically motivated talk of "transforming" schooling and promoting "best practice" or "expert practice" (as distinct from "good practice") in fact undermines teacher morale and steady, reliable growth in effectiveness. Marisa, a teacher of Grades 1/2 and in her fifteenth year observed: "The advice I would give to a new teacher is: 'Don't sweat the small stuff, and don't worry, your programme does not need to be perfect'. At the beginning that was a really big thing for me, but over time I've learned that it doesn't need to be perfect".

Similarly, John, in his fourteenth year and teaching health and physical education and dance in Grades K-6 remarked:

> In recent years I've become more patient with myself. I've taken a bit of the advice that I've been pouring into my students over the years. I've stopped trying to be that perfectionist and am allowing myself to be vulnerable. If you don't achieve it this year, there's always next year. We always look at children through their development and what they're capable of, and I feel that adults are the same. Maybe it's your mind-set, your current situation or other factors, but sometimes today is not the right day; maybe it has to be tomorrow.

Complexity

In life. Life is very broad and complex. Accordingly, people need a complex way of life in order to achieve wellbeing, one that includes intellectual, social, emotional, physical, occupational, and other elements. There is no such thing as "the simple life", at least not in a good way. Many conditions have to be fulfilled if we are to experience even a moderate degree of happiness.

Too often just one or two principles of living are stressed when talking about wellbeing: focusing, thinking positively, financial success. But according to Oettingen (2014), we have to think about many things to achieve our wishes, and this requires knowledge of and involvement in many things. Similarly, Dolan believes that a broad set of conditions have to be fulfilled to be happy. He describes his life approach as "context-focused, rather than cognition-driven" (2014: 153), explaining that although particular mental strategies are important, a whole way of life is needed to achieve happiness.

In teaching. In line with this general insight about life, teachers should themselves develop a complex life approach. This will both enhance their wellbeing and make them better teachers. If they spend too much of their time focusing on preparing lessons, marking papers, etc., they will have less wisdom and insight to share with their students.

Maintaining a solid work/life balance and gaining wider life experience should be seen not as neglecting teachers' responsibilities but placing them in a better position to help their students. They should see it as something they "owe to their students". Maria, in her fifteenth year and teaching Kindergarten observed: "I don't think teachers realize what they are getting into when they take up teaching. It's just based on so many different things, there are so many factors". And Dina, also teaching Kindergarten and in her twelfth year commented: "I'm less stressed now because I can manage teaching a bit better. I'm not as disappointed, because I know there are so many balls in the air and I can only do so much; and I'm confident that what I am doing makes a difference".

In the teaching programme and the general culture of the classroom, many aspects of life should be emphasized rather than just the narrowly academic. This is difficult given current pressures to just "cover the curriculum" and prepare for standardized tests; but as discussed in earlier chapters, it is possible to "do both" – teach a great deal of subject content *and* address "real-world" and way-of-life matters.

Routines

In life. Given the complexity of life and the constant change both in us and our circumstances, we often have to make adjustments to how we live. But while change is very important, it should normally take place gradually, against a backdrop of considerable continuity. Because we have been carefully designing our life from early childhood to the present, there are bound to be many good things in it that we should hold onto. This is in line with the ideas of Heath (2014) and Kennedy (2010), who oppose "sudden", "over-the-top" change. Not only should we respect the good in our past decisions, but also because life is so complex we cannot intelligently change everything at once.

In accordance with a gradualist approach, our lives should contain many routines, recurring activities, and ongoing arrangements that we continually modify but seldom change all at once. Having such continuing elements is important because, as just noted, it gives us many proven satisfactions to hold onto as we experiment with new directions. It also makes change more rational as we make incremental adjustments, see the results, and then revise them again. And it means that at any given time, we do not have to do *too* much reflection, thus undermining our enjoyment of life.

In teaching. One implication of this gradualist approach to life is that teachers should feel they can have habits, routines, etc. Sometimes it is suggested that teachers should be amazingly creative and constantly find radically new ways to teach, rather than returning year after year to the same set of topics, issues, and readings. However, while steady refinement of teaching is necessary, considerable continuity is also appropriate. Having routines and recurring activities reduces the workload, gives a sense of security and predictability, and provides a solid basis for fine-tuning. As in life generally, if we try to change everything at once rather than making adjustments to what has worked before, things can go seriously wrong.

Turning to the student experience, regular routines and recurring activities can also give a sense of familiarity and security. And rather than constantly asking "what am I supposed to be doing", students can focus on the issues and content at hand (in line with Csikszentmihalyi's concept of flow). Moreover, they can learn valuable study practices and "habits of mind" (Meier et al., 2015) that they carry with them for the rest of their lives. Jeannie, a Grade 3 teacher in her thirteenth year, talked about the need for students to have some predictability: "It helps kids to get a schedule when they come in the morning; and I always try to give them advance notice of things, like if I'm going to be out of the classroom at a workshop or meeting". And Jessica, in her twelfth year, working in the library and teaching K-6 prep and special education, reported:

> I had a student from a very traumatic home experience who suffered from anxiety. And he liked playing with cars and I had a basket of them in the library. So we had a routine where he could play with the cars at certain times and then we put them back in the basket and locked the cupboard door. And after doing his work in the classroom, he always knew he had that to look forward to, because he would come back to the library with me to do it; and it would help him self-regulate.

Self-care

In life. In earlier chapters and sections, we stressed that individuals need to look after themselves more than in the past. The lack of emphasis on self-care in traditional morality, education, and politics has done great harm, both by discouraging individuals from developing their own way of life and by increasing inequalities in wealth, privilege, and so on. Certainly we should help others a great deal, as discussed elsewhere; but if we do not look after our own interests, things are likely to go badly for us and for those dependent on us.

Even where a balance between self and others has been advocated, it has often been poorly thought out. The idea has been that we should put others first and leave our own wellbeing partly to the generosity of others and partly to natural processes: "just let it happen". But self-interest is a basic human inclination, and trying to ignore or suppress it leads to confusion and even psychic damage (Freud's return of the repressed). And besides, the generosity of others is not something we can always rely on, partly because it is often not strong enough and partly because others do not know us or our needs well enough to provide for them.

In teaching. Teachers need to model an appropriate level of self-interest and self-esteem by maintaining their own work/life balance, with many interests and enjoyments within and beyond the profession. If they see themselves in a purely self-sacrificing role, as "super-teachers" and "healers of society's woes" (Kosnik, 1999), they will not set a good example of how to live to their students and will likely burn out quickly; they may also be too hard on their students because of unconscious resentment about their situation. Rachel, a teacher of K-3 music and drama in her twelfth year, spoke of the need for work/life balance: "One challenge I find is just keeping my own mental health and not running myself down. And what I do is make sure I have my own interests and take time for myself, putting myself first sometimes and learning to say no". And Jessica, in her seventh year and teaching Grades 2–8 English as a second language (ESL) observed:

> I try to teach my students to self-advocate, to see that their ideas are valuable, they have something to contribute. And a lot of my ESL students come to me and they can understand me, hear me, even communicate with me; but there is a silence because it's almost like, what am I saying, is what I'm saying valuable, does it make sense? But by the end of the course you can see the change in confidence. And a lot of the books I use with them are about building confidence and self-advocacy.

Relationships with and caring for others

In life. To this point we have talked mainly about designing our *own* complex, integrated way of life that is enjoyable and satisfying. However, a happy life also typically involves relating to *other people* and working in part for *their* wellbeing. There are several reasons for this: interacting with and helping other people is a major source of enjoyment in itself; we need the support of others; we can learn a lot from others; and most people care about others and want to help them. Designing our life, then, usually involves much effort to establish and maintain good personal relationships and community connections.

Apart from the enjoyment they bring, a major advantage of relationships lies in how much we learn from them. As relationships deepen we learn steadily more about ourselves, those we relate to, and people in general; and as we converse with people, we learn things they already know about the world. With the emphasis today on "expert" knowledge, there is a tendency to underestimate how much we can learn from ordinary people with their varied backgrounds and experiences.

In teaching. As discussed in Part 2, the classroom should be a genuinely social place in which people enjoy and celebrate each other and care for each other. The emphasis on relationships in life in general should be reflected in the classroom. This is in line with the thoughts of Peterson (1992), who observes that so many school activities involve a fairly large group of people relating to each other in a space not much larger than a living room. To prohibit conversation and social interaction in that setting makes no sense, and renders the classroom – in which children spend so much time – quite alien to ordinary life.

Lucy, now a coordinator but having previously taught Grades 1–3, spoke in her seventh year about how she brings care for others into the classroom:

> I have much more compassion for students now, whereas when I first became a teacher I was a really strict, even rough teacher. After the years of experience and having kids of my own, my attitude is, they're just kids. Expectations definitely need to be there but when a kid's going through something you kind of have to take that into account. And I've realized that a lot of misbehaviour either reflects on your own teaching or on the fact that something else is going on. Kids aren't like that for no reason.

Paul, in his fourteenth year and a teacher of Grades 7/8, talked about the need for more enjoyment and social interaction in school, for teachers and students alike.

> One of the things I've realized is that staff and students are really stressed these days, and there's not enough joy in the school. And part of my focus next year – and this is hard for me because I'm not an extrovert, I'm not Mr. Social – but I feel like someone needs to provide some leadership in terms of just having some fun together. I'm hoping to get people to have lunch together more, because when you eat lunch together you chat and catch up on things and plan things.

This led Paul the following year to establish the Joy Lunch Club: "It meets weekly and has just two rules: make sure you and everyone around you are enjoying themselves, and we don't use phones or other technology. And it's been really great".

Inclusion

In life. In the previous sub-section we discussed the contribution of relationships to both our own wellbeing and that of other people. We now wish to note that, in choosing relationships and engaging in them, it is important to be inclusive of people who differ from us in race, ethnicity, gender, sexual preference, abilities, socio-economic status, etc. Once again, such inclusion is in our own interests as well as that of other people: it should not be seen as something we do just out of a sense of duty.

As emphasized in Chapter 9, people have a great many commonalities across categories of race, ethnicity, gender, etc., and the differences *within* such categories are typically far greater than *between* them. Most differences between people simply do not run along such lines. Important differences (in intellectual interests, social behaviour, political views, etc.) occur at an individual level, *within* race, gender, etc. Hence, stereotyping people according to such categories leads to many misconceptions and does a great deal of harm. Besides, in our rapidly globalizing world, an increasing number of people no longer belong to a single race, ethnicity, etc.

In teaching. As discussed in earlier chapters, classrooms need to become more inclusive for the reasons just noted about life in general. Through study, discussion, and experience in the classroom, teachers and students can learn how the differences between categories of people have been greatly exaggerated, resulting in enormous bias and discrimination. They can also learn how to enjoy relationships with people previously thought to be "different" from themselves. It might be thought that if the classroom is more friendly and inclusive than the "real world", students will develop unrealistic ideas and not be able to function in everyday life. But being exposed to a different way of thinking and interacting can in fact leave students better informed, more optimistic, and *more* able to function in the real world.

One problem in schooling is that with so much focus on learning subject content, there is not enough time left to discuss issues of bias, discrimination, and inclusion. However, this problem can be overcome partly by having a discussion of inclusion *within* subject study, especially literature, history, and social studies. Even in mathematics, data analysis activities can be included that show, for example, how certain categories of people are discriminated against. Another crucial strategy is to ensure that *all* students in the class are heard from in presentations and discussions, so everyone can see for themselves the range of talents and personality traits found within all categories of people.

In Chapter 9, we gave examples of how teachers in our longitudinal study attempted to promote inclusion in the classroom. Here we note just one example, that of Wanda teaching Grades 5/6 in her tenth year, who described how she approaches this area:

> One of my basic beliefs is that we are all pretty much the same, and so all deserve to be treated with respect and kindness. We all have a place and a purpose, and we have to recognize that in each other. And if we treat each other kindly and with respect, it just makes the world an easier and better place to be. So if I treat my students that way and live that value with them, they will do the same with me, creating camaraderie and a stronger community and better people … As I say to the kids, we are a puzzle, and if one piece is missing the whole puzzle falls apart.

Chapter summary

Connecting teaching to life – and life to teaching – in the 21st century is in many ways the basic theme of this book. The world, including the total physical and life environment, and our lives within it are changing at such a rapid pace that education must change dramatically to enable young people now and as they grow older to live well in the broadest sense and help sustain the environment in which we all exist.

To live well in the long run, young people need to develop a comprehensive way of life that brings them wellbeing and supports the wellbeing of other individuals and groups and the world environment. This requires relating education to life as a whole rather than keeping it as a detached academic exercise, as has happened too often in the past. This is important for teachers and students alike.

Good teaching, then, must have many of the same characteristics as sound living beyond the school. Both teaching and life need to be characterized by, for example: enjoyment and satisfaction, realism, complexity, routines, self-care, relating to and caring for other people, and inclusion. This is a small sample of the necessary connections between life and teaching, but they are key ones and serve to illustrate the importance, possibility, and challenges of linking the two domains.

Connecting life and teaching is challenging, but teachers already do it to some extent and going further in this direction can bring many rewards to teachers – both personal and professional; and with time it can become more feasible. Indeed, keeping the two realms separate is perhaps more difficult given the toll it takes on student engagement, effective teaching, teacher interest and motivation, and the wellbeing of both students and teachers.

Questions for reflection and discussion

1 Why should teachers work to connect life and teaching?
2 What are key areas of such connection?
3 What are some key strategies teachers can adopt to increase the connection between life and teaching?

References

Allen, C. (1989). The primacy of *phronesis*: A proposal for avoiding the frustrating tendencies in our conceptions of rationality. *Journal of Religion*, 69 (3), 359–374.

Ananiadou, K. and Claro, M. (2009). *21st Century skills and competences for new millennium learners in OECD countries*. EDU Working Paper no. 41. Paris: OECD Publishing.

Banks, J. (2009a). Introduction. In J. Banks (ed.), *The Routledge international companion to multicultural education* (pp. 1–5). New York: Routledge.

Banks, J. (2009b). Multicultural education: Dimensions and paradigms. In J. Banks (ed.), *The Routledge international companion to multicultural education* (pp. 9–32). New York: Routledge.

Banks, J. (2009c). Diversity, group identity, and citizenship education in a global age. In J. Banks (ed.), *The Routledge international companion to multicultural education* (pp. 303–322). New York: Routledge.

Banks, J. (2016). Civic education in the age of global migration. In J. Banks, M. Suarez-Orozco, and M. Ben-Peretz (eds.), *Global migration, diversity, and civic education: Improving policy and practice* (pp. 29–52). New York: Teachers College Press.

Beck, C. (2017). Informal action research: The nature and contribution of everyday classroom inquiry. In L. Rowell and J. Shosh (eds.), *Palgrave international handbook of action research* (pp. 37–48). London: Palgrave.

Bellanca, J. (2010). *Enriched learning projects: A practical pathway to 21st century skills*. Bloomington, IN: Solution Tree Press.

Belova, N., Stuckey, M., Marks, R. and Eilks, I. (2015). The idea of filtered information and the learning about the use of chemistry-related information in the public. In I. Eilks and A. Hofstein (eds.), *Relevant chemistry education: From theory to practice* (pp. 185–203). Dordrecht: Sense.

Boaler, J. (2016). *Mathematical mindsets: Unleashing students' potential through creative mathematics, inspiring messages and innovative teaching*. San Francisco, CA: Jossey-Bass.

Bransford, J., Darling-Hammond, L. and LePage, P. (2005). Introduction. In L. Darling-Hammond and J. Bransford (eds.), *Preparing teachers for a changing world: What teachers should learn and be able to do* (pp. 1–39). San Francisco, CA: Jossey-Bass.

Bulfin, S., Parr, G. and Bellis, N. (2016). Literacy teacher education and new technologies: Standards-based reforms and the technologizing imperative (pp. 119–133). In C. Kosnik, S. White, C. Beck, B. Marshall, L. Goodwin, and J. Murray (eds.), *Building bridges: Rethinking literacy teacher education in a digital era*. Rotterdam: Sense Publishers.

Burnett, B. and Evans, D. (2016). *Designing your life: How to build a well-lived, joyful life*. New York: Knopf.

Carr, W. (1995). *For education: Towards critical educational inquiry*. Buckingham: Open University Press.

Chapman, L. and West-Burnham, J. (2010). *Education for social justice: Achieving wellbeing for all*. London: Continuum.

Cochran-Smith, M. and Lytle, S. (1993). *Inside/outside: Teacher research and knowledge*. New York: Teacher College Press.

Cochran-Smith, M. and Lytle, S. (2009). *Inquiry as stance: Practitioner research for the next generation*. New York: Teacher College Press.

Collins, A. (2017). *What's worth teaching: Rethinking curriculum in the age of technology*. New York: Teachers College Press.

Collins, A. and Halverson, R. (2018). *Rethinking education in the age of technology: The digital revolution and schooling in America* (2nd edition). New York: Teachers College Press.

Csikszentmihalyi, M. (1990). *The psychology of optimal experience*. New York: Harper & Row.

Day, C. and Gu, Q. (2014). *Resilient teachers, resilient schools: Building and sustaining quality in testing times*. London: Routledge.

Dewey, J. (1916). *Democracy and education*. New York: Macmillan.

Dewey, J. (1938). *Experience and education*. New York: Collier-Macmillan.

Dolan, P. (2014). *Happiness by design: Change what you do, not how you think*. New York: Plume.

Dolan, P. (2019). *Happy ever after: Escaping the myth of the perfect life*. London: Allen Lane.

Dolby, N. (2012). *Rethinking multicultural education for the next generation: The new empathy and social justice*. London: Routledge.

Duckworth, E. (2016). *Grit: The power of passion and perseverance*. New York: Collins.

Falk, B. (2009). *Teaching the way children learn*. New York: Teachers College Press.

Florian, L., Black-Hawkins, K. and Rouse, M. (2017). *Achievement and inclusion in schools* (2nd edition). London: Routledge.

Gardner, H. (1999). *Intelligence reframed: Multiple intelligences for the 21st century*. New York: Basic Books.

Gee, J. (2015). *Literacy and education*. New York: Routledge.

Gill, S. and Thomson, G. (2012). *Rethinking secondary education: A human-centred approach*. London: Pearson.

Gillies, R. (2016). *Enhancing classroom-based talk: Blending practice, research and theory*. London: Routledge.

Goleman, D. and Senge, P. (2014). *The triple focus: A new approach to education*. Florence, MA: More Than Sound.

Gorman, A. (2021) Tweet, February 14.

Heath, J. (2014). *Enlightenment 2.0: Restoring sanity to our politics, our economy, and our lives*. Toronto: HarperCollins.

Holt, M. and Grills, A. (eds.) (2016). *Critical issues in school-based mental health: Evidence-based research, practice, and interventions*. New York: Routledge.

Kabat-Zinn, J. (2013). *Full catastrophe living: Using the wisdom of your body and mind to face stress, pain, and illness* (revised edition). New York: Bantam.

Kennedy, M. (2010). Against boldness. *Journal of Teacher Education*, 61 (1/2), 16–20.

Kosnik, C. (1999). *Primary education: Goals, processes, and practices*. Ottawa: Legas.

Lortie, D. (1975). *Schoolteacher: A sociological study*. Chicago, IL: University of Chicago Press.

Martin, J. (1992). *The schoolhome*. Cambridge, MA: Harvard University Press.

Martin, J. (2011). *Education reconfigured: Culture, encounter, and change*. New York: Routledge.

Meier, D. (2002). *In schools we trust: Creating communities of learning in an era of testing and standardization*. Boston, MA: Beacon Press.

Meier, D. (2015). Reflecting on Mission Hill School's early years … and before. In D. Meier, M. Knoester, and K. D'Andrea (eds.), *Teaching in themes: An approach to schoolwide learning, creating community, & differentiating instruction* (pp. 9–26). New York: Teachers College Press.

Meier, D., Knoester, M. and D'Andrea, K. (eds.) (2015). *Teaching in themes: An approach to schoolwide learning, creating community, & differentiating instruction*. New York: Teachers College Press.

Miller, J. (2019). *The holistic curriculum* (3rd edition). Toronto: University of Toronto Press.

Murphy, S. (2019). *Fostering mindfulness: Building skills that students need to manage their attention, emotions, and behavior in classrooms and beyond.* Markham, Ontario: Pembroke.

Nieto, S. (2009). Multicultural education in the United States: Historical realities, ongoing challenges, and transformative possibilities. In J. Banks (ed.), *The Routledge international companion to multicultural education* (pp. 79–95). New York: Routledge.

Nieto, S. (2016). Education in a globalized world: Challenges, tensions, possibilities, and implications for teacher education. In J. Banks, M. Suarez-Orozco, and M. Ben-Peretz (eds.), *Global migration, diversity, and civic education: Improving policy and practice* (pp. 202–222). New York: Teachers College Press.

Noddings, N. (2013). *Education and democracy in the 21st century.* New York: Teachers College Press.

Oettingen, G. (2014). *Rethinking positive thinking: Inside the new science of motivation.* New York: Current/Penguin.

O'Meara, J. (2010). *Beyond differentiated instruction.* Thousand Oaks, CA: Corwin.

Paley, V. (1992). *You can't say you can't play.* Cambridge, MA: Harvard University Press.

Peterson, M. and Hittie, M. (2003). *Inclusive teaching: Creating effective schools for all learners.* Boston, MA: Allyn & Bacon.

Peterson, R. (1992). *Life in a crowded place.* Portsmouth, NH: Heinemann.

Phillippo, K. (2013). *Advisory in urban public schools: A study of expanded teacher roles.* New York: Palgrave Macmillan.

Piaget, J. (1968). *Structuralism.* London: Routledge & Kegan Paul.

Pollard, A. et al. (2019). *Reflective teaching in schools* (5th edition). London: Bloomsbury.

Santoro, D. and Cain, L. (eds.) (2018). *Principled resistance: How teachers resolve ethical dilemmas.* Cambridge, MA: Harvard Education Press.

Schleicher, A. (ed.) (2012). *Preparing teachers and developing school leaders for the 21st century: Lessons from around the world.* Paris: OECD Publishing.

Schön, D. (1983). *The reflective practitioner: How professionals think in action.* New York: Basic Books.

Seligman, M. (2002). *Authentic happiness: Using the new positive psychology to realize your potential for lasting fulfilment.* New York: Atria.

Shirley, D. (2017). *The new imperatives of educational change: Achievement with integrity.* New York: Routledge.

Smith, E. (2012). *Key issues in education and social justice.* Los Angeles, CA: Sage.

Smith, M. and Wilhelm, J. (2002). *Reading don't fix no Chevys.* Portsmouth, NH: Heinemann.

Stiglitz, J. (2012). *The price of inequality: How today's divided society endangers our future.* New York: Norton.

Swartz, L. (2020). *Teaching tough topics.* Markham, Ontario: Pembroke.

Thaler, R. and Sunstein, C. (2009). *Nudge: Improving decisions about health, wealth, and happiness.* London: Penguin.

Tomlinson, C. (2001). *How to differentiate instruction in mixed-ability classrooms* (2nd edition). Alexandra, VA: ASCD.

Tranter, D., Carson, L. and Boland, T. (2018). *The third path: A relationship-based approach to student wellbeing and achievement.* Toronto: Nelson.

Trilling, B. and Fadel, C. (2009). *21st Century skills: Learning for life in our times.* San Francisco, CA: Jossey-Bass/Wiley.

UK Department for Education (DfE) (2019) *Character education: Framework guidance.* DfE-00235-2019. London: DfE. Available at: https://assets.publishing.service.gov.uk/government/uploads/system/uploads/attachment_data/file/904333/Character_Education_Framework_Guidance.pdf.

VanSledright, B. (2011). *The challenge of rethinking history education: On practices, theories, and policy*. New York: Routledge.

Waring, M. and Evans, C. (2015). *Understanding pedagogy: Developing a critical approach to teaching and learning*. London: Routledge.

West-Burnham, J. and Coates, M. (2005). *Personalizing learning: Transforming education for every child*. London: Continuum.

White, J. (1991). *Education and the good life: Autonomy, altruism, and the National Curriculum*. New York: Teachers College Press.

Yandell, J. (2016). The impact of policy on teacher education and literacy education in England: Notes from a corner of a small island. In C. Kosnik, S. White, C. Beck, B. Marshall, L. Goodwin, and J. Murray (eds.), *Building bridges: Rethinking literacy teacher education in a digital era* (pp. 31–42). Rotterdam: Sense Publishers.

Zeichner, K. (1995). Beyond the divide of teacher research and academic research. *Teachers and Teaching: Theory and Practice*, 1 (2), 153–172.

Zeichner, K. and Liston, D. (2014). *Reflective teaching: An introduction*. New York: Routledge.

Index

technology *see* information
communication technology
Tranter, D. 6, 60, 161
Trilling, B. 5–6, 16, 43–4, 52, 80, 116, 132, 141

VanSledright, B. 90–1, 116–17

wellbeing (students) 30–2
equity and inclusion 77
strategies for promoting 33–7
theory and research on 32–3

wellbeing (teachers) 179–80, 187–8, 191
challenges of promoting 180
strategies for promoting 181–7
theory and research 180–1
West-Burnham, J. 68–9, 181
Education for Social Justice 33
Wilhelm, J. 33, 68, 165, 181
work/life balance 182–3, 192, 194, 196
workload, teaching 79, 164, 195

Zeichner, K. 79, 172